The Leftouts

Disadvantaged
Children
in Heterogeneous
Schools

The Leftouts

Disadvantaged Children in Heterogeneous Schools

SANDRA A. WARDEN

Michigan State University

HOLT, RINEHART AND WINSTON, INC.

*New York   Chicago   San Francisco   Atlanta   Dallas
Montreal   Toronto   London*

To Frank, Mike, Lynda, and Greg
who cooked, cleaned, cajoled, and commiserated
but never laughed

Preface

Compensatory programs intended, at least in part, to aid socioculturally disadvantaged children have burgeoned in the last three or four years. Probably the best known and most generally admired of these programs are VISTA and Project Head Start, conducted under the auspices of the federal government and aimed at the child of the ghetto—isolated from his more advantaged age-mates. In 1965, President Johnson called for the establishment of a National Teacher Corps of especially trained teachers to work in urban slums and areas of rural poverty. Tutorial programs established and run by college students now proliferate. In addition, literally thousands of state, community, church, and independent projects are being conducted.

The vast majority of these compensatory educational programs deal with children who attend relatively homogeneous schools in more or less isolated "poverty" areas. This effort is a worthy one, but our principal concern will be with educationally disadvantaged children in heterogeneous school situations. Of course, many of the problems are the same, but they are simply intensified when the child must attend school with those who *are* prepared to cope with the demands of the school system.

It seems obvious that money and help are readily available—but equally obvious that more than good intentions and financial support is needed for effective compensatory education. Cooperative planning, coordinated activities, and a great deal of research and training seem necessary, all of which should begin with a thorough understanding of the problems of socioculturally disadvantaged children. The social-psychological problems of the Leftouts most especially need attention because they are often indeed "left out" of much current compensatory educational planning.

Analysis points to a number of at least theoretically supported relationships, which are worthy of concentrated research efforts. Part of the analysis of the particular problems of Leftouts, generated by their specific social situation in the heterogeneous school, has relied on research and theory only indirectly related to the specific problems at hand, for the simple reason that no one to date has considered the problems of disadvantaged children in heterogeneous schools as they might differ from those of disadvantaged children in homogeneous schools. It seems obvious that many of the Leftout's problems will *not* differ from those of any disadvantaged child in the school system, yet it is the consequences of this disadvantage *in a particular kind of social setting* that are suggested to make the Leftout's problems different. In our analysis we attempt to indicate the probable consequences of sociocultural disadvantage for the Leftout.

It is with the consequences of the values, attitudes, and behavior of teachers and more advantaged age-mates in this unique social setting that we are primarily concerned. Thus, this analysis relies heavily on social-psychological theory, on child development literature, and on such empirical research as seems relevant. The analysis seems reasonable enough in light of this kind of evidence, but far more *directed* research is indicated.

It is important to my argument that both teachers and peers are potentially significant "others" for an elementary-age child, especially for a disadvantaged child in the heterogeneous school situation. Thus, important areas for directed research must be those of: the general significance that teachers and more advantaged age-mates have for the Leftout; the relative influence of parents, teachers, and peers on the Leftout's development of value orientations and behavioral expectations; and the specific nature of the consequences for the Leftout of parent, teacher, and peer conflicts in demands.

It is assumed in the bulk of the discussion that the Leftout has both the physical and intellectual potential needed for successful social and academic adjustment, given appropriate compensatory training. Thus, other crucial areas for research must center on: the truth of this assumption; appropriate ways of meaningfully measuring physical and intellectual capacity among disadvantaged children; and the design and evaluation of appropriate compensatory programs.

My contention is that academic, social, and emotional factors in the heterogeneous school situation are interdependent and equally important for the Leftout's potential for successful school adjustment. Thus, research efforts also need to be directed toward investigating more fully the relationship between these variables for the disadvantaged child in a heterogeneous school situation.

Finally, I strongly suggest that the particular social situation in which the Leftout finds himself both compounds his general disadvantage and, at the same time, offers the means for overcoming it. Research is urgently needed to show whether in fact the Leftout's unique social situation has differential consequences, and to explain the specific nature of any observed differences. I attempt to offer cogent, theoretically oriented guidelines for each of these areas of research.

Education needs to be considered in the context of broad societal values and goals. Formal education is one aspect of the socialization process. This implies socializing for something—usually for performance in a variety of adult roles.

This notion raises two important issues. The first issue centers on the nature of the relationship between academic achievement, as measured by grades and standardized test scores, and career success, critical thinking, intellectual curiosity, creativity, and a host of other personal and social goals. The second issue relates to the normative values of the larger social system and the role of the school in what might be called "citizenship training."

What are the goals of education in our society? What ought they to be? Perhaps these are the essential questions toward which research and theory construction efforts might best be directed.

East Lansing, Michigan   S. A. W.

August 1968

Acknowledgments

David Gottlieb was instrumental in my undertaking this project, but Denton Morrison's encouragement and criticism spurred it to completion.

Although the ultimate responsibility for the quality of this work rests with me, I am indebted to Wilbur Brookover, William Faunce, and Eugene Jacobson whose support and suggestions were invaluable to the final product. I am also grateful to Lucy Rau Ferguson for her careful reading and thoughtful criticism of Chapter 3.

This investigation was supported in part by a Public Health Service Fellowship #5 F1 MH–24, 016–02 (BEH) from the National Institute of Mental Health.

Contents

The Leftouts

**Disadvantaged
Children
in Heterogeneous
Schools**

1

The Leftouts:
Who, What,
Where, When,
Why, and How?

The United States philosophically is devoid of class bias and traditionally
has been seen as having a uniquely open and fluid society. It also has been
argued that in this century, notable for its rapid technological expansion,
the social structure has exhibited a tendency toward becoming more rigid.
This rigidity is based partly on such factors as regional and occupational
categories, but most particularly on educational categories. The contemporary social scene is being influenced by an emphasis on ideological
liberalism and by the increasingly large role that government agencies at
several levels are playing in educational concerns. "Equality of opportunity for all" is evolving from a philosophical tenet into a concrete goal,
and active efforts, supported in part by governmental financing, are being
made to reduce educational barriers to social mobility. Many social scientists, including this author, feel that the possibility of upward social
mobility in the contemporary United States rests primarily within the
educational system—and specifically within the public school system.

In the United States, philosophical and educational traditions affirm
the public school's task of unifying a diverse society without creating
uniformity among its citizens. Whatever problems may be associated with
such a complex demand and whatever the results of its efforts, the public
school is most certainly a highly significant agency of socialization. With
an ideological command to provide "education for all" and with the task

1

of socializing children of broadly divergent backgrounds, the public school system has done a highly admirable job. Historically, through repeated influxes of immigrants, the school system in the United States has done a commendable job of assimilating and acculturating children from many dissimilar cultural backgrounds, while allowing for the preservation of distinctive cultural heritages. Today the problems faced by the public schools are somewhat different. The "culturally disadvantaged" child of our era is apt to be a native-born citizen, with at least nominal English as his native tongue, and without a deeply rooted cultural heritage. The threat of what has been called the "tyranny of conformism" hangs as the sword of Damocles over the social theorist who would argue that the problem can no longer be focused on maintaining cultural diversity, but must focus on raising *all* citizens to a minimum level of literacy, competence, and even common value orientations—conformity if you must.

The culturally disadvantaged child of today usually comes from the lower socioeconomic strata. However, large numbers of children from low socioeconomic backgrounds are able to adjust to school and classmates without giving evidence of being essentially different from other children. A full understanding of what is involved in the culturally disadvantaged child's adjustment, or lack of adjustment, in the public school system requires an acquaintance with some theory and research seemingly far removed from the central problem.

PURPOSE AND APPROACH

This book represents an attempt to tie together these diverse endeavors and to elict from them, as parsimoniously as possible, a set of explanatory principles that may lead to further research. It is fortunate that the literature related to this subject is extensive, and unfortunate that it is so widely scattered and so lacking in theoretical perspective. The literature in this area of interest tends to be fraught with an abundance of mystical pronouncements and seemingly unrelated findings. The attempt here will be to review critically some of the major works extant, to synthesize a number of findings that relate to the problem, and to develop clear analytical statements in a consistent way, which will aid in understanding who the Leftout is, where, when, and why he got to be that way, and how compensatory measures may foster his successful adjustment to school. A framework that is at least potentially capable of dispelling some of the ambiguities surrounding the causes and consequences of children's "cultural disadvantage" as this term is understood in the mid-twentieth century, will be offered.

The fact that the journalistic dictum serves as the title of this introductory chapter does not imply a journalistic approach. In the pages to come we will explore, in a scientific frame of reference, these questions—who, what, where, when, why, and how—as they relate to the Leftouts. The general area of concern is that of the impact of the social system on personality—as it develops and as it must change to cope with the demands of the interpersonal environment.

Of special interest is the impact of the social subsystem of the public school on those children who have variously been termed "deprived," "disadvantaged," "without," and so forth. Even more specifically our attention will be focused on the "Leftout." ⟨A Leftout is defined as an organically normal, socioculturally disadvanted elementary-school child who attends a heterogeneous school, a school in which the majority of his age-mates are significantly better prepared than he is to meet the academic and social demands of the school situation.

The approach of this book is social-psychological; that is, it is assumed that the majority of what any individual thinks and feels, and a great deal of how he acts and reacts, is the direct result of his interaction with other people. The fundamental theoretical assumption is that the most basic characteristic of human life is its *social* quality. Because human beings are inherently social—because they continuously live, work, and play together—they come to share an understanding of the meaning of a tremendous array of sounds, symbols, postural cues, and overt actions in their interpersonal environment. The individual's interpretations of the meanings for himself of each of these things is the basis upon which he chooses his own actions and decides what he thinks and feels about himself, his situation, and other people.

It is assumed, further, that the major sociological concepts relating the social system to personality are those of socialization, social roles, cultural value systems, and reference groups. Each of these concepts will be considered in some depth in succeeding chapters; here the purpose is to lay the theoretical foundation on which later discussions will be erected. The social psychologist's definition of personality is based on the idea that the personality is a social product, the result of social learning acquired during the socialization process. This process is one of learning and internalizing beliefs, values, attitudes, world views, and a conception of self from those with whom the "neophyte" interacts. Note the use of the term "neophyte." Much of the psychoanalytically-oriented thinking about socialization centers on the neo*nate*,[1] but for the social psychologist, socialization is an ongoing process that is not complete at puberty, adulthood, or any other point in time, but continues with new experiences. Thus, the social psychologist may speak of socialization in as widely divergent contexts as toilet training an infant or the kind of role learning

---

[1]*Neophyte* refers to someone new to a particular situation, a newcomer to the group. *Neonate* refers to the newborn, the unsocialized child.

required of a man who is today "a banker" and tomorrow "a retiree." Social psychologists do not imply that early experiences are unimportant, but only that later ones are important too.

The social-psychological view of socialization has been heavily influenced by George Herbert Mead's thinking about the development of the "social self" (Mead, 1934) and symbolic interactionism, the "interpersonal" approach of Harry Stack Sullivan (1953), other neo-Freudian thinking, and learning theory. Mead emphasizes the reciprocal nature of human interaction on the basis of shared symbolic meanings and learned mutual expectations. Sullivan stresses the importance of interpersonal interaction for personality development during the process of socialization. Some of Piaget's work on the development of intelligence (more thoroughly treated in Chapter 3), especially the importance of a stimulating environment, has also had a fairly direct influence on contemporary social-psychological thinking about socialization. Parson's (1951) discussions of "anxiety," and Merton's (1957) discussions of "alienation," follow fairly closely Karen Horney's (1945) conceptions of "basic anxiety," that is, a generalized fear of separateness and aloneness. The interpersonal-social-learning approach to socialization and personality development is exemplified in the more current work of Bandura and Walters (1963)—a work that will be cited several times in the ensuing discussion. This position might be described as a wedding of the elements of classic learning theory (stimulus, response, reinforcement) with notions of the specific importance of *people, social* rewards, and how the individual perceives and interprets the actions of those with whom he interacts.

Those elements of Freudian psychoanalytic theory that have been retained in the contemporary social-psychologically-oriented view of socialization are: (1) a generalized conception of an internally organized personality structure of interrelated parts, which have some bearing at least on overt behavior; (2) the importance of early experience; and (3) identification as the facilitating mechanism by which socialization attempts can successfully influence the internalized personality development. Social psychologists have added to these ideas: (1) the importance of later experiences; (2) the tremendous influence of other people, the situation, and social expectations; (3) the ideas of social learning through identification with role models and reference groups; and (4) the great importance of communication in general (broadly defined) and language acquisition in particular.

It would seem that the social-psychological approach to the concept and content of socialization improves upon the psychoanalytic view because: it is more nearly demonstrable by research; it relies less heavily on introspective reports; it accounts for both individual differences and individual similarities without postulating some biologically inherited social past; and, most importantly, it moves the whole area of interest into the realm of the conscious and observable and does not rely on untenable and untestable propositions about unconscious motivations and unobservable defenses. Social psychologists have also contributed the conception of man as an *inherently* social animal and rejected the notion that "civilization" is merely a thin veneer painted over what is basically a Darwinian brute.

We take as axiomatic that the values, beliefs, and attitudes, that are learned during the socialization process are, in large part, consensually shared by the already existing group of which the neophyte is a member. To some extent then, his value orientation and behavior will be like that of *all* other men (to paraphrase Kardiner, 1939). However, the group with whom any individual interacts in his lifetime is, necessarily, a subsegment, not only of the total human species, but also of those who comprise any particular society. Thus, the value orientations and behavioral proscriptions and prescriptions to which he is exposed may differ from those prevalent in some other subsegment or those "modal" to the total system. Therefore, any individual's value orientations and behavior are, to some extent, like those of only *some* other men. And, of course, some specific experiences, and surely the combinations of particular experiences, will be idiosyncratic for any given individual. Thus, to some extent, his value-orientations and behaviors will be like those of *no* other man.

Within any social system or subsystem, each individual occupies one or more positions, or roles, which are accompanied by normative expectations of how a person in that position should think, feel, and behave. One of the major products of the socialization process is that of knowledge of role expectations. Since any social system is comprised of identifiable and interrelated positions, it is possible to talk of social "structure." From the viewpoint of the social system, roles are differentiated and role expectations are developed in keeping with what is regularly required for the maintenance of the structure *qua* structure. In much the same way, an individual may be said to possess a personality system and a cognitive structure. From the viewpoint of the individual, roles are delineated and expectations accompanying them are internalized and "fitted into" the developing personality in a way which will help maintain that structure *qua* structure. We might also speak analytically of a cultural structure—a structure of interrelated normative regulations for beliefs, behavior, perception, and so on, which must also seek to maintain itself as a structural whole and preserve a patterned way of life. However, the individual is not wholly a product of the social or cultural structure of which he is a member. Primarily, the influence that the social or cultural system may have on the developing individual is most directly felt only at the point at which the needs of the social structure, the cultural structure, and the personality meet. Not all behavior is included in this area—for a variety of reasons.

Consider, for example, the degree of differentiation that can occur among social and cultural systems. In large, complex, highly differentiated social and cultural systems and subsystems, the range of roles is wide, and so too is the range of socialization practices. Thus, in anything as broad as a "social class" for instance, one would expect a wide range of possible personality orientations. A second kind of consideration is the degree of integration among the components of a system or subsystem. In a highly integrated system, in which the roles are extensively inter-related, influence on the developing personality should be greater than in a situation in which various roles are less well integrated and, thus, no *one* set of role expectations and obligations taken alone has the power to influence the system as would an integrated role complex. For example, consider the differential influence that a teacher in the subsystem of a public school might have among children who, on one hand come from families whose values and behavioral expectations coalesce with those of the school and, on the other hand, who come from families whose value orientations are antithetical to those of the school.

A third limitation to the influence of the social and cultural systems on personality is that of the degree of structuring per se, that is the number of normative rules setting behavioral limits that may be present in any system of roles. Some subsystems and roles may be accompanied by more of such normative regulation than others. Thus, some may have a more clearly definable influence on developing personality than those which permit a wider range of behavior and interpretation. Consider, for example, the role of "child" as opposed to that of "student." Each permits a fairly broad interpretation, but the role of student is accompanied by basic expectations concerning diligence, motivation, promptness, respect for teachers, and so on, which are not included in the more loosely structured role of child.

We can conclude that the effectiveness of the social and cultural systems on the development or the changing of personality systems always is modified by the degree to which these can influence the socialization process and maintain control in the face of many experiences and situations. Reference groups, which are selected by the individual, have a mitigating influence on the development of personality. That is, those people in the interpersonal environment to whom the individual elects to attend may support and strengthen the general social and cultural structures, or they may undermine and weaken their effects by devaluing those things that are valued in the larger system. It is with these basic theoretical considerations that we approach the more specific problem at hand.

During the last two decades, and particularly at present, there has been a burgeoning interest in the relationship between sociocultural disadvantage and school achievement, motivation, and general social and emotional adjustment among children. Adjustment is defined for our purposes as continual adaptive learning in the face of new experiences. A great deal of the literature in this area deals with more or less geographically isolated "poverty pockets," for example, urban slum areas and isolated rural areas, in which the vast majority of the children in a given school system may be designated as disadvantaged. Little attention has been directly focused on the even more common phenomenon of the disadvantaged minority who must attend school with age-mates who are prepared. Rapidly increasing moves toward consolidation of rural schools and integration of racially or residentially segregated urban schools tend to expand this kind of situation even further. Therefore, special attention will be directed toward the socioculturally disadvantaged child who, *in comparison with his more advantaged classmates,* is disadvantaged.

Concern will be centered on those youngsters whose background suffers by comparison to their classmates in terms of adequate prior training and experience to prepare them for the demands of the school system; that is, on those children whose subcultural socialization patterns have been inadequate to equip them to reach successfully goals typical of the expectations of their teachers and their more advantaged age-mates.

The contemporary American public school system is the "given" in this discussion. Obviously, individual schools differ from each other in many ways, for example, teacher or classmate attitudes and behavior toward children of socioeconomic, ethnic, racial, or religious minority groups may be negative, positive, or neutral; a specific teacher's methods and personality may aid or hinder the disadvantaged child's adjustment; and the particular social "climate" in any given school may foster academic achievement or may impede it. Nevertheless, all public schools in our society exhibit basic similarities in that: (1) the students are separated by age groups and into roughly equivalent grades or achievement groups; (2) a variety of detailed cumulative records are kept concerning each child's academic rating, his scores on standardized intelligence and achievement tests, his social adjustment to his classmates, and his general physical and emotional health—all of which serve as the basis for evaluation of his level of success and determine with which group he shall be placed; (3) the basic orientation of the instruction and testing is intellectualism, with a strong verbal focus; and (4) the primary content of the instruction centers on the development of uniform academic skills such as reading, writing, arithmetic, and on acquisition of knowledge of the white, Anglo-Saxon Protestant historical heritage and the contemporary core-cultural values of this group. These similarities are what we refer to when discussing *the* school system. Thus, while there will be occasion to discuss the specific adjustive and maladjustive factors in *a* school system, we typically refer to the Leftout as disadvantaged in relation to the goals and practices of this generalized school system.

It has been widely suggested that fundamental changes are required in this generalized system if it is to cope adequately with educating the socioculturally disadvantaged child. Indeed, this may well be the case. However, it does not seem feasible to attempt to effect changes until those variables which are maladjustive in this system have been identified. In order to identify the maladjustive variables in the system, an analysis of the causes and consequences of the Leftout's disadvantage must be available.

Schools that serve heterogeneous (or worse, dichotomous) student bodies often enhance the discrepancies in background—to the increased detriment of the child who is lacking. Class work in such schools is geared, necessarily, to the child who has had at least an average preparation for school, and who, from teachers and the family, receives, as a matter of routine, encouragement and support toward academic and social success. In this kind of setting, a child who is ill prepared or poorly motivated, or both, may indeed be left out. It should be noted that there is no intended implication that heterogeneous or integrated schools are inherently inferior to more homogeneous ones, although it is postulated that the range and scope of both social adjustment problems and achievement potential in heterogeneous schools may prove greater. In such schools, problems require careful attention, and tendered solutions demand skillful planning.

For the disadvantaged child, the discrepancy between his own position and that of the majority of his classmates may create severe conflicts and frustrations. While discussion will focus on those children who are most severely disadvantaged, it will not exclude those whose disadvantage is less extreme or those who might even be classified as "advantaged" if they were compared to some other group than the one in which they are interacting. What is suggested is that sociocultural disadvantage ranges along a continuum, and this is the reason for insistence on a definition of "disadvantage" specifically in comparison with those children with whom the Leftouts are actually in contact in a heterogeneous school system. It is possible, of course, when speaking of comparative disadvantage to take into account the larger society with whom the child will one day interact; so that the slum child in a homogeneous social setting where he is not disadvantaged in comparison to his classmates could be seen from the perspective of his eventual contact with those whose ability, motivation, knowledge, and experience are substantially greater than his own. However, we will focus our attention on those children who are in daily contact with their more advantaged age-mates.

The primary objectives in future chapters are to examine how the Leftout differs from his age-mates and to analytically connect the variables of how and why the Leftouts get to be that way in their particular school situation. It is clear from the definition of the Leftout as socioculturally disadvantaged in comparison to his classmates, that part of his potential adjustment problem in the school situation must center on this cultural alienation from the expectations of the majority group or on his economic disadvantage, or both.

The term "culturally deprived child," which has been prevalent in the literature until recently, is coming to be supplanted by "socioculturally disadvantaged child" and related variants. In any attempt to define this cultural disadvantage or alienation from the cultural expectations of the majority group, it is necessary to consider the concept of "culture." Several considerations help to clarify the concept. In the first place, culture—as social scientists employ the term—is a universal attribute of all social groupings, and variations among cultures cannot properly be interpreted as differences in amount or in value, but only as differences in *kind*. Thus, no individual is "deprived" of a culture, and cultural disadvantage or alienation must be considered in relation to some other kind of culture than his own. In this case, culture refers to the established pattern of norms and values of some group. Those who are "culturally alienated" are alien to (foreign, outside of) the mainstream of the "core" culture of the majority group in any society and, by definition, are minority group members (sometimes in the more accepted use of that term too, but not always).

Although all groups in our society share to some extent in the prevailing "middle-class core culture," there are many different patterns of culture, reflecting more or less distinct ways of life among particular nationality, religious, ethnic, social-class, geographical, and other subgroups within the population. These may be characterized as "subcultures." Ethnic, racial, and other criteria for distinguishing subgroups often do play a part in sociocultural disadvantage, but "minority group status" in the usual sense is unsatisfactory alone for use as a criterion of those who are Leftouts.

These subcultures vary in the extent to which their socializing influences, that is, intrafamily relationships, child-rearing practices, language patterns, intellectual pursuits, behavioral norms, values, outlooks, and so forth, equip children to adjust successfully to the middle-class core-cultural patterns that prevail as the ideal in the larger society and that are taught in the schools. Thus, children who are socialized in subcultures markedly different from the prevailing standard may or may not find themselves disadvantaged in the schools, where core-cultural values and behavioral patterns are commonly required for successful academic and social adjustment.

The term culture also has a second common meaning. In this sense, culture may relate to experience with and appreciation of art, music, drama, and other such cultural accouterments. The common denominator of those children whose socializing influences have been largely alien to the demands of middle-class norms of cultural appreciation is relative poverty and social discrimination. The children involved live mainly in urban and rural slums, in substandard housing, with poorly educated parents, and with little opportunity to develop an interest in things cultural. Thus, in this sense, those who are culturally alienated are also alien to the trappings of society, which, given limited economic facilities, are foregone as unattainable or unknown luxuries. From this perspective, and at a very common sense level, cultural alienation is linked to economic disadvantage.

Economic disadvantage is not nearly as sticky a problem as cultural alienation as defined in the first instance, for economic disadvantage can be measured largely in terms of dollars and cents. The only real trick here is to avoid any kind of rigid classification into specific states of deprivation. Again, each empirical instance must be measured in comparative terms, that is, in direct comparison to those with whom the individual interacts. For example, the federal government's definition of poverty relates to an annual income of approximately $3,000. While such an income may be adequate to avail a child of the cultural opportunities offered in Hazard, Kentucky, or Bay Mills, Michigan, it is hardly adequate for minimum subsistence in Los Angeles or New York City. The kind and depth of compensatory programs offered by the schools to economically disadvantaged children must take into consideration the range and availability of cultural activities offered outside the classroom.

It should be emphasized that the concept of sociocultural disadvantage is *not* used here as a stereotype for all children nurtured in subcultures of poverty and ethnic discrimination. Although large numbers of such children find it difficult to cope with typical school tasks, this is by no means universally the case. Such children exhibit a wide range of individual differences, and part of our concern will be to suggest answers to the question of why some of these children adjust successfully to typical school demands and why some do not. The following chapters seek to explore the bases of sociocultural disadvantage among school children and draw implications concerning the impact of various kinds of deprivation on the developmental and adjustive process in heterogeneous schools. We will examine deprivation in the areas of achievement motivation, general knowledge, specific experience and training in language, and such disadvantage as may be inherent in the social situation in which the Leftout finds himself. The primary purpose of this study is to undertake a systematic synthesis of research findings and theories relating to the academic and social adjustment of the socioculturally disadvantaged child in the heterogeneous school situation.

Discussion will center on the particular age group found at the elementary-school level. We will limit our concern in this way for two reasons. The first of these is based on a belief in the hoary proposition that "an ounce of prevention is worth a pound of cure." The second is based on a belief that the influence of family and other adults, directed at molding behavior to accepted social standards, is greatest in the child's early years.

As we will see, research indicates that problems intensify and multiply with increasing age. Research findings also suggest that feelings of isolation and social rejection arise from everyday experiences, which indicate to the child that he is, indeed, alone and left out. If the child holds his teachers and classmates in the position of a reference group (and many elementary-age children do), then failure to establish successful interaction with teachers and classmates may have crushing repercussions on the child's social and emotional adjustment to the heterogeneous school situation. By the time the child reaches adolescence, after several years of frustration and unhappy experiences, it is quite possible that the Leftout may *not* perceive his teachers and more advantaged age-mates as a reference group.

It is evident both theoretically and by only superficial observation that Leftouts may form their own subculture within the school and look to each other as a reference group. That this happens particularly in the adolescent period is beyond question. Thus, our concern will be specifically with preadolescent children among whom clique boundaries have not been as rigidly drawn and from whom it is both possible for the Leftout to gain acceptance (given the proper compensatory experience and training in social and academic skills) by the majority group and probable that he wishes to do so.

By junior high school, and certainly by high school, programs aimed at academically and socially integrating the Leftout are extremely difficult to devise, if not doomed to failure. They are doomed, not because his personality is permanently formed and not amendable to change, but because the Leftout has by this time so radically altered his initial goals, self-concept, and reference group identification that only with extreme difficulty, great patience, and many rewarding experiences can he possibly be induced to revive the goals and interests with which he has entered the social subsystem of the heterogeneous school. Our interest, then, lies in trying to understand and perhaps to suggest ways of "short circuiting" the connection between sociocultural disadvantage and academic and social maladjustment among elementary-school children.

WHAT

The "what" of our interest is the dual concern with social and psychological perspectives and how they are inter-related in the comparatively disadvantaged child's personality development, academic achievement, and social growth within the social subsystem of the heterogeneous school. Burton (1953) claims that two challenges have been issued to American education: "to develop a minimum literacy and simple fundamentals of citizenship" and "to develop cultural unity within a diverse society simultaneously with full development of individual talent." Throughout our society, public school programs and curricula as they now exist appear to accomplish both of these goals relatively well for a large proportion of American school children. It has been argued that approximately one half of the children who enter the public school system successfully adjust to the current program and social climate and emerge as responsible, well-trained young adults (Bloom, Davis, and Hess, 1965). By the same token, of course, approximately one half of the children who enter school experience at least some difficulty or failure in successfully adjusting to the social and academic demands of the public school. Obviously the reasons for adjustment problems are many and varied, and some of them lie outside our specific interest area. On the other hand, a large proportion of Leftouts will be numbered eventually among those who fail to successfully complete high school.

The successful completion of public school training through high school is ever more increasingly the determining criterion of status, economic opportunity, and successful entry into the responsibilities and privileges of adulthood in the larger society. In a nation such as ours, with a highly developed technological economy and a highly literate, socially conscious populace, the child who does not complete secondary school training is denied admission to an ever expanding sector of the occupational hierarchy and is increasingly more disadvantaged as a citizen. In the past, when there was sufficient opportunity in the economic system for unskilled workers with a minimum of education and when even such daily living requirements as driving an automobile, rearing children, voting on bonding and legislative issues, shopping for food and furniture, and the myriad of other tasks that face all modern families were less complex and demanding, the schools could operate on the principle of weeding out the less able and selecting the most capable for advanced education and specialized training. However, we are in the midst of a time of far-reaching basic social changes, which are affecting the entire society, and which will increasingly place pressures on all aspects of the educational system. Our rapidly developing, complex, urbanized, industrial society requires that every functioning member be literate, responsive to rapid changes in every aspect of life and work, and capable of learning and relearning relatively complex skills and ideas as minimal prerequisites for economic security, social responsibility, and mature independence. The public schools must bear the major burden of training children to be functioning members of such a society. The public schools, therefore, cannot be selective, but must be particularly concerned with the life and career potentials of those youngsters who are adversely affected by the present school program and social climate. The contemporary focus of the educational system must emphasize raising both the aspiration and the achievement levels of the group of children who have been ignored, rejected, or placed in a marginal position relative to their more advantaged classmates.

It is a happy commentary on our society to note that educational planning and concern is currently being directed toward precisely these kinds of goals. It is this author's feeling, however, that too little attention is being directed toward an analysis of where and when the disadvantaged child's troubles begin, why some children of apparently similar backgrounds and intelligence successfully adjust and achieve in school while others do not, and how compensatory programs may be designed to reduce the disadvantage of the Leftouts. It is hoped that this work raises some of the theoretical issues underlying the problem, explores their interrelationships, and arrives at a reasonably sound analysis of the "where," "when," "why," and "how."

Compulsory attendance laws bring into the school children who are poorly motivated, ill prepared, and who have little concern for the goals of the school. Our interest will be largely limited to the particular concern of the child as he relates to the social subsystem of the school. However, the consequences of membership in the specific subsystem of the school are partly determined by preschool and nonschool related influences, particularly those of the family and the child's socioeconomic subculture. Thus, it is necessary to consider the initial preparation, value orientations, and motivation to achieve that the school-age child has developed prior to and outside of school, and the amount of school-oriented support he may receive from other sources. While we may discuss analytically the problems perpetrated or perpetuated within the specific subsystem of the school, there is in fact no clearly defined point of separation between school influences and those of parents, peers, or general subcultural experiences. Therefore, nonschool issues must be raised.

The "what" here is threefold: (1) to arrive at a clearly delineated picture of the Leftout's social and academic problems, which entails discussion of what is meant by the lack of academic and social adjustment and a look at how the Leftouts differ from other children in apparently similar circumstances; (2) to garner from the extant research and theoretical literature those variables relevant to an analysis of how and why the Leftout gets to be that way; and finally, (3) to systematically present a frame of reference that will account for the Leftout's academic and social maladjustment, and from which suggestions related to both theoretical concerns and to practical problem-solving programs may be derived.

Extensive, albeit somewhat impressionistic, experience already underlies our concern with socioculturally disadvantaged children's adjustment—or lack of it—to the heterogeneous school situation. For some eighteen months this author had the privilege and responsibility of setting up and administrating Michigan State University's Student Education Corps.[2] Exercising this responsibility required meeting at length with school administrators and teachers in some thirty heterogeneous schools in Michigan. Each of these schools is intimately concerned with how best to approach educating socioculturally disadvantaged children. In addition, this author's experience included personal observations of "problem" classrooms, as well as contact with a minimum of 400 university student volunteers who were working directly with disadvantaged children. This author also had the privilege of participating in two intensive conference sessions, which afforded contact with people from all over the nation who are concerned with variants of this problem. These experiences have pointed up the very real need for the type of analysis undertaken here.

WHERE AND WHEN

As for the "where" and "when" of the problem, one of the sources of difference in school adjustment among children is that of the differential backgrounds they have as a result of membership in various socioeconomic strata. As a broad generalization, to be extensively qualified in Chapter 2, upper- and middle-class children adjust well to school, while lower-class children in varying degrees tend toward maladjustment and failure. Part of the "where," then, is located in the subculture in which the child is reared, and part of the "when" of the development of disadvantage occurs prior to entry into the school. In our analysis the antecedents of particular kinds of value orientations, social behaviors, and communication skills among school-age youngsters will be examined. One obvious source of such antecedents is the child's socioeconomic background—and

[2]For a discussion of the program, see Warden (1964).

Chapter 2 is partially devoted to exploring the truth of that proposition.

Already mentioned is a basic theoretical proposition that underlies this exploration—that value orientations, behavioral expectations, and symbolic systems are learned in social interaction. Another basic proposition, as specified in Homans' (1961) theoretical formulation, is that the more rewarding men find the results of an action, the more likely they are to take this action. Translated into the specific interests of this study, these two propositions suggest that if there is acceptance of the teacher as a "significant other" by the child, contingent on the teacher's acceptance of him, and if he finds the learning situation a rewarding one, then he learns. If he does not accept the teacher's values and goals, and if the learning situation is not rewarding, then he does not learn. Thus, we must examine what factors influence mutual acceptance between teacher and student, and how school situations, values, goals, and so forth, come to be perceived as rewarding by some students but not by others.

In keeping with what has been said about the general relationship between the social system and personality development, it is expected that there are individual differences in susceptibility to social influence. However, we must assume that it is possible to predict that certain rewards will be effective in the learning process for most members of a particular group, since the group members will share many common experiences. It is especially useful to know something of the subcultural, age, and sex differences among children in considering continuities in personality. Bandura and Walters (1963) note that since children from diverse backgrounds experience different reinforcement contingencies and are exposed to widely differing social models, there are marked group differences at any age level. There is often marked interindividual variability due to biological, socioeconomic, ethnic, and cultural differences and to variations in the child-rearing practices of families. These factors are likely to remain relatively constant throughout much of the child's earlier life, and one would expect a considerable degree of intraindividual continuity in value orientations and behavior at successive age periods, even if these change in the face of new demands from other socializing agents. Thus, social-learning approaches to personality development lay stress on interindividual differences and on intraindividual continuities. The subject of Chapter 2 will be an exploration of what is known of the influence of social class and subcultural differences on value orientations, on perceptions of the reward value of school, and on social acceptance among children.

This kind of approach to social learning relates to external stimuli in the form of behavioral examples and patterns of reinforcement for guiding and modifying the responses of the child. However, internalized sanctions (conscience formation), the child's self-conception, his generalized conceptual schema, and other intraindividual factors play important roles in guiding and modifying his responses. This internalized discriminative activity is also socially developed, largely within the influence sphere of his primary family group through fear of significant others' disapproval. Thus, the role of the family as an agent of social influence and as a prerequisite model to the development of internalized discriminative activity must be considered. In Chapter 3 the role of the family in the maladjustive development of socioculturally disadvantaged children will be explored.

WHY AND HOW

The task of defining disadvantage in comparative terms demands an explication of the general process of normal, that is, typical of or acceptable to the larger social system, sociocultural growth. Maladjustive behavior patterns and value orientations cannot be defined or evaluated independently of some description of a well-adjusted developmental pattern. Thus, theory and research aimed at general child development and personality development within the family becomes not only relevant, but crucial. We do not assume that we can cope with the obviously impossible task of explaining the behavior of every individual child. This study does hope to develop an analytical framework which will explain why large numbers of individuals placed in similar circumstances, having similar backgrounds, facing similar demands, and sharing similar social experiences are apt to behave in similar ways—and why the consequences of this behavior are likely to be similar. What constitutes "similarity" will also be explored. Some children of apparently similar subcultural backgrounds adjust successfully to school, while others do not. This indicates that subcultural criteria of similarity may be too broad for very accurate or reliable predictions and explanations of sociocultural disadvantage. Thus, Chapter 3 will examine the variability among children, which has its antecedents specifically in the family and in such individual developmental factors as language acquisition and the choice of role models.

In discussing the social-psychological development of the organically normal school-age child who is the primary focus of interest, it is important to note that at this age the child regularly spends seven to ten hours daily outside the home, away from his parents' direct influence, and is therefore, subject to influences from many sources. Note that of the fourteen to seventeen hours the child *does* spend at home, a minimum of eight of these are given over to sleep, so hours of outside influence equal if not surpass hours of parental control. The value orientations, behavioral expectations, and self-concept developed in the family setting may or may not be reinforced by these other influences and, of course, the child may or may not hold these others in the position of a reference group, depending on whether or not he perceives that it is rewarding to do so. One possible source of nonfamily influence is that of teachers and other adults, who largely fulfill the role of parental surrogates. However, many of the skills and values acquired during the socialization process are learned in peer groups, which freely supply a variety of rewards for appropriate, approved, social behavior. The child has little or no incentive to deviate from the expectations of his peers, whose approval may be more rewarding to him than that of his parents or other adults, unless he cannot fulfill their expectations and is rejected by them. A child's social acceptability by his peers is an extremely important influence in directing and modifying his value orientations and his behavior. The nature of his reception by his classmates in school will undoubtedly influence his general attitudes and behavior. Similarly, the child's self-concept—already partly determined by experiences prior to and outside of school, as well as by the teacher's attitudes and his level of academic success—will be further modified by his perception of social acceptability among his peers. The nature of this self-concept, in turn, will have consequences for the child's total adjustment to school. In Chapter 4 we will explore something of the character and consequences of peer group influences and will examine the idea of self-concept and how it relates to maladjustment in school. This study will take the theoretical position that self-acceptance and social acceptance are positively related, and that an adequate self-concept is a necessary prerequisite to successful adjustment in school.

The examination of socioculturally disadvantaged children's adjustment to heterogeneous schools suggests the necessity of a threefold criterion of "adjustment to school." One dimension is relatively clearly defined in terms of academic performance, as measured by standardized tests, grade point averages, and so forth. A second dimension of adjustment, not as easily defined, relates to social acceptance. This dimension is most often measured in terms of affective social relationships, sociometric rankings, accessibility of participation in valued activities, and so on. These two elements of adjustment, the cognitive and the social, might be termed "outer-directed" and discussed in terms of relationships with objects and people. A third dimension of adjustment, emotional adjustment, deals with the "inner-directed" element of self-concept as held by the Leftout. Measurement of this dimension is typically done in terms of standard personality tests and clinical reports.

A somewhat eclectic approach to the development of this analysis seems indicated, since no single extant theory or research effort takes into consideration all, or even the majority, of the many areas of maladjustment and disadvantage, as it has been defined here, that are prevalent among the Leftouts. The basic theoretical framework that has been employed is the general social-psychological one already discussed. The specific analysis, developed within the broad context, will synthesize formulations derived from many sources.

It is perhaps necessary at this point to draw a distinction between the analysis and the theoretical frame of reference. The latter refers in this case to the generalized social-psychological perspective, that is, the particular approach to the problem at hand, which serves to suggest the kinds of variables that should be considered as relevant. On the other hand, the analysis consists of a series of statements relating what is known or suspected about the explicitly posed issue at this particular point in time. The issue is represented by the Leftout, a particular kind of student in a particular type of school. What we ask of the analysis is that it offer tentative suggestions concerning the causes of the Leftout's disadvantage, the consequences of his disadvantage, and what variables seem to offer the greatest potential as a means to overcoming his disadvantage.

In this case the frame of reference is extremely important. The particular selection of means for approaching the problem directs the selection of observations that will be utilized in the initial steps of the development of the analysis. The frame of reference represents a conscious effort to orient the direction of problem exploration in a meaningful way. For this reason time has been taken to explicate the theoretical frame of reference both at the beginning of this chapter and elsewhere as indicated in the body of the work.

The term "analysis" refers to a set of inter-related propositions, containing explicit definitions, and offering a tentative explanation of the empirical phenomena examined; that is, the Leftout's potential maladjustment in the heterogeneous school situation. The analysis is developed inductively from the findings of prior empirical investigations that are assumed to relate logically to the potential theory on the basis of the generalized theoretical perspective. The crucial role expected of the analysis is that of clarifying the nature and extensity of the problem under study. For example, the analysis argues that the academic, social, and emotional adjustment of an elementary-school child are all equally important in determining his total adjustment potential in school. Furthermore, these three dimensions of adjustment are rather directly inter-related. The suggestions derived from this analysis indicate the most obvious theoretical causes, consequences, and potential "cures" for the Leftout's particular adjustment problems. At the same time, the general analytical framework should prove capable of extending an understanding of the success or failure of any child's adjustment to any school situation.

It is clear that the analysis may be put to a test by further deducing research hypotheses, conditional statements, which specify the conditions that are to be taken as lack of confirmation, testable in the empirical world, and that are subsequently accepted or rejected on the basis of empirical data. This step has not been taken for two major reasons. The first of these centers on a concern with examining the very broad range of research felt to be relevant to the Leftout's problems. Such a bringing together of diverse materials and integration into a coherent whole is a major undertaking in itself. Secondly, the very scope of the derived suggestions virtually precludes any empirical test by a single researcher, or the development of any single "critical hypothesis" upon which the whole analysis might rest. In one sense, the empirical evidence has already been collected—for this is, after all, the basis for the development of the analytical framework. What remains to be tested of course, is the particular analytical *combination* of suggestions offered. It is hoped that the synthesis will generate a great deal of empirical research.

Both this author's experience and a critical exploration of current theoretical and research literature, strongly suggest that one crucial variable, which is both antecedent to and a consequence of sociocultural disadvantage in general, and the Leftout's maladjustment to the social subsystem of the heterogeneous school in particular, is lack of communication skills. Comparative ineptness in communication skills required in the school and by the larger society is seen as a consequence of inadequate language acquisition based on stimulus deprivation, that is, an environment that affords comparatively little opportunity for constructive stimulation. Comparative lack of language skill is also seen to be directly related to conceptual ability, measured intelligence, and difficulties in learning formally taught academic skills and more informally taught social skills. Thus, Chapter 5 will briefly examine the theoretical and empirical contributions of the work of Martin Deutsch and others who have directed their special attention to the consequences of stimulus deprivation.

The analysis also indicates a number of other variables of crucial importance in any effort to understand and explain the Leftout. Therefore, Chapter 5 will be concerned with a final pulling together, from various theoretical and empirical works, of those ideas that relate to the Leftout's deprivation in the areas of: (1) general knowledge of the core-cultural expectations; (2) achievement motivation and functional anxiety; (3) experience and training in social skills; (4) general ability to adjust; and, (5) self-concept. We will consider Wilbur Brookover's theoretical and empirical work, as it relates to the antecedents and consequences of a low self-concept of ability. The analysis will deal with the three levels of concern, which are analogous to the three dimensions of adjustment—academic, social, and emotional—and with how each of these intrapersonal areas are influenced by the social and value structures of the school as a subsystem of teachers and peers. The "what" of this work, then, is a systematic look at what is known about Leftouts, and the organization and synthesis of this knowledge into a coherent whole, presented in Chapter 5. The analysis deals with the "where," "when," and "why" the Leftout gets to be that way. It also concerns itself with the consequences of such deprivation for the disadvantaged child in a heterogeneous school.

In the chapters to come a number of contemporary research efforts serve as the basis for the analysis. This study has been concerned primarily with empirical research reports, which are relevant to the over-all problem area or some specific aspect of it, and which hold implications for both theory and practice. A complete summary of all the research relating to sociocultural deprivation and its impact on children or on the educational system is not offered. The research that seems to bear most directly on the development of an analytical framework has been selected for presentation in these chapters. The "truth" of the analysis can come only from extensive and intensive testing of the many interrelated propositions it presents. The analysis can serve as a framework within which many otherwise nontheoretical studies can be subsumed, and as a beginning point for directing future studies at many levels.

Chapter 5 will present the suggested directions for future research, which are typical of and almost obligatory in an analysis such as this. However, the purpose of making such suggestions has something more than the usual fervor behind it, because the need for directed, controlled research in this problem area is urgent and critical. The current pressure of public concern and the availability of research funds for work in this area (including great quantities of government money) have contributed to a proliferation of programs, many of which have something less than a fully adequate analytical and methodological basis. The issue of the socioculturally disadvantaged child's maladjustment to the heterogeneous school situation is pressing. Common humanity demands that quick solutions be found for what are highly complex problems. It is hoped that one significant contribution of this analysis will be toward the understanding of the Leftout, and that with understanding will come constructive ideas for corrective measures.

2

The Role
of "Social Class"
in Differential
School Adjustment

In one sense, the Leftouts represent a "class" of disadvantaged children. The Leftout is defined in comparative terms. That is, in comparison to others with whom the Leftout must interact in the school system—and, eventually, the larger social system—he falls at the bottom of any scale of those who have the ability, motivation, knowledge, social training, and financial resources to approximate the ideal behavioral values of his particular group. Note the phrase "approximate the ideal." It suggests that *no* group of human beings live up to the ideals they espouse in full measure. However, every group does develop norms of behavior that specify more or less clearly the bounds of acceptable divergence—and it is these norms that the Leftout must learn and observe if he is to successfully adjust to the interactional demands made upon him in the social subsystem of the school in its present form.

In another sense, this discussion is *not* primarily concerned with social class in the usual meaning of the term. The term Leftout is *not* limited only to children whose ethnic identity, social-class status, or economic background falls into some standardized classification system. This discussion does not address itself to the problems of social class per se, but always as these, and other factors, relate to the development of social skills, acquisition of role-knowledge, development of value orientations and achievement motivation.

The concept of social class has played a large part in the history of social scientific concern with children's adjustment to the educational system in the United States. Unfortunately, this concept is probably one of the most misused and abhorred sociological clichés extant. It is, at one and the same time, abhorred because it implies the negation of a strong cultural ideal of equality for all men, and misused because it is often employed to stratify rigidly, and sometimes artificially, social groups. It is, at its best, an ambiguous concept virtually devoid of agreed-upon definable parameters and, at its worst, a rigid stereotype that does grave injustice to the individuals pigeonholed within class categories.

Despite these drawbacks, the notion of patterns of social stratification has been widely used—and not entirely uselessly. Properly employed, the concept of social class is an analytical tool for codifying data of individual and group differences. It is apparent to any interested observer of the world around him that ethnic, economic, educational, occupational, and subcultural value differences *do* exist among men. Furthermore, these differences may be recognized as crucial variables in understanding the dynamics of many social situations. Therefore, while social scientists may not agree on the precise meaning of social class, or on how it is best measured, there is general agreement in the literature that relatively clear, stable, definable subgroup differences do exist, and, moreover, that these differences account for at least some of the variation in human behavior insofar as they influence the socialization process. It is assumed that just as the attitudes, value orientations, beliefs, and behaviors of the individual members of the child's family may have an important influence on the socialization process, so too may the broader subcultural values typical of the particular socioeconomic stratum in which the child is reared. This assumption leads us to the necessity of a brief consideration of the relationship between individual variables and broader social-systemic variables.

Differences in individual acceptance of socialization attempts have been known and noted by man since primitive time. However, efforts to observe, compare, and contrast similarities and uniformities also have a long and distinguished history. The ancient Greeks differentiated among the structural characteristics and resultant member personalities of their several city-states by drawing comparisons between Athenians and Spartans. It is axiomatic then, that there are definable sets of system-wide beliefs, values, and behavioral norms and that these sets vary between subcultures. One of the fundamental attributes of any "social system" qua "system" is that it is normative. That these norms are essentially arbitrary and differ not only among systems, but also within the same system over a time is clear. Nevertheless, certain uniformities tend to persist, and for this reason the reciprocal and interdependent interaction of individuals who are members may properly be said to constitute a social system. One of the primary functions of a social system lies in providing the means and content of the socialization process through which neophytes become full-fledged members.

It is assumed that this process of socialization to system-wide beliefs, value orientations, and so on, begins in the family and is strengthened by secondary contacts. The concept of value orientation, as used here, refers to the generalized theme that is representative of the complex of an individual's beliefs concerning that which is to be valued and the means by which evaluations are to be made. It is a tacit or explicit theme that finds expression in each of the role and life-style choices an individual makes. This notion of social "choice" implies selection from among a perceived set of finite, concrete, and available alternatives. The social system influences individuals, to the extent that it places limits on available alternative choices, that it supports and strengthens early family experiences, and that it offers alternatives in such a way as to be perceived as choices by the individual. However, the role played by the social system in shaping and developing an individual's outlook may be overemphasized. Many factors can affect the acceptance of influence attempts during the socialization process. The intensity and extensity of the interaction of social-systemic and individual psychological variables is always delimited, to the extent that the social unit is able to: (1) influence the socialization of the individual while value orientations are developing; (2) maintain some degree of control against change, through a system of sanctions, once the individual has developed a value orientation; and (3) serve as the reference group for the individual and hence command his ego involvement in internalizing commonly shared values.

In much of the literature dealing with the interrelationships between social class and scholastic achievement, social class is treated as a determinant of behavior. It is here postulated that social class, as typically defined in this literature, does not constitute an integrated social system that can *specifically* define and delimit alternatives, control behavior, or serve as a reference group. At best the social stratum, of which the individual is a member, can only imperfectly function in this way and have only a generalized influence. Thus, individuals who are nominally members of the *same* social class may have different experiences.

Neal Gross (1953) has expounded some specific criticisms of using social class as a determining variable in educational research. He argues that social stratification phenomena are but one important factor useful as a predictor or explanatory variable in educational research. He warns that social class is inadequate as the single explanatory "cause" of educational problems and specifically urges guarding against confusing causation with statistical association. He notes the lack of agreement on the "proper" way of classifying the various social strata, for example, race, income, education, occupation, ecological area, prestige, and so forth (though it should be noted that many such factors covary), and emphasizes the importance of considering the conditions under which two factors are related. For example, if social class can be shown to be related to some educational phenomena under condition A there is no reason to assume that the relationship will hold under conditions B, C, and D. Gross also notes that techniques employed to determine social class are often highly questionable on methodological grounds. For example, the way in which the questions are asked is highly influential to responses, and, in addition, social class may have no generally recognized meaning among members of the subcultural group.

Gross is not alone in his criticisms of the use of the concept of social class. Other criticisms can be mentioned: tendencies toward overgeneralization, uncritical acceptance of research findings, confusing value propositions with validated research, and artificial forcing of evidence into prearranged class categories. Research of this kind is prey to all of the evils discussed—and probably more. This is why emphasis has been placed on *relative*, *general*, and *comparative* patterns, and the burden is on the reader to bear this in mind as he considers the influence of social class on the developmental and adjustive process.

HISTORICAL DEVELOPMENT OF INTEREST IN SOCIAL CLASS AND EDUCATION

At least four sociological classics have dealt with the relationship between social stratification and education in the United States. Major studies by the Lynds, Warner, Davis, and Hollingshead have been widely read and have had an impact on critical thinking about the American educational system. The Lynds (1929) in their extensive study of "Middletown" draw two major conclusions: all Middletown parents, regardless of social-class level, recognize the value of education for their children; and lower-class children are penalized within the school system, since they do not come to school with an experiential background that adequately equips them to deal with the verbal symbols, attitudes, and behavioral characteristics most valued by the dominant middle-class group. Warner's (1944) conclusions are similar: for all but the upper class in the community, the school may serve as the means to upward social mobility, by teaching those skills that are essential for both high status occupational preparation and the acquisition of those socially rewarded values and attitudes typical of the middle class; but the child with a lower socioeconomic background is penalized in the social system of the school, because he is not prepared to conform to the school's middle-class standards and expectations.

Davis, in the 1948 Inglis Lecture delivered at the Harvard Graduate School of Education, briefly summarizes Warner's data on middle-class and lower-class subcultures and urges that consideration be given to social-class influences on children's learning. He argues that the schools currently have a built-in bias in curriculum, teaching method , and intelligence tests based on linguistic aptitudes that favor the middle-class child—to the detriment of the lower-class child. Hollingshead (1949) also concludes that opportunities for attaining desired rewards vary positively with the child's position on the social-class "ladder." He proposes that the socialization process, typical of the working class, is not satisfactory preparation for the child's educational adjustment. He also argues that the middle-class adults in the school, teachers, supervisors, and so on, force their class values on the children in their care, and that they reject or ignore those children who do not or will not conform to these class values.

Davis (1948) emphasizes basic differences in socialization patterns as they are found in middle-class and lower-class subcultures. His work—and that of other thinkers in this period—has been the impetus for a great deal of research and the target of much criticism. On the positive side, in 1953 the *Harvard Educational Review* devoted an entire special issue to research related to the impact of social stratification on education. Loeb, writing in that issue, employs the concept of core culture to discuss the American class system and its implications for personal and social development. He characterizes the middle-class core culture as the official culture of the society. He notes that its major features are: (1) an emphasis on "success" in the form of upward social mobility, which often requires severing established affective ties; (2) an emphasis on "propriety" in the form of observance of both overt and covert normative guides to behavior; (3) an emphasis on the ownership of material goods, cleanliness, avoidance of overt aggression, particularly physical aggression, active participation in organizations, and so on; and (4) an emphasis on delayed gratification of needs and desires. These cultural values have elsewhere been caricatured as the "Boy Scout virtues"—and the reading of the Boy Scout "Laws" quite literally affords a clear insight into the core-cultural prescriptions that Loeb has suggested is the culture taught in American schools. For Loeb, the teacher serves as the mediator between the child, whatever his specific background, and this established core culture.

The basic ideas inherent in the concept of social class are that, first, people who share a common position in the economy are apt to be in prolonged interactional relationships, which foster the development of characteristic subcultural norms. These norms serve to guide behavior, perception, cognition and affective ties; in short, a consensual value system develops that differentiates subcultures. Secondly, these behavioral patterns and value systems (subcultures) are differentially evaluated and hierarchically ranked on a system-wide basis. Status is accorded in terms of this stratification. Upward social mobility refers to changes in behavior and value orientations required of those individuals who would seek to raise their status evaluation. Loeb suggests that if there is a conflict between parental class culture and the core culture taught in the school, anxiety may result and the child may rigidly and dependently cling to established modes of behavior, rather than exhibit motivation toward social mobility. As the reader will see in the next chapter, the child not only learns certain behavior from significant others during the socialization process, but also comes to invest them with what Loeb refers to as positive feelings of "belongingness." Loeb argues that if the child lacks a feeling of sufficient social security, he will cling to the affective ties with family and neighborhood, and the value orientations that are familiar, and he will experience anxiety if he is forced to give them up for other people and other values. The child is, in effect, incapable in this situation of changing his behavior or adapting his value orientations to new demands. This failure to seek upward social mobility in the school often results in his being characterized in the classroom as a nonlearner. Or, if his behavior is highly deviant and rebellious or aggressive, he may be labeled a delinquent.

Loeb suggests that the school system represents a major pathway to social mobility, but he argues that for lower-class children much of school learning falls under the headings of meaningless content, conflicting motivations (for example, immediate versus delayed gratification), and incomprehensible goals. Burton, writing in the same special issue, argues that the schools have been geared typically:

> . . . . to the aims, ambitions, moral, or ethical standards of the white, prosperous middle class, Protestant Anglo-Saxon population. . . . The school is not organized to capitalize upon the *nonverbal* types of intelligence often found among children who have not had access to or constant contacts with books. The school often does not recognize the emergence of high intelligence and creative behavior in forms other than the abstract verbal type long fostered by the school.[1]

Loeb, with regard to this last comment, also discusses the problem of testing. He notes that standard school administered achievement and intelligence tests assume motivation on the part of the child to do his best. Unfortunately, this motivation may not exist at all for the lower-class child and, even if it does exist, such tests often involve behavior that is neither familiar nor meaningful in his evaluation. Motivation and school achievement will be considered at greater length in subsequent sections and chapters. The purpose at this point is to explicate the historical generalization that American public schools support a dominantly middle-class value

---

[1] Reprinted from William H. Burton, "Education in the United States," *Harvard Educational Review*, **23** (Fall 1953), 248.

orientation and are controlled by a middle-class administration. This approach has been termed "historical" despite the fact that it is still found in the literature, because it has given rise to much criticism that has succeeded in modifying the social-class approach.

Such criticisms can be, and have been, leveled at these studies for generalizing from research done in a few relatively small communities to all of American society. It has been argued that the data fail to fully support the hypotheses that curriculum selection, participation in extracurricular activities, achievement levels, sociometric friendship patterns, school dropout rates, and so forth, are wholly determined by social-class position or by unjust school policies, which literally barricade the road to upward social mobility for the lower-class child. Among others, Charters (1953), Brookover (1953), and Hernandez (1963), writing a decade apart and nearly thirty years after the Lynds' initial work, indicate that the subject of social class and education is still far from being a dead issue. What has died—or, at least, suffered mortal wounds—is the uncritical acceptance of social class as a unitary explanatory principle. Charters questions the assumption that all individuals internalize, to the same degree, the value orientations of "their" social class. He notes that the impact of social-class background may be profoundly altered by subsequent experience with other subcultural groups and by shifts in reference group identification. Implicit in Charters' argument is the theoretical position already explicated that personality and value orientations are open to modification throughout life by changing social influences and new experiences.

Charters analyzes the evidence for a dominant social-class control of the school and concludes that such control has not been demonstrated. Brookover (1953) also critically examines research evidence relating to the social-class position of public school teachers and the impact of various social-class teacher models on children's levels of aspiration, general personality, and behavior. He argues that the evidence is not sufficient to allow conclusive generalizations about the teachers' position in the stratification system, or to show how this position might affect the children under their direction. In a later work, Brookover (1961) notes that research evidence indicates that teachers tend to encourage achievement and mobility of certain children, not on the criterion of their measured social class per se, but rather, on the basis of the teachers' perceptions of the child's behavior and value orientations in relation to the teacher's *stereotypes* of social class.

Many thinkers have criticized the "one factor" method of analysis, which stops with the exploration of a single variable such as social class, as being an inadequate approach to a complex problem. Hernandez (1963) bluntly proclaims that the concept of social class is being misused in the field of education and points to the dangers of pursuing social class as a fixed determinant of individual values. He concludes that "individual behavior cannot be predicted from socioeconomic status." Perhaps *that* conclusion is as broad an overgeneralization as the concept he criticizes, but we would agree that knowledge of an individual's position in the stratification system alone is not enough if we are to understand the values and attitudes of that individual. What appears to be the case is that subcultural variations in the socialization process produce a typical, but not universal, set of attitudes indicative of value orientations, which are related to the demands of the school situation. These attitudes may or may not correspond to the general value orientations of the subsystem of the school or those specific to particular teachers and administrators.

It is important at this point to consider the definition of "attitudes," for it has significant implications for considering the interrelationship between individual outlook and behavior of both the school child and his teacher. The definitions of attitude are legion in the literature, but the point worth noting is that attitudes may be defined either in terms of cognitive organization, that is, regularities in feelings and thoughts, or in terms of behavioral motivation, that is, predisposition to act in a specific way—or both. The most fruitful approach to defining the concept of attitude appears to be this last integrative one. For the purposes of this study, then, attitudes are defined as ways of organizing and evaluating cognitions about people, experiences, physical objects, and abstract ideas, which affect the likelihood that an individual will behave in a way that is consistent with these organized evaluations, given conditions which permit their expression, and arouse the motive to do so. When attitudes are defined in this way, it allows for talking about generalized attitudinal value orientations that may or may not influence actual overt behavior, depending on the nature of the situation. Thus, even if all members of a given social-class category were socialized in an identical manner—which they are not, of course—and developed identical value orientations, these attitudes would not necessarily be reflected in behavior. At best, we can speak only of "general," "typical," or "usual" patterns. However, to the extent that these generalized sets can be distinguished, they are useful for providing some information about differences among and between people, provided that they are not taken as the *only* explanatory variable. Thus, however cultural alienation and adjustment to school are evaluated, simple equation with social class, as defined by such criteria as father's occupation, level of family income, area of family residence, parent's level of educational achievement, and so forth, is not the total picture, but only one fragment. However, this fragment may yield important clues and guidelines to completing the entire puzzle.

One element common to the description of class differences that have been noted is the theme of deviance from some norm taken as a standard.

"Deviation" has come to be a heavily value laden term connoting a general "badness," which may or may not be accurate. Deviance, literally, means different from some standard, a lack of conformity to some law, rule, value, attitude, or behavioral characteristic held as "proper" by a majority group. Whether or not this is "bad" is a matter of judgment. Some kinds of deviance are obviously bad in that they would be so defined by consensual agreement of all the members of a social system, for example, murder of an in-group member. Other kinds of deviance are consensually "good," for example, innovations that produce increased rewards for all members of the system. Most kinds of deviance have no such clearly consensual definition as good or bad, and "bad for whom or what?" becomes the central question. The Leftouts may be defined as deviants, and in doing so it is explicitly assumed that such deviance is, for these children, bad. That it is, in fact, bad for them becomes an empirical, rather than a purely judgmental, question when their goals are specified. In this case one assumes that at least the initial goal of any individual, including the Leftout, in the school setting is twofold in that it involves some degree of personally defined success in educational achievement and social acceptance. Thus, any deviation from the accepted means of achieving these goals within the group is bad, or, if you prefer, maladjustive. It has been shown that, in this society, attractive rewards are freely available to some members and denied to others. Some highly valued rewards are permitted only to those who have attained a certain status because of age, social position, prestige, ethnic background, and so forth. Barriers to attaining such rewards may arise from personal limitations, intellectual or physical factors, and other fortuitous factors over which the individual has little or no control. Lack of skill, knowledge, and opportunity may also lead to deviancy. This deviancy from the accepted paths to success is reflected in differential distribution of rewards.

Abrahamson (1952) has investigated the relationship between the child's social-class level and the awarding of scholastic rewards. His sample of 705 students in the early junior high grades was drawn from two urban, two suburban, and two rural schools. Rewards were defined in terms of selection for participation in extracurricular activities, prizes received, and academic grades. In all cases he finds that middle-class students receive a disproportionate share of high grades, occupy the majority of class and school offices, and are the primary participants in extracurricular activities. Abrahamson does not consider the IQ scores of the students, or such factors as whether or not they are required to work at home or elsewhere after school, thus limiting their ability to attain rewards. However, his research does permit the conclusion that more scholastic rewards are obtained by children of higher socioeconomic background—for whatever reason.

It has been suggested earlier that one of the prominent features of the socialization process is the tremendous amount of variability that occurs within each of the social-class levels. Normative behavior is not a simple concept. Much of the research literature has failed to distinguish possible subpatterns within the lower socioeconomic class. Cohen (1964) suggests that, while most human behavior is learned through experiences in a particular cultural setting that offers particularistic norms, in a complex urban industrial society alternatives are numerous and available enough to make predictions of individual behavior hazardous. Some rural and geographically isolated subcultures with more narrowly defined populations afford more limited alternatives, but variations at the family and individual level are still wide. Added to this problem of variation in subcultural patterns, Cohen points out that the cultural norms vary in their specificity. Some areas of behavior may be culturally undefined, or the social sanctions applicable to deviancy may be unclear, thereby increasing the opportunity for variation. When it is not possible to deal with idiosyncratic variations, and patterns of response only must be the basis of analysis, it is important to distinguish how various aggregates within a social class respond. Cohen, among many others, notes that the interaction between personality and social structure plays an important role in any behavioral picture and that circumstances nurturing particular kinds of development must be identified. He distinguishes between two subcultures in the lower socioeconomic strata: a "lower-class culture of poverty" and a "working class."

He argues that members of the "poverty-culture" have little opportunity for mastery of skills and that lack of skill is anxiety producing. A sense of shame is also seen to accompany limited opportunity. Often this anxiety and shame act together to produce hostile aggressiveness, lack of trust in others, feelings of inadequacy, withdrawal, and a generally suspicious and negative attitude toward the social environment. On the other hand, working class members have the opportunity for skill mastery, pride in achievement, and some social power (derived through labor union membership), which serve as anxiety-reducing functions. Cohen argues that working class life nurtures family cohesion and stability. Assuming that children learn through contact with and observation of their social environment, this kind of psychological setting obviously would provide a qualitatively different kind of socialization background for the school child from that of the lower-class poverty-culture.

Miller (1964) has outlined an even more detailed analysis of subcultural patterns within the lower classes. He identifies four possible subgroups, using economic security and family stability as subdividing variables. Type I, the "Stable Poor," is characterized by economic and family stability; the principal wage earner is regularly employed but in a low skill occupation. The majority of families falling in this class are white, rural, and southern. The aged and the downwardly mobile are over-represented in this group. Negro families with higher social class than their white counterparts are also included. Children from these families are those most likely to be upwardly mobile in the educational system. Type II, the "Strained," is characterized by a secure economic pattern but an unstable family one. This category is more influenced by individual variation and is cross-sectional in terms of demographic variables. Children from these families tend to be anxious and adjust less easily to school demands on the basis of their personal insecurity. Type III, the "Copers," is characterized by economic insecurity and family stability. This group increases appreciably during periods of economic contraction and contains the largest share of urban, northern, and Negro families. Children from these families are sometimes withdrawn from the school to help supplement family income, or because family finances are inadequate to provide appropriate clothing, lunch money, and so forth. These children do poorly in school, because of frequent absences or residential mobility engendered by a search for economic stability. Type IV, the "Unstable," is characterized by economic insecurity and family instability. Miller points out that not every family in this category is a hard core case, but that there are degrees of strain and instability. In general, this category contains unskilled irregular workers, broken families, the physically handicapped, and mentally disturbed poor. The families in this category are typically, chronically dependent on some sort of welfare agency because of sickness, alcoholism, prolonged periods of unemployment, and high rates of illegitimacy. Children from these families are those least likely to successfully adjust to, or derive many advantages from, the educational system. Miller suggests that, for Type IV, a concentration of public assistance funds on compensatory education for children might be of more value than diffuse efforts to remedy family stability.

It is clear that the historical development of concern with the interrelationship between social stratification and education has shown a progressive and profitable modification; and every indication in the literature suggests that it will continue to do so. Social class is no longer the unitary concept it once was. With this modification in mind, the following sections will review several of the specific findings that have come out of social-class research, which help, at least in part, attempts to understand the Left-out.

NEGRO VERSUS WHITE:
A SPECIAL CASE OF STRATIFICATION

The discussion of "color caste" in contemporary society has been the central interest in a rather large body of separate literature. There is neither time nor sufficient space to review it here. However, the special case of the Negro in our social system cannot be completely ignored. The central issue in this chapter is that of social class, which is not the same as that of caste. The Negro in society, irrespective of his economic, occupational, educational, or other achievements, has been the object of discrimination. While other ethnic groups have been assimilated successfully into the core culture, following relatively short problem-fraught periods, the Negro, because of readily identifiable physical characteristics, has been largely excluded and forced to remain as a separate caste. Within this color caste a somewhat parallel system of social-class categories have developed that are recognized by other Negroes but, until very recently, have been given only occasional and scant recognition by whites. In the majority of studies that will be reviewed, when color distinctions are made, the Negro child is relegated to the lower-class categories. This is justifiable by and large because social discrimination functions as both a cause and a consequence. That is, social discrimination directed toward Negroes has caused nearly insurmountable barriers to generally recognized means of upward mobility. These barriers, in turn, result in keeping the typical Negro family in the lower socioeconomic strata and in preserving among them the behavioral characteristics and value orientations that serve as the rationale for discrimination against them. Neither the relatively few individual Negro families who have managed to escape this vicious circle, nor recent antidiscrimination legislation have had far-reaching positive influence to date on the social evaluation of Negroes in general. Desegregation in the schools is not yet complete. Even in those schools where it is complete, or where segregation per se never existed, there is still something less than "integration," in the ideal sense, between Negro and white students. Physical proximity is not equivalent to social acceptance, and lack of segregation is not tantamount to integration.

In the U.S. Department of Labor Report to the President (1965), it is emphasized that the most difficult fact for white Americans to understand is that the circumstances of Negroes in contemporary society have been getting worse, not better. The Report suggests that indices of average income levels, standards of living, and educational achievement levels are deceptive. Individually, Negro families are reaching higher levels of social status than ever before achieved. Collectively, in a stratification system in which a few get much and many get little, Negroes are in the lowest socioeconomic strata. The Report argues that the gap between Negroes and most other groups in American society is widening.

> The fundamental problem, in which this is most clearly the
> case, is that of family structure. . . . The evidence—not final, but
> powerfully pervasive—is that for the Negro family in urban ghettos
> the fabric of conventional social relationships does not exist. . . . So

long as this situation persists, the cycle of poverty and disadvantage will continue to repeat itself.[2]

Moynihan (1965), addressing himself to this same point, postulates that the family structure is not only the product of social causes, but is itself, as the primary socializing agent, a significant and dynamic element in the creation of culture, of social character, and of social structure. He argues that while there is no universal family pattern to be found among urban, poor Negroes, there is a tendency toward high incidence of broken homes dominated by women, in which children never acquire any stable relationship with male authority, and never acquire any rational expectations about the future. These problems are not exclusively Negro problems. It should not be presumed that the problems of Negro children are in any way different from those of white children, except insofar as they are increased by the factor of negatively evaluated skin color. It is this factor that constitutes an additional social handicap, and one over which the child has no possible control. Gottlieb (1964) argues that there is considerable evidence that both white and Negro teachers respond differentially to white and Negro children, as well as to children of different social classes. This differential treatment takes the form of negative evaluation of children with dark skin color or perceived lower socioeconomic status, or both. In this context it is important to consider briefly whether there are objective differences to be found among groups on the basis of race.

Several studies yield evidence to support a hypothesis that social structural factors are more significant in differentiating between Negroes and whites than is the variable of skin color. These studies indicate that, in many cases, there is no particular reason for emphasizing race as a crucial variable. Dreger and Miller (1960) have critically reviewed psychological studies of Negroes and whites published during the period from 1943 to 1958. They find that, in general, there is a great deal of psychological similarity between the value systems of Negroes and whites. While religion is highly evaluated by Negroes—in keeping with the prevalent racial stereotype—this element also ranks high with white females. They find marked differences in self-concept among Negroes and whites, with Negroes' feeling less adequate. Related to this is the finding that there is a higher incidence of mental illness among Negroes than among whites. However, it is suggested that both of these findings can be explained on the basis of social structural differences, which keep the Negro in a position of inferiority, discrimination, and highly limited opportunity. Dreger and Miller have found many reports of intelligence differences—with Negroes

[2]Reprinted from U.S. Department of Labor, Office of Policy Planning and Research, *The Negro Family: The Case for National Action.* (Washington, D.C.: Government Printing Office, March 1965), p. 13.

ranking lower than whites—and research evidence shows that educational achievement differences largely correlate positively with the pattern of intelligence test differences. They argue, however, that environmental, rather than hereditary factors, can explain these differences—and that is precisely the view supported by our theoretical position. In reviewing studies of temperament, Dreger and Miller find that differences have been noted, but that evidence is insufficient to determine the cause. They also point out that cross-race similarities are more typical than cross-race differences. They conclude that differences found between Negroes and whites in leadership styles, family patterns, child-rearing practices, fertility rates, and so forth, all seem to conform to social structural differences, rather than to racial differences. Thus, in the areas of social-psychological concern, social-learning variations are shown to serve more clearly as the basis for differentiation among people than racial differences.

Lott and Lott (1963) also have explored the value systems and goals of Negro and white high school children, particularly as these are relevant to their educational and vocational choices and plans. They find no significant differences among Negro and white children in the area of need for affiliation. The dominant goals for both groups are a desire for popularity, a desire to attain security, and a desire to obtain knowledge and achieve success. The authors find that, despite Negro children's awareness of the problems of discrimination and prejudice, they are generally more optimistic about their futures than are white children. It can be argued, of course, that by this age (late adolescence), the more pessimistic children will have left the system. The authors indicate some evidence that points to the relatively high status in the school system of the "successful" Negroes, those who have become school leaders. The socioeconomic background of the Negro leaders is higher than that of their white counterparts. The parents of Negro leaders are better educated than the parents of most other Negro students and are at least as well educated as those of the white leaders. Negro leaders are found to be more motivated to achieve financial security and social respectability, while white leaders are motivated toward more idiosyncratic sources of success.

Lott and Lott also find generally that white students have greater economic and home stability than do Negro students. It would appear to be clearly the case that racial differences per se do not play a major role, but that the social structural dynamics already mentioned, of discrimination, economic disadvantage, and structural instability in the family, are the variables that cause Negro versus white differences. Approximately thirty years ago Frazier was writing about the pattern of family disorganization prevalent among Negroes and was noting its results. He argued that the most important problem resulting from family disorganization was an economic one: reliance on the meagre earnings of the mother or female head of the family. More recently Frazier (1950) points out that financial support programs, such as Aid to Dependent Children (ADC), have alleviated the economic problem to some extent but have left untouched the devastating social problem.

> As a result of family disorganization a large proportion of Negro children and youth have not undergone the socialization which only the family can provide. The disorganized families have failed to provide for their emotional needs and have not provided the discipline and habits which are necessary for personality development. Because the disorganized family has failed in its function as a socializing agency, it has handicapped the children in their relations to the institutions in the community. . . . Since the widespread family disorganization among Negroes has resulted from the failure of the *father* to play the role in family life required by American society, the mitigation of this problem must await those changes in the Negro and American society which will enable the Negro father to play the role required of him.[3]

Frazier goes on to draw an important distinction between "unorthodox" family patterns and "disorganized" patterns, which is applicable to our concern with understanding the Leftout regardless of his skin color. He suggests that disorganized patterns are especially prevalent among the lowest socioeconomic strata, Miller's Type IV, and are characterized by: (1) a lack of family traditions and kinship ties; (2) a lack of discipline within the family unit; (3) a lack of "familiness," for example, eating meals together and family forms of recreation; and (4) a lack of socialization to specific values but, rather, socialization to superficial admonitions to "be good," "honest," "sexually pure," and so on. Frazier points out that high rates of desertion and illegitimacy are found among Negroes. However, these rates are *not* equivalent to disorganization if unmarried couples function as a family unit or if children are absorbed into existing family units, for example, are reared by grandparents or other relatives. He points out that it is not the child from an unorthodox home, but from a disorganized and inadequate one, who reaches the school, which teaches values not previously taught or at odds with those already learned, and finds it dull, uninteresting, unintelligible, and anxiety-producing. Further, because of a general lack of discipline training, self-control, and value training, the

---

[3]Reprinted from E. F. Frazier, "Problems and Needs of Negro Children and Youth Resulting from Family Disorganization," *Journal of Negro Education,* 19 (Summer 1950), 277.

child will seek to escape whenever possible. This escape may be either in the form of physical absence or psychological withdrawal.

Jenkins (1958) specifically studies the relationship between illegitimate birth status and school, personal, and social adjustment of Negro children. His study of forty-five Negro children in grades four through twelve attempts to determine whether illegitimate children of economic status similar to their legitimate classmates differ significantly from them in adjustment to school. "Adjustment" is based upon a combination of IQ scores, age-grade placement, number of absences, teacher's ratings, cumulative grade records, and scores on the California Test of Personality (CTP). Jenkins finds that, while illegitimate children tend to rank lower than legitimate children in every area except that of number of school absences, significant differences of at least .05 are found only on teacher's ratings and IQ-age correspondence. CTP scores fail to show significant differences in any of the various areas, although the scores consistently favor legitimate children. Jenkins concludes that his data suggest that birth status affects the school adjustment of Negro children.

Jenkins argues against a belief, claimed to be prevalent among many social workers and other professional people (which may be derived from Frazier's position), that illegitimacy is accepted as a normal status in the Negro subculture and that this acceptance precludes stigma or social ostracism from operating adversely on the personality of the illegitimate Negro child. Jenkins maintains that these assumptions are invalidated by his research. We would agree that these assumptions may have been called into question by Jenkin's study, but his evidence hardly serves as proof to the contrary, since statistically significant differences are found in only two areas. The fact that teacher's ratings are found to exhibit significant differentiation particularly suggests that perhaps the teacher's personal values against illegitimacy may influence perception of the illegitimate child's adjustment. Jenkins does not state whether or not the teachers are aware of the children's birth status, but, if birth status is to be an influence on social relationships at all, we assume the status must first be known. There would seem to be no theoretical or intuitive explanation for birth status differences in the case that Frazier suggests, that is, where the unmarried parents act as a family unit or the illegitimate child is taken into an existing family unit unless the fact of his illegitimate status is known to those who disapprove.

Jenkin's findings also indicate that in comparison to their legitimate classmates, younger illegitimate children consistently rate higher than older children. In addition, there is found to be a significant negative correlation between age and IQ. The author hypothesizes that this lower ranking is due to increasing social stigma that comes with increasing age. He offers no further explanation, but it is suggested here that the reason pressures increase with age is that social contacts expand with age, and that some of these social contacts lie outside of the Negro subculture, which has accepted the fact of the child's illegitimate birth status. Thus, it seems plausible at least to consider Frazier's argument that unorthodox families and family disorganization are not necessarily equivalent in their consequences. This kind of argument again suggests the necessity of considering disadvantage and lack of adjustment in the light of multivariable determination.

Bloom, Whiteman, and Deutsch (1963) undertook a study, in order to separately analyze the factors of race and social class, among a sample of 292 pairs of parents and their first- and fifth-grade children. The data were derived from interviews with the children and from parents' responses to questionnaries. Three social-class groupings were used, on the basis of educational achievement level and occupational prestige ratings of the family's main wage earner. There were similar proportions of Negro and white children in each class level. The dependent variables considered in the study included housing conditions, educational and occupational aspirations, family life-styles, and others. Bloom *et al.* find that, by and large, Negroes are similar to whites in the lowest class group. This group is characterized by a high frequency of residence in substandard housing and by absence of the father from the home.

In this study, in which race and social class are independently treated, it is found that lower-class Negro parents report higher educational aspirations for their children than lower-class white parents, and that Negro children aspire to higher levels of occupational prestige than white children. It is found that for lower-class families housing is more crowded, mothers are more often employed outside the home in relatively menial tasks, and there is a tendency for mothers to be away during meal times (especially breakfast), and that children more often have inadequate breakfasts—but Negro-white differences in these areas are nonsignificant. The authors of this study conclude, as we have done, that general cultural, social, and economic handicaps associated with low position in the stratification system seem to be more influential in predicting behavioral and attitudinal factors than race.

SOCIAL CLASS
AND ACHIEVEMENT MOTIVATION

It will be seen in the next chapter that children's achievement motivation is heavily dependent on parental attitudes. If these attitudes are positive, and if they are supported by the child's secondary contacts in his more general social environment, then these attitudes will support the child's motivation to achieve in the school situation. However, if parental attitudes or those of the subcultural environment, or both, are negative toward educational achievement, the child may lack both initial motivation to achieve and subsequent support for any motivation that may be aroused by his teachers and classmates. Several studies have been aimed at differentiating value orientations toward educational achievement prevalent in various subcultures. Some of these issues have already been raised in connection with our consideration of the historical development of social class and education. We turn now to some more specific findings that have contributed to knowledge in this area.

Hieronymus (1951) has studied the nature of differences in social and economic expectations and attitudes toward education among different socioeconomic strata. He has administered a battery of attitude, socioeconomic, expectation, intelligence, and performance scales to 610 ninth-grade students in four schools. Socialized anxiety for education was considered to be the major variable in both educational expectations and performance. Hieronymus concludes that perception of social-class status is more closely related to levels of expectation than tested intelligence or performance scores. He finds a correlation of approximately .30 between socioeconomic status and attitudes toward education. This correlation is in the expected direction, that is, lower-class children hold less positive attitudes toward education.

Employing Hieronymus' own concept of "socialized anxiety for education," we would suggest that this correlation between socioeconomic status and attitudes toward education might have been higher and more useful had he separated those children in the lower classes, whose families are stable and supportive, from those whose families are disorganized and negative or indifferent toward educational achievement. A study by Kahl (1953) points out that lower-class parents who are discontented with their own status tend to train their sons from the earliest years of schooling to take it seriously and to use educational achievement as a means for upward social mobility. However, Kahl notes that only those children who *internalize* such value orientations are sufficiently motivated to overcome cultural, social, and economic handicaps, perceive the need for academic achievement, and develop what Hieronymus has termed "socialized anxiety for education."

Rosen (1956) examines the idea that social-class differences in attitudes toward and concern with achievement and upward striving for social mobility exist in our society. He hypothesizes that there are class differences in two components of the achievement attitude: an internalized personality factor termed "achievement motivation," and value orientations that define and implement achievement-motivated behavior. Note the closeness of his formulation to our definition of an attitude, in that it contains both internal organizational and external behavioral components. Rosen's sample consists of 120 white boys, ages fourteen to sixteen, with middle and lower social-class backgrounds. Thematic Apperception Tests, scored for achievement motivation, and a questionnaire to measure value orientations have been administered. Responses that are future-oriented, activistic, and individualistic are taken to represent those values most likely to define and implement achievement motivation and striving for upward social mobility. Rosen finds that lower-class boys score lower on achievement motivation and are less likely to express achievement-oriented values than middle-class boys. It is found that a personality factor of achievement motivation is positively related to high academic grades, but that achievement-oriented values per se are not. On the other hand, educational aspiration is related to value orientations, but not to motivation scores. In short, actual achievement—in this case, high grades—requires behavioral motivation, not just high attitudinal evaluation.

Rosen has shown that achievement *value* and achievement *motive* are independent, though they often and ideally occur together. (It is further suggested that while values may not be accompanied by motivation to act on them, it is doubtful that a child who is motivated will lack the relevant value orientation.) For our interests, this suggests that in order to produce motivation toward academic achievement, producing positive values toward education is not enough; behavior aimed at goal achievement must be elicited. Thus, lower-class parents who place high cognitive value on education still may socialize their children inadequately if they fail to provide a role model or some other actual motivation training. Rosen suggests that achievement value orientations are conceptual and are probably acquired through relatively complex verbal communication. On the other hand, motivation probably has its beginnings in parent-child interaction and identification and is likely to be unverbalized, yet internalized, by the child. Middle-class children are more likely to be taught the motivation that makes achievement possible, because middle-class parents are better able to serve as adequate role models.

Whether or not lower-class children actually do place a value on educational achievement and occupational mobility has been the subject of several research studies, and the findings are somewhat in conflict. We will briefly consider two studies as examples of the problem.

Sewell, Haller, and Strauss (1957) examine the general hypothesis that children's levels of educational and occupational aspiration are associated with the socioeconomic status of their families. The subjects of their study were 4167 randomly selected nonfarm students, who were carefully controlled by level of intelligence. Data were gathered on the basis of a questionnaire, which was designed to elicit information concerning the present occupation of parents, the level of educational aspiration, and actual occupational plans. The responses were arranged in five equal-sized, rank-ordered categories on the basis of prestige of parental occupation and the level of student intelligence. The findings support their hypothesis, and the authors conclude that for both boys and girls, when intelligence is controlled, there is a significant positive relationship between both educational and occupational aspirations and the level of parental socioeconomic status.

Contrary evidence is supplied by Bennett and Gist (1964). They have studied the educational and occupational aspirations of 800 urban students in relation to their social-class background and types of family influence. Social class is determined again on the basis of the prestige ranking of the father's occupation. These researchers find that educational and occupational aspirations show little variation among classes. Only specific occupational plans vary significantly by social class. It should be noted, at this point, that both of these studies deal with high school seniors who are above the age of compulsory school attendance—a fact that suggests the possibility that poorly motivated students from the lowest and most unstable socioeconomic levels may already have been eliminated. We suggest that many children from Type II and Type IV families (in Miller's terms) have already dropped out by the senior year of high school and, therefore, most of the lower-class children represented in these studies have been socialized to and found support for high levels of achievement in their homes. Weiner and Murray (1963) attempt to account for this kind of conflicting evidence about aspiration levels and social class in terms of the parents' ability to help their children attain desired goals. They suggest that parents from different socioeconomic strata may have the same level of aspiration for their children, but that the higher status groups are more certain that their aspirations will be fulfilled. In a study in Westchester County, New York, these authors find that the majority of parents and children, regardless of social class, aspire to professional occupations. However, whereas 100 percent of the middle-class children are enrolled in college preparatory courses aimed at reaching this goal, only 37 percent of the lower-class children are taking such courses. In short, Rosen's distinction between achievement value orientation and actual motivation would appear to be a significant one.

The work of Sewell et al. suggests that controlling for intelligence is also an important factor. The reader will see in the next chapter that measured intelligence reflects social stimulus and training. It can be hypothesized that those who receive the least stimulation, poorest training, and least support at home are also those children in the lowest groups on the basis of tested intelligence, and that very low socioeconomic rating, low intelligence ranking, and low educational aspirations are not wholly independent but tend to vary together. However, this tendency may be mitigated by an unusually stimulating family background or a stable family that allows for and supports training for their child outside the home. By the same token, of course, high socioeconomic status does not offer an unqualified guarantee of environmental stimulation or parental training and support. Therefore, it is hardly surprising that low aspiration and low socioeconomic status go together in some cases but not in others.

In this context it is important that Bennett and Gist have considered types of family influence. They find that these types of influence vary dramatically with social-class ranking. Maternal influence, relative to paternal, appears to be both stronger and more effective at lower-class levels, regardless of race. Both Negro and white lower-class children attribute to their mothers stronger attempts to influence their opinions. The authors hypothesize that in the lower classes the low social prestige of fathers' occupations will lead to matricentrism in the family. They suggest that mothers, regardless of social class, have nearly equal opportunity to measure up to general societal expectations for their roles, but that lower-class fathers typically fall short of cultural criteria of success as reflected in the mass media and the value orientations prevalent in the school. Bennett and Gist argue that the lower-class fathers' recognition of their own role failures causes them to renounce responsibility for influencing their children. This is to be expected in terms of the theoretical position on family roles, which we will discuss more thoroughly in the next chapter. We will also point out that when the mother devalues the father, as may be the case in this situation, she will see her own role as the dominant one. This is, of course, also the case in father-absent families.

Pressures toward motivation to achieve may have drawbacks unless they are accompanied by specific training to the socially approved means for attaining success. In the absence of clearly articulated means-training, the motivated child may attempt to employ normatively disapproved avenues to success or he may develop deep-seated anxiety because of the lack of knowledge of the appropriate means to his ends. Either of these modes of achievement motivation are maladjustive in terms of our definition. Davis (1944) has considered this particular problem of the difference between adaptive competition and ambition, and maladaptive rivalry and aggression. In his theoretically-oriented work he postulates that successful socialization of the child to achieve depends upon the degree of adaptive anxiety to which he has been socialized. While this kind of concept is difficult to define operationally, the implication is that a certain level of anxiety is necessary to motivate achievement behavior. This anxiety leads to ambition and socially approved competition for rewards and concern that these rewards will not be obtained. On the other hand, overanxiety leads to aggression and disapproved means of striving for rewards. Davis argues that children learn the consensual behavioral expectations and value orientations of the subculture to which they belong and in which they are socialized. The middle-class child is better prepared to achieve in the school setting than is the lower-class child, because the middle-class subculture approves of adaptive ambition and the lower-class subculture approves of maladaptive aggression. The author concludes that the problem of American public education is one of learning how to motivate lower-class children to socially adaptive anxiety and the generally acceptable means to achievement. He implies that lower-class children must be resocialized to these means, which often seem remote from their goals, and convinced of the reality of the end rewards.

Bandura and Walters (1963) point out that achievement demands are highly variable among subcultural groups, but that in a society in which upward mobility is an ideal, great pressures are exerted on children to at least equal—and preferably surpass—the attainments of their parents. However, high degrees of social approval are contingent upon both achievement striving and the observance of normative prescriptions and proscriptions designed to prevent this striving from having socially harmful consequences. Compliance with social expectations thus involves a considerable amount of discriminative learning and the exercise of self-control. Any radical change in effort to correct the child's antisocial behavior may threaten the social and material rewards associated with his deviant career, unless he perceives that he will be provided with satisfying substitute rewards. The persistence of deviant behavior can be accounted for in terms of social learning. Persistence of disapproved behavior appears to result from intermittent positive reinforcement, such as would be derived from those behaviors and value orientations rewarded by parents, peers, or subcultural groups when they are in conflict with those taught in school. However, if this conflict can be overcome, the principles of social learning can be used to foster socially approved response patterns and establish self-control. The authors note that research evidence indicates that devaluation of goals that are not readily attainable is one learned way of maintaining self-control. An equally important means of learned self-control is the placing of high evaluation on unpleasant means to a highly desired goal.

Such a position clearly indicates that environmentally learned social behavioral patterns must be considered when interest is directed toward understanding the acquisition of achievement motivation and self-control over the means employed. Again the reader is cautioned that these patterns are not universal within any socioeconomic status category; individual differences as the result of socialization practices and experiences in specific families may obviate the pattern. Nevertheless, there is a tendency for lower-class children to be statistically more often socialized to a pattern of aggressive competition, which is maladaptive as the basis for successful achievement motivation. Achievement motivation implies *active* but not aggressive efforts on the part of the child to attain rewards. As we have noted, this differs from simply placing high evaluation on such rewards as academic success, social acceptance, occupational prestige, and so on.

Several other factors are related to achievement besides those of high evaluation and actual efforts. One of the most important factors in educational achievement is intellectual ability. We will discuss, in the next chapter, the high theoretical relationship between language acquisition and the development of tested intelligence. A number of studies have dealt specifically with language and intellectual differences among the various social classes, some of which we will explore in the next section. Other factors in achievement include actual mental capacity, time orientation, and the use to which leisure time is put. Differences in each of these bases of achievement have been related to socioeconomic level. We turn now to a brief consideration of each of these prerequisites to successful achievement.

SOCIAL CLASS AND
THE BASES OF ACHIEVEMENT

It would appear to be unlikely that the child who is severely handicapped in the area of language skills would be highly motivated toward educational achievement unless, or until, such a handicap is overcome. An element that recurs in almost all of the social-class literature on educational achievement is that of the lower-class child's relative disadvantage in this area of communication skills. The lower-class child's cultural handicap typically includes the lack of books in the home, little emphasis on reading or verbal communication, and the dialect that he learns from his family and peers. Ample research evidence clearly indicates differential socialization to language exists at different class levels. Bernstein (1961) discusses two linguistic codes, the "elaborated" and the "restricted," which he sees as a function of different social structures. He discusses differences in family structure and activities that relate to these particular types of language development and usage. We will not consider here the specific origins of language disadvantage but will limit our concern to its consequences.

John (1963), in her study of language deprivation among Negro children, studies the impact of early social environment on the patterning of intellectual skills at three levels of socioeconomic status. That this study deals only with Negro children seems irrelevant to our concerns, in keeping with the theoretical assumption we have expressed, that social environment supersedes race as a crucial variable. She examined patterns of verbal and cognitive behavior among a sample of sixty-nine first-grade and 105 fifth-grade children. Three major levels of language behavior were analyzed: labeling, relating, and categorizing. Consistent social-class differences in these language skills are found to emerge among children of different socioeconomic levels. Some initial differences are noted but, by the fifth grade, lower-class children are significantly less skilled in all communication areas. She finds that middle-class children surpass their age-mates in that they possess a larger vocabulary and a higher nonverbal IQ. She finds trends toward this pattern at the first-grade level, but points out that all children at that age are primarily occupied with the acquisition of language skills. The gap, however, grows wider with age, so that by the fifth grade, middle-class children are far better at tasks requiring precise and abstract language.

Middle-class children are more skilled in such verbal behavior as the use of descriptive and integrative language and the use of language as a conceptual tool. John suggests that lower-class children, because of their relative poverty of language, may also experience difficulty in pooling and processing varied experiences. This is in keeping with the theoretical position explicated by Bruner that we will discuss more fully in the next chapter. John sees this as the source of the lower-class child's disability in the area of accepting delayed gratification.

Several such studies show that children from lower socioeconomic backgrounds employ shorter and more fragmented sentences than do their middle-class age-mates. Typically these children have more limited vocabularies and are less articulate. Newton (1962), as director of the Reading Skills Clinic at North Carolina College at Durham, has collected considerable evidence concerning the background of the child who is deficient in language skills. She points out that the foundation for the child's verbal development is laid subtly, but inexorably, in: (1) the general cultural level of his home, (2) his parent's language patterns, (3) the language patterns of his peers, (4) the general level of culture in his community, and (5) the educational resources available to him in school and outside of school. Thus, the standard English usage of teachers, textbooks, and more advantaged age-mates is virtually alien to the Leftout. If the child has not grown up in an environment that affords both breadth and depth of educationally stimulating activities, he will not have the background concepts to which to relate verbal symbols. Newton catalogues the socioeconomic status, personal characteristics, and language patterns typical of the "verbally destitute" child. He is:

1. usually a member of a family in which there is less than two full generations of literacy;
2. often the product of a small, substandard, public school system located in communities barren of cultural opportunities, or of a large, overcrowded, outmoded public school system located in ghetto-like urban areas;
3. frequently a racial or cultural minority group member or a resident of a geographically isolated place, or both, or he is a migrant;
4. during his formative years communicating customarily through nonstandard English, characterized by: (a) casual observance of standard inflections, (b) simple words, (c) frequently mispronounced and uncorrected words, (d) rare use of descriptive or qualifying terms, (e) simple sentences or sentence fragmentation in both oral and written expression, and (f) speech heavily infused with vernacular expressions;
5. usually performing two or more years below grade expectancy on verbal tests, but frequently demonstrating adequate scholastic potential on nonverbal tests;
6. generally disenchanted with all types of book-centered learning, which he displays through aggressive, defensive, or indifferent attitudes in the classroom;
7. generally experiencing difficulty in relating present activity to future goals.

The author's own experience with disadvantaged children substantiates this view, but it is regrettable that these studies are not derived from a theoretical approach to language and cognition. We will attempt, in the next chapter, to bring a theoretical perspective to bear on this problem. Luria and Yudovitch (1961), for example, have provided part of the explanation for cognitive deficit exhibited by speech retarded children. Our general hypothesis is that this lack of language skills is created by restriction in the child's social environment—either by lack of educational stimulus or monotony of stimulus.

Deutsch (1963) has outlined the main factors that affect the disadvantaged child's readiness for the demands of school. One such factor he cites is the lack of variety of visual, tactile, and auditory stimulation in the lower-class home. This position has been criticized by Riessman, and we will consider his arguments and other theoretical positions in Chapter 5. Here we simply want to note that Deutsch argues that the lower-class home contains few objects that aid in the development of visual discrimination skills, and that lack of manipulatable objects reduces tactile development. He points out that a lower-class environment affords much noise, but little direct communication and feedback. In such circumstances, the child is apt to learn skills of inattention in an effort to drown out indiscriminate noise. Thus, the lower-class child is deprived of meaningful experience and constructive feedback. Deutsch concludes that differences in life-styles among various socioeconomic strata provide different training patterns. If language acquisition is taken as the prerequisite to concept formation and problem solving, as suggested in the next chapter, then this deficit has a tremendous effect on intelligence and the capacity to successfully adjust to school achievement demands.

In a later work, Deutsch (1964) more extensively reports his data on language and cognitive variations among a sample of 292 white and Negro children in the first and fifth grades. He explores the interrelationships between socioeconomic status, race, grade in school, and language skill. Comparative disadvantage is significantly correlated with race more frequently among children in the fifth grade than in the first grade. The language variables of abstraction, verbalization, and experientially dependent enumeration are those found to be correlated significantly with race. The number of significant correlations with socioeconomic level remain relatively constant at each grade level. The general language disadvantage evident by both social-class and race standards reflect a deficiency in abstract and categorical use of language, as opposed to labeling and denotive usage. His data indicate that social-class differences in perceptual abilities and general orientation to the environment decrease with age, while language differences tend to increase. Thus, his data clearly support the "cumulative deficit" hypothesis that he advanced in his previous work and that is also supported by the work of Vera John noted earlier. Deutsch argues that, even considering the disadvantaged child's initial inadequacies, the decline in his comparative performance brings into question the adequacy of the school system. We would suggest that before all the blame for increasing comparative disadvantage is placed squarely on the shoulders of teachers and institutional administrators, certain other factors should be considered. Undoubtedly poor school practices are partly responsible, but we suggest that other factors also play a part in cumulative deficit.

Deutsch's own work suggests at least one supplemental hypothesis. He notes that social-class differences remain relatively stable but that racial differences especially increase with age. This would appear to point up the fact that the role of social acceptance by peers plays an increasingly large role as age increases. (We are assuming that fifth-grade teachers, on the average, are no more discriminatory in their practices than are first-grade teachers.) One big change in social environment that does occur during the period between first and fifth grade is an increase in racial discrimination among children. Several studies have indicated that children of first-grade age, six or seven, make racial distinctions but are not highly discriminatory in their behavior. However, by age ten or eleven, peer groups are apt to become more sharply racially divided. If the Negro child lacks social acceptance by his more advantaged peers, then we would hypothesize that he also lacks positive significant interpersonal support and suffers from a lowered self-concept. Furthermore, he may also lack a role model for learning, which keeps him in a position of lower relative ability. Therefore, the peer group may also be partly responsible for cumulative deficit. There will be more to say of this subject in a later chapter.

The particular language pattern found in many disadvantaged homes may be also a contributing factor. Many Negroes—and whites living in similar circumstances of cultural isolation—speak a nonstandard English dialect with common characteristics: (1) slurring words, for example, "smothertam" for "some other time"; (2) certain omitted letter sounds, for example, "hep yo sef" for "help your self"; and (3) some transposed letter sounds, for example, "bofe" for "both"; as well as those features already noted, of poor grammar, inadequate sentence formation, and a dearth of elaborate abstract and categorical terms. This kind of dialect can be so pronounced that it is tantamount to a foreign language. Disadvantaged children may lack support for "school English" in the home and neighborhood and thus, in essence, be required to speak and learn two languages.

The problem is not confined to Negroes. Many Leftouts are in the position of having to learn two languages that are not apt to be complementary. In situations of true bilingualism, the introduction of fundamental educational material in the original language provides the basis for developing competence in the new language. However, in the Left out's situation, at least three variables operate to reduce the child's potential for true bilingualism: (1) because it is usually assumed that the child speaks English as a native language, little or no emphasis is given to initial teaching of formal language as functional but, rather, the emphasis is given to "expansion" and "correction," which places the disadvantaged child in the position of being inferior, wrong, and often criticized; (2) rarely, if ever, are nonstandard dialects employed in the school system as a teaching tool for developing skill in formal language; and (3) much of the archaic language typically employed in schools, for example, "wraps," "cloakroom," "monitor," "pupils," and so forth, are terms that are employed nowhere else and only detract from the child's efforts to learn more important things.

In this situation, the disadvantaged child's alienation is also apt to be increased by the text and pictures usually found in elementary readers. For example, Dick and Jane romp on their green lawn, while

Spot gambols off through the blooming rose bed to greet Father who, neatly dressed with brief case under his arm, stands near his automobile and smiles at Mother who is waving a welcome from the cool, screened veranda. The Negro child, the child who has never seen his father, the child who lives on the third floor of a deteriorating apartment building, the child whose "playground" is an empty warehouse, a rubbish-filled vacant lot, or a city street often can neither recognize these scenes, nor identify with people in them. This problem of the intricacies of "foreign" words and pictures clearly contributes to his relative disadvantage. Initially, at the first-grade level, *all* children are relatively lacking in language skill, but the child who becomes as adept as his peers by the fifth grade must also have support for his formal school-taught English outside the classroom. This may be absent in the home environment and unattainable from more advantaged peers who discriminate against the disadvantaged child, partly on the basis of the "funny way he talks." Social distinctions among dialects are made, not on linguistic grounds, but in terms of status considerations. Thus, the family and general subcultural environment may also be partly responsible for cumulative deficit.

A third nonschool factor, which may contribute to cumulative deficit, lies largely at this point in the realm of speculation, although some limited research would indicate that it cannot be overlooked. We are assuming, in the bulk of this discussion, that the disadvantaged child has, for all practical purposes, both the physical and intellectual capacities needed for social and scholastic adjustment. Unfortunately, this may not be the case. Eventually, we will rule out any practical effect on the basis of heredity, but it must be recognized that environmental deprivation conceivably can have also physically limiting consequences; and the disadvantaged child may be the victim of irreparable damage that no amount of compensatory education can wholly overcome. We caution that this suggestion probably applies to a limited segment of severely handicapped children and in no way is to be interpreted as a rationale for not providing compensatory programs for disadvantaged children in general. It is only suggested that these programs may also have to provide for nonacademic training of those children who may not be capable of achieving successfully in the standard school program.

Hunt (1961) has accumulated research evidence to show that various deficiencies in maternal diet and care during pregnancy associated with low socioeconomic levels can produce complications in both pregnancy and parturition, which result in intellectual retardation and behavioral disorders in children. Severe retardation or behavior problems exclude the child from our area of concern. However, we assume that these problems are arranged along a continuum of severity and, insofar as the disadvantaged child is functioning adequately enough to be regarded as "normal" and enrolled in the public school, they may affect our specific concerns. In addition to the factor of maternal diet and care during pregnancy, the disadvantaged child may himself be subject to inadequate diet and lack of medical care, which can result in health problems that carry over and influence social adjustment and academic ability. In January of 1966 the American Association for the Advancement of Science held a two-day symposium on "Behavior, Brain, and Biochemistry." One major discussion question centered on whether learning and memory could be retarded or improved by chemicals. The contemporary neurobiological theory of learning holds that memory depends on a process in which molecules of ribonucleic acid (RNA), a protein derivative, are coded to record particular events and then become lodged in specific nerve cells in the brain to be summoned up when required. Experimental work with infrahuman animals indicates that a relatively large supply of protein in the diet increases actual ability to learn. Protein derivative tests (in the form of administering a "smart pill" with the trade name of Cylert) are just beginning to be made on human subjects. However, theoretically, protein-rich diets can increase memory and ability to learn and, presumably, protein-poor diets can restrict this ability. Probably hot-lunch programs and school sponsored medical and dental clinics can help compensate, at least in part, for this kind of physically based deficiency. However, some even more disturbing physiological evidence was presented at this symposium.

Experiments on rats by Mark Rosenzweig, a psychologist at the Berkeley campus of the University of California, have shown that rats reared in a richly stimulating environment are not only better off chemically (RNA level), but also have a cortex, which controls voluntary action and thought, that averages 4 percent heavier than that of rats raised in an environment of low stimulation. The researcher concludes that brains literally grow and improve with use. In short, with infrahuman animals at least, it is possible to produce tangible, measurable differences in actual brain size by altering environments. The limiting factor of a poor environment can place the organism in a position of relative disadvantage, which it never can overcome, and which will only increase over a time, if environmental stimulation remains at a comparatively low level. Rosenzweig himself translates his findings into human terms when he suggests that "the more richness an individual experiences, the more his brain expands."[4] We are taking the view that socioeconomically disadvantaged children are apt to have a high poten-

[4]*Newsweek Magazine* (January 10, 1966), p. 45.

tial for school maladjustment unless compensatory efforts are made. Contemporary neurobiological research confirms this view and, in addition, by showing that the effects of a poor environment affect the very structure and chemistry of the brain, the research suggests that the socioeconomically disadvantaged child is not only less well socialized, but is also less capable of learning and remembering. In this case, a cumulative deficit is expected, quite apart from any inadequacy in the educational institution.

We have been suggesting here that social-class differences in evaluation of education and child-rearing practices in fostering motivation, of socioeconomically based factors of health, nutrition, and actual ability all play a role in the social and academic adjustment of the disadvantaged child to school. Other factors associated with socioeconomic differences in life-style, such as how leisure time is used and attitudes of time orientation, may also influence the child's motivation and ability to achieve. Several studies (Davis, 1948; Macdonald et al., 1949; Lewis, 1959; and Schorr, 1964) have provided evidence to show socioeconomic differences in the leisure time activities of children—with higher status children being more active in formal organizations with constructive goals and lower-class children active primarily in nongoal directed leisure behavior. Significant socioeconomic differences are also found in the amount of leisure time devoted to family-oriented activities. Again, the highest socioeconomic strata engage in the most family activity. The number of persons, both children and adult family members, who read books, increases with increases in socioeconomic level, while movie attendance and hours devoted to watching television decreases with increases in socioeconomic level.

These and other studies, for example, LeShan (1952) also give evidence to support the view that individuals in the higher status levels are characterized by a deferred gratification pattern and, conversely, that those in the lowest socioeconomic strata are oriented toward an immediate gratification pattern. These studies argue that among the lowest classes, when it is impossible to satisfy basic needs in any adequate or dependable way, the satisfaction of immediate goals becomes more important to both children and their parents. They develop a fatalistic attitude that generalizes to alter their pattern of living in such a way that there is little energy available for long-range planning or for developing distant goals. Present-time orientation is more central in their conceptual schema than future-time orientation. Their ability to cope with the environment and to plan for the future is impaired. A general attitudinal orientation of passivity, defeatism, and hostility results. Since much of what goes into the adjustment demands of the school system requires a time orientation of deferred gratification, the child who does not possess or cannot develop such an orientation is again placed in a position of disadvantage.

While this kind of pattern may be more prevalent statistically among the children of the lowest socioeconomic strata, it is certainly possible for any child to develop such maladjustive orientation in the face of unfulfilled basic needs. The lack of successful adjustment to school, based on present-time orientation and a generalized pessimistic personal outlook can, over a period of time, do much to present the child with a self-fulfilling prophecy in which he expects his basic needs to be frustrated. His expectations, in turn, determine his view about himself and his relationships to his environment, which, if repeatedly verified, have personality consequences in the form of a low or inadequate self-concept. In the succeeding chapters we will explore more thoroughly the influence of family and individual personality factors on school adjustment and the interrelationship between these social, structural, familial, and individual factors.

PATTERNS AND THEMES
IN THE SOCIAL-CLASS LITERATURE

Our investigation of the theoretical relationship between socioeconomic status and potential adjustment to the social subsystem of the school has been predicated on two assumptions; that children do not always reflect the value orientations and behavioral expectations of their social class and, therefore, that knowledge of social-class background alone will not allow for prediction about the attitudinal orientations held by specific children. Social class per se is a poor criterion for prediction, since between-family and within-family variations in interpersonal environment, as well as differences in individual orientation, are found within the full range of social classes in our contemporary society. There is a difference between patterns that are statistically representative and actual individual behavior that must not be overlooked. However, statistically identifiable patterns can help us understand what there is apt to be in the child's socioeconomic status background that can lead to disadvantageous variations in attitudes, values, and behavior. Social class is probably the best *single* predictor of behavior currently available in the social sciences.

Toby (1957) has undertaken an analysis of middle-class and lower-class orientations toward education in an effort to determine the factors leading to lack of school success for the lower-class child. This social, structural approach to the bases of disadvantage views the child as the passive victim of situations over which he has no personal control. Toby

notes that one prevalent theme in the literature is that of teachers hold-
ing middle-class value orientations and penalizing, consciously or un-
consciously, those children who do not or cannot hold those value orientations as a result of their pattern of socialization. This theme suggests
that the child who is identified as a member of the lower socioeconomic
strata is handicapped in his chance for development because of
stereotyped discrimination. A second theme prevalent in the literature
relates directly to the social and economic disabilities of the child's
family. Toby points out that the middle-class parent not only expects his
child to get an education, but is in a position to help with studies; the
environment pattern is one of pressures toward academic achievement
and social acceptance. He notes that lower-class patterns may support
values and behavior that are maladaptive for achievement and acceptance in the general culture. The teacher is a good parent surrogate for
the middle-class child because parent-teacher roles are comparable in
content. The middle-class child learns that scholastic competition is
somewhat analogous to his social and preschool preparation, for he is
exposed to wider vocabularies and abstractions in everyday life. He
achieves higher status in school and exerts even further efforts to maintain that status.

The parents of the lower-class child may not support the value
orientation of the school. Even if they do, the parents probably have less
education and are less able to make schoolwork meaningful for the
child. Parents of low socioeconomic status often lack the incentive,
training, and ability to encourage and help their children. The child then
is disadvantaged, and repeated failures may result in lack of interest in
school. Because schoolwork is cumulative, in a few years the lower-class
child is retarded in basic skills. The consequences of a child's lack of
training, ability, or interest in school are not all immediate. For those
who have lost hope in social mobility, school is a symbol of competition
in which they believe they cannot participate, and their self-concept suffers.

The lower-class child's verbal skills are not highly developed. The
lower-class parent is more adept in operating concrete objects than symbols in his occupational role and, thus, is a poor role model for the
development of complex verbal skills. However, since the school system
gives an advantage to those children who exhibit verbal skills, the lower-
class child is at a disadvantage. Because verbally-oriented intelligence
tests are geared to higher socioeconomic groups, they are not necessarily
a good measure of intellectual ability in the lower-class child; however,
such tests are quite highly predictive of academic accomplishment, and
lower-class children do comparatively poorly on them.

The notion that the occupational role of parents may influence their value orientations and, hence, the manner in which the child is socialized is one that needs some brief comment. Kohn (1963) has argued that class differences in parent-child relationships are a product of differences in parental values, with middle-class parents' values centering on self-direction and working-class parents' values centering on conformity to external prescriptions and proscriptions. He suggests that these value differences stem from conditions of life, particularly occupational conditions, with which the parents must contend. He notes that those occupations that are typically evaluated as "middle class" require a greater degree of self-direction than "working class" occupations, which more often require that the individual follow explicit rules set down by someone else in a position of authority. Kohn's interpretive model is, in essence: social class results in certain conditions of life which, in turn, are reflected in value orientations and behavior. We would agree with this kind of analysis as far as it goes, but it doesn't go far enough for our purposes.

The subtypes to be found within the lower classes, such as Miller has suggested, carry the analysis to a finer level of abstraction. However, variations in reference group orientation, in self-concept, in family patterns and expectations, and many other factors may account for some of the school-related differences in achievement, social acceptance, and emotional adjustment that have been attributed to social class alone. In the following chapters we will explore some of these "intervening variables." We are suggesting that social-class background is important if it can tell us something of what the child's general attitudes, value orientations, and behavior is apt to be. Patterns typically, though not universally, found among Negroes, unstable lower socioeconomic groups, comparatively poorly educated or low income families, and so on, can suggest what kinds of disadvantage to look for and what types of compensatory programs are indicated.

It is perfectly possible that lower-class children are well-adjusted in school and, of course, that higher status children are poorly adjusted. Social class is not regarded as a totally overwhelming influence on personal development. It is only a rough guide.

SUMMARY

The basic ideas inherent in the concept of social class are first, that people who share a common position in the economy are apt to be in prolonged interactional relationships that foster the development of characteristic subcultural norms. These norms serve to guide behavior, perception, cognition and affective ties—in short, a consensual value system develops that differentiates subcultures. Secondly, these behavioral patterns and value systems (subcultures) are differentially evaluated and hierarchically ranked on a system-wide basis. Status is accorded in terms of this stratification.

This chapter has dealt with how socioeconomic and racial status relate to the development of social skill, acquisition of role-knowledge, development of value orientations, and achievement motivation. It has been suggested that one possible kind of disadvantage a Leftout may experience is a lack of development in these areas within the normative range acceptable to the core culture. The general pattern of a Leftout's social-class background is one crucial variable in the effort to understand how he has come to be left out in the heterogeneous school situation.

Lack of opportunity for developing acceptable skills produces anxiety and shame when the child is faced with age-mates more experienced than himself. If there is a conflict between parental class culture and the culture taught in the school, anxiety may also result, and the child may rigidly and dependently cling to established modes of behavior, rather than exhibit motivation toward social mobility.

There is clear historical evidence that socioeconomic status and educational achievement are inversely related. There is also an abundance of historical evidence to suggest that part of the cause is centered within the school system itself, which traditionally has had a built-in bias favoring upper- and middle-class children. This bias is evident in the selection of curriculum, teaching methods, and intelligence tests based almost solely on verbal skills. At the same time, the public school system traditionally has been and still is regarded as a source of training to assure social acceptance and cultural assimilation to children with lower-class backgrounds.

For the Negro child, social-class problems are multiplied because of the factor of prejudice against the color of his skin, his dialect, his too often unorthodox or disorganized family pattern—all of which bring increased discrimination against him. The evidence is clear, however, that general cultural, social, and economic handicaps associated with a low position in the stratification system are more influential than race in predicting behavioral and attitudinal factors. The problems of Negro children are in no way different from those of other children, except insofar as they are augmented by the factor of a negatively evaluated skin color.

A child's social-class background, while it may well expose him to typical patterns of behavior and normative expectations, does not fully explain his own behavior or value orientations. The influence of social class is limited by its very nature, and its impact may be profoundly altered by subsequent experience with other subcultural groups and by shifts in reference group identification.

It appears to be the case that subcultural variations in the socialization process produce a typical, but not universal, set of behaviors and attitudes indicative of value orientations toward academic achievement, self-control, time and its uses, verbal skills, conformity, and other things, which are related to the demands of the school situation. These value orientations may or may not correspond to the expectations of administrators, teachers, and age-mates. When they do not, the child is considered deviant. This deviance places him at a disadvantage in succeeding either academically or socially and, thus, is "bad" in the sense of being dysfunctional in the heterogeneous school situation.

It is clear that social class alone is a poor criterion for predicting who will be a Leftout and who will not. Between-family and within-family variations in interpersonal environment, as well as differences in individual orientation, are found within the full range of social classes in our society. There is a difference between patterns that are statistically representative and actual individual behavior that must not be overlooked. However, statistically identifiable patterns can help us understand what there is apt to be in a child's background that can lead to disadvantageous variations in attitudes, values, and behavior. One possible cause of the Leftout's academic, social, and emotional disadvantage and potential for failure to adjust to the heterogeneous school situation is clearly a relatively low socioeconomic background, with attendant learned deviant values and behavioral expectations.

3

The Developmental
Process
and the Role
of the Family

The social subsystem represented in the school situation, and its impact on the developing child, is the central focus of this book. However, the tremendous influence exerted by other social subsystems to which the child is exposed cannot be ignored. Each child brings to school an already developed collection of values, beliefs, attitudes, and behavior patterns through which these values and meanings are expressed. These cognitions and behaviors are based on preschool experiences gained largely from the home situation. Thus, in order to understand the background of the Leftout, it is necessary to know something of how his early experiences and training influence his present thinking and behavior. For this kind of concern, the family is the critical focus of attention, since it is the family that serves as the first agent of socialization. This chapter, and to some extent the preceding one dealing with the influence of the social stratification system, consider the family and its strengths and weaknesses in influencing the developing child.

The Leftouts with whom we are centrally concerned have experienced an abnormal and comparatively disadvantaged socialization pattern. The task of drawing together the particular abnormalities and disadvantages is the focus of Chapter 5. However, the definition of comparative disadvantage demands an explication of the general process of normal sociocultural growth, since maladjustive patterns cannot be evaluated in-

57

dependently of some criteria of a normal developmental pattern and its consequences. Thus, the large body of literature relating to child development in general, and intellectual and personality development in particular, becomes not only relevant, but crucial. The sections of this chapter will be devoted to a consideration of some of the more widely known theories of the developmental process in children.

THE DEVELOPMENTAL PROCESS IN CHILDREN

For our purposes, "personality" is defined as an analytical construct, based on the observation of overt behavior (including test-taking behavior), which is consistent with the hypothesis that internal, systematically (but not necessarily logically) organized cognitions and affective relationships influence many overt behaviors in a relatively stable manner. "Intellect" is defined, for our purposes, as the observable aspect of this internal cognitive ordering. Intellect is the result of the individual's mental operation upon information from internal and external sources, in order to change that information into productive thinking aimed at problem solving, analytical and logical inductions and deductions, as well as creative actions. Our approach to the general developmental process is a social-psychological one, which conceives the basis of personality and intellectual development to be social learning in an interpersonal environment. Human beings live in a social world, a world that requires knowledge of consensually shared values, beliefs, meanings, and attitudes of its members. As the newborn infant develops into the mature adult, an ongoing intensive and extensive process of social learning must occur. This social development includes the learning of language, a vast body of empirical facts relating to the physical and social environment, a variety of specialized skills, the acquisition of moral values and standards of evaluation for self and others, and the normative "rules" concerning the ways and means of relating to other people. This entire, complex social-learning process is subsumed under the rubric of "socialization."

The primary agents of this process of socialization are other persons; parents, teachers, siblings, peers, and others who are significant to the child. For the preschool child, whose social contacts are apt to be limited, the family, particularly parents and siblings, is the principal source for social learning. It is primarily the adults or older siblings in the family who stimulate the child's early intellectual and social development.

Social-learning theories, supported by a great deal of research, pinpoint the elements of the family environment that appear to be most significant in influencing the general social learning of the child, as well as such more specific factors as measured intelligence, school achievement, social acceptance, and so on. In very general terms these elements may be delineated as: (1) providing the tools, stimulation, opportunity, and reinforcement for general learning; (2) providing role models for social learning; (3) providing help and guidance in language development; and (4) providing stimulation, concern, and support for achievement and learning outside the home, especially in school.

Theoretical analyses and empirical investigations help to reveal the dynamics of the process of interactional learning between the developing child and his social environment. Development refers to change that occurs over a period of time, and there is a wide range of theories extant in the literature concerning the process of intellectual and personality development—not all of which are as emphatically social in orientation. The central controversy found among these theories relates to the question of whether or not development proceeds in a sequential and invariant order, that is, in "stages" or "levels," and relates to the role played by heredity and physical maturation in the developmental process. While the work of Piaget exemplifies the position that the developmental process is sequential, invariant, and biologically based, there is much of value to be learned from his work which has bearing on a more social orientation.

The theoretical analyses of Jean Piaget reflect the detailed observations of his own three children, in addition to thirty years of work with his collaborators at the Rousseau Institute in Geneva, Switzerland. Because Piaget has devoted a professional lifetime to studying the development of intellectual functions and logic in children, it is with his work that we begin. For Piaget, intelligence is a special case of general interactive adaptation to the environment. Two complementary processes: "assimilation," corresponding to internal cognitive organization and "accommodation," corresponding to external behavioral adaptation, are seen as basic to the developmental process. Assimilation occurs whenever the child incorporates anything from his environment into his cognitive framework. Piaget assumes that the child always acts in terms of a Gestalt-like, centrally organized structure that is mediated by any memories he may have of previous experiences with the same or similar events and objects in his environment. Accommodation is the complementary process and occurs whenever the existing cognitive structure must be modified to meet the demands of variations in environmental circumstances. It is in these two ways that the environment is seen to influence the child.

Piaget describes the development of the behavioral aspects of intelligence in terms of stages. These stages are seen as sequential and the order in which they appear, as fixed. He analytically separates the stages in terms of transition points but repeatedly emphasizes that the development of intelligence is a process of continual change. Since the child is in continuous interaction with his environment, he must constantly adapt to external environmental demands and progressively modify his internal cognitive organization. Thought processes develop through gradual internalization of action, are "decentered," and eventually come to dominate over both direct perception and action. This is made possible by the concomitant development of the central neural system. Piaget argues that within the limits imposed by the genetic capacity for development of the central neural system, intelligence is capable of indefinite extension into time and space.

Note that this formulation of environment-child interaction through accommodation and assimilation considers both heredity, through limits on the development of the central nervous system, and environment. Hunt in reviewing Piaget's work, points out that several principles may be derived from his formulation. Especially important, for our purposes, is the principle that appropriate environmental stimulation and the opportunity to exercise developing thought processes are required if the thought process is to survive. Equally important is the idea that new accommodative modifications and new assimilative cognitive combinations are sources of *pleasure* to the child. In other words, new experiences are seen as inherently rewarding to the child. Another important derived principle is that continuous and progressive changes take place in the structures of behavior and thought, but the nature of this accommodation (adaptive change to environmental circumstances) implies that the *rate* of development is largely a function of the diversity the child encounters in his environment. On the basis of these principles, Hunt derives the hypothesis that the more new things a child has seen and heard, the more he is interested in seeing and hearing. In addition, the more variation in environment with which he has had to cope, the greater his capacity for coping. Hunt modifies this latter hypothesis with a warning that the child may be presented with too much too fast, become bewildered, and fail to cope at all.

Thought processes are conceived as originating from a process of internalizing actions. Intelligence, for Piaget, increases as thought processes are loosened from their bases in direct perception and action and, thereby, have the capacity to become reversible, transitive, associative, and symbolic. The impact of language and the development of conceptual thinking becomes crucial at this point. The development of conceptual thinking is of vast importance for creating order out of perceptual and environmental chaos. Conceptual thinking refers to thought processes that employ symbols and categories of classification for ordering information. This kind of thinking is a critical link between the environment and the individual, since these concepts are learned. Language acquisition provides the basic tool for both facilitating and directing the learning process. The learning of concepts and the development of conceptual thinking are complex dynamics involving basic processes of perception, discrimination, transposition, and generalization, all of which are mediated and facilitated by language in the form of consensually shared symbols.

Bruner (1964) takes the position that the development of human intellectual functioning is directed by a series of "technological" advances in the use of the brain—by mastery of techniques that are transmitted, with varying efficiency and success, by the culture or subculture of which the child is a member. For Bruner, language acquisition is the primary technique employed in intellectual development. This is so because children, as they grow, must acquire ways of representing the recurrent regularites of their environment (representation) and must learn to transcend the events of the moment by developing means of linking past, present, and future (integration).

For children in the age group we are considering—roughly five to twelve years—language comes to play a powerful role as a technique for knowing, representing, and integrating. Language serves the function of integrating intellectual activity into coherent, organized sets. Language is internalized as a program for ordering experience. Thus, if the child is deficient in his experience with language skills or has had inadequate language training, he is disadvantaged indeed.

The importance of language acquisition for intellectual functioning raises some questions concerning a fixed level of intellectual potential based on biological characteristics for the physically normal child. The conception of a fixed level of intellectual development potential is based on, and receives supplemental support from, the assumption of genetically predetermined development, which may be traced rather directly to Darwin's theory of natural selection and other such theories prevalent in the late nineteenth and early twentieth centuries. This kind of orientation is seen in Freud's work, in Piaget's formulations, and culminates in Thorndike's conceptions of learning by trial and error and stimulus-response theories of problem solving. However, it is with both the order of "stages" of transition, and the invariant nature and physiological basis of this order that other thinkers have disagreed with Freud and Piaget. There is a wealth of support for the idea that stage-theories of developmental sequences are not theoretically adequate, and a conception of normal intelligence potential as biologically limited under the environmental circumstances available to the vast majority of people also is inadequate.

The critics of this position oppose the view that various inherited abilities unfold along a growth continuum in ordered stages of biological maturation, with modification by environmental circumstances given only a secondary and relatively minor position of influence. These thinkers hold that the child's personal and intellectual development is the product of learning experiences, that is, differential levels of ability, knowledge, and skills are a function of these experiences. In these formulations, stages are not to be regarded as universal but, rather, particular to particular classes of situations. A stage theory is not necessarily contradictory to a theory of environmental influence, although the assumption that developmental sequences are biologically determined is contradictory. Experience can function to move the individual from one stage or level to the next, or to retard his movement.

For Hunt, intelligence is thought of as a central neural operation for the processing of information, which is developed in the course of encounters with the environment. He presents the findings of a large number of research studies, which quite clearly support the position that experience with the environment is the major influence on the development of tested intelligence and conceptual thinking. He emphasizes that it is environment interaction that affords the opportunity for genetic potential to be achieved. He points out that only rarely, if ever, is the experiential environment so rich and stimulating that hereditary limits are reached for the normal child. Thus, in effect, heredity is not an influencing factor in fixing the level of intelligence as it is commonly measured.

Many studies have confirmed the fact that deprivation of experience affects the rate and extent of intellectual development. Hunt reviews a large number of such studies with both infrahuman and human subjects that relate to the role of experience in shaping intellectual development. Typical of those he mentions is the Berkeley Guidance Study, which finds variations of thirty or more IQ points in a period of six to sixteen years among 10 percent of a sample of 222 children. In 3 percent to 4 percent of the cases, positive changes of a magnitude of three standard deviations (sixty IQ points) occur. Developmental curves of this range suggest unequivocably that measured intelligence is modifiable through experience. Hunt concludes that perceptual capacity demands a background of conceptual experience, which is then generalized to new experiences. Experience continually adds to the developing child's intellect a hierarchy of operations for processing information and for coping with and adjusting to new or changing environmental circumstances. It is clear from the evidence surveyed by Hunt that early impoverishment of experience can retard the development of tested intelligence. In terms of the traditional measurement of intelligence, this means a reduction of IQ scores for the disadvantaged child. With this kind of a conception of intelligence, the assumption that intellectual development is fixed and predetermined by genetic factors is untenable. Assuming the absence of any gross organic defect, inadequate intellectual development is relatively permanent only insofar as there is failure to take active measures to compensate for early deprivation.

Hunt argues that a number of externally manipulatable factors participate in controlling the depth and permanence of the negative influence of deprivations in childhood experience. He notes that one crucial element appears to be the duration and frequency of the deprivation. On the basis of research evidence, he finds that another important element is the opportunity available for experiences calculated to correct early disadvantages and deficiencies.

A third critical factor, as Hunt suggests, is the opportunity for verbalization in the home. He cites evidence to support the view that conceptual thinking and such school-oriented dimensions of intellect as reading readiness are a function of language experience. Thus, the impact of language skills, developed through interpersonal interaction, and its basic relationship to the very processes of thought and intellectual development, has clearly come to the fore as a major theoretical concern in our analysis of the disadvantaged child. We take the view that language acquisition is more than just a tool to be used in conceptual thinking.

Watson (1960) points out that language development in early childhood clearly demonstrates that both egocentric and socially-oriented functions are served by its acquisition. Any uniformity in the "real world" is known only through the experience of those who observe; and "objectivity" may be defined as uniformity of observation. The attainment of the common perspective essential to the establishment of observational uniformities relies on the symbolic equipment, the language and normatively consensual signs, of the observer, and on the possibility of communication between observers. Thus, symbolic systems serve a dual role. First, from the perspective of the individual, systems of shared symbols serve as objects of orientation for, and as internalized components of, personality systems. Secondly, from the perspective of the social system, symbols appear as institutionalized patterns in the form of language and serve as the vehicle for the transmission of shared value and belief systems. Complementarity of expectations and perceived reactions is necessary for human interaction—a complementarity that would not be possible without relative stability of shared meanings made possible through symbolization. Thus, symbolic systems provide the basis for the maintenance and elaboration of human interaction, and it is necessary to examine the function of language in studying any aspect of the development of human behavior.

Watson points out that not only does the size of the vocabulary normally increase during the early developmental years of childhood, but this same period is typically characterized by changes in clearness of articulation, in the integration of words into sentences, in the length of sentences, in the relatively increased use of grammatical parts of speech, and in the development of introspective and time-oriented responses. These external signs of developing language skill are normally found to show greater elaboration and maturity with increases in chronological age. For Watson, as for other thinkers that have been mentioned, the development of understanding is viewed in terms of concept formation and language skills, and speech rests firmly on the social-learning process. He points out, however, that this leads to the expectation of individual, group, and sex differences in language skill and intellectual development on the basis of diversity in environmental experience.

Luria and Yudovitch have intensively investigated the relationship between deprivation in language training and the development of the child's mental processes. They report the findings of an experimental investigation into the speech and productive thinking development of a set of identical twins. The theoretical position underlying the study (stripped of its overtones of Russian political ideology) closely follows that which we have been examining. They argue against reducing the complex forms of children's mental activity to a combination of elementary motor habits and sequential steps of physical maturation. They postulate instead that intellectual development relies on three fundamental propositions: (1) all mental processes are complex functional formations which are built up as a result of concrete forms of interaction between the child and his environment; (2) development occurs in stages only insofar as changes in these concrete forms of activity, made possible by physical maturation, present the child with new problems and new demands which, in turn, necessitate the development of new forms of action or cognition for adjustment; and (3) the child's mental activity is the outcome of manipulable social circumstances, such as opportunity for communication with the members of his interpersonal environment.

Luria and Yudovitch hypothesize that in infrahuman animals the development of higher nervous processes in each species is the outcome of individual experience but, for humans, language is essential to intellectual development. The child acquires from adults the experience of many generations through intentional instruction (speech) and incidental learning acquired through imitating role models (consensual symbols). They argue that, for the child, language is crucial for both the transmission of knowledge and the formation of concepts—the latter being the central process of the child's intellectual development. Interpersonal communication is of decisive significance, because the acquisition of language allows for abstraction, isolation, generalization, and perceptions of relationships among objects in the external environment—a systematization of experience. Language introduces forms of analysis and synthesis into the child's perception, which he would be unable to develop by himself in the absence of consensual symbols.

With this theoretical basis, Luria and Yudovitch set out to test its implications in the situation in which language development is abnormal, that is, retarded and inadequate for the demands of the social situation. They selected for study a set of five-and-a-half-year-old identical twins whose speech development was severely retarded. The twins were able to communicate with each other and make their needs known to their parents, but were quite inadequately prepared to cope with the communication demands of the school situation that faced them. Their pretest behavior indicated poor mental structuring in terms of a generalized inability to plan their actions, to direct them toward abstract or future goals, and to detach words from objects and actions. In keeping with their theoretical formulations, the researchers experimentally separated the twins and established conditions such that it became necessary for the twins to employ language. Concurrently, a program of intensive language training was instituted with one of the twins.

Within a three-month period, both twins developed nearly normal speech for their age group (with only minor problems of a grammatical nature). For the twin who was intensively language-trained, there was also evidence of cognitive restructuring in depth. His speech reflected narrative and planned elements; he could formulate the aims of his activity verbally; he engaged in goal-directed play and other productive and constructive activities. In addition, he evidenced the new-found ability to carry through a series of intellectual operations in order to solve a problem, and there was evidence of discursive thinking—all significant changes in the structure of his cognitive activity. This experiment not only demonstrates that language acquisition is important for more complex mental processes but, also, that while intellectual development is handicapped by deprivation in the area of language skills, it is possible to induce rapid and deep-seated changes in a relatively short period of time, given the necessity of employing speech, and training in its use. Thus, perception and attention, memory and imagination, consciousness and action, are not regarded as simple, innate mental properties, but as the product of complex *social* processes that directly influence the formation of complex human activity.

Bruner (1961) has examined the long-term cognitive consequences of early experiential deprivation. He presents a probabilistic metric for understanding the development of normal, environmentally appropriate cognitions, beliefs, values, or attitudes. He suggests that it is necessary to take into consideration the set of environmentally *possible* stimulating states that might occur at any given time, and the degree of bias in their likelihood of occurrence. He argues that the basic learning problem for a child is to reduce the complexity of his environment to the level at which he is able to cope with it; in other words, to match his cognitive programming to the likelihood and the significance of particular experiences in his environment. Bruner's formulation reflects a contemporary shift in psychological studies of perception away from a rigid model of neural activity to a functional emphasis, wherein perception is seen as directly related to the ongoing activities of the individual in interaction with his environment.

The implications of this kind of approach for our concerns with the effect of sensory deprivation are many. In general, Bruner's findings support others that have already been cited, that an impoverished background—one with little heterogenity of experience and with little opportunity for situational manipulation and diverse experience with discrimination—produces a child with: (1) reduced abilities to discriminate; (2) dysfunctional modes of coping with problems requiring complex or future-oriented solutions; (3) little interest in exploratory, creative behavior; and (4) a notably reduced tendency toward cognitive organization aimed at coalescing disparate elements in his environment. Thus, a certain amount of differentiated sensory stimulus seems necessary for normal orientation to his environment and even for mental adjustment in the child. Bruner concludes that to operate effectively in, and successfully adjust to, his environment, the child must develop during the socialization process an adequate implicit model of that environment—for two reasons. In the first instance, this implicit cognitive model of the environment, this "world view," functions to conserve information in the form of concepts or universals. Secondly, it serves as the basis for extrapolating or interpolating from partial information and incomplete experiential cues. Without such a model, learned in early childhood, and adequate for the adjustive demands made by later environmental contacts, the control functions of the central nervous system are without a basis for predicting that certain events are more likely to happen than others (or for precluding others); there is no basis for selectivity among stimuli.

The unhampered operation of this evaluation process is essential to the adjustment, the continuing adaptation, of the child. This is true for both the long-range development of adequate cognitive and social functioning, and for the directing of here-and-now behavior. Bruner suggests that one of the prime sources of anxiety lies in the individual's being placed in a state in which his conception and perception of environmental demands do not "fit" into his previously learned conceptual model. Thus, he has no basis for prediction of the environment in a manner that makes reasoned action possible.

> It follows that when an organism is prevented from monitoring the fittingness of his percepts and his cognitive structure, he is cut off from one of his principle sources of maintaining adjustment.[1]

This kind of division between what is familiar and what is novel is precisely the situation which faces the school-age child who has been inadequately socialized to the demands of the school situation. Early experiential deprivation prevents the formation of adequate models and

---

[1] Reprinted from J. S. Bruner, "The Cognitive Consequences of Early Sensory Deprivation," *Sensory Deprivation*, (Ed.) P. Solomon. (Cambridge, Mass.: Harvard University Press, 1961), p. 207.

means of coping with the environment of the school. The problem is one which centers on the transferability of learning, especially nonspecific transfer of experiential learning, for example, the establishment of generalized models, constructs, or concepts that represent the environment in such a way that when a new task or situation is encountered, it is possible to cope with it as an examplar of familiar concepts that are already associated with socially appropriate responses. Such model formation involves the learning of normative ways and means for dealing with relatively common features of the child's environment. Early experience with a comparatively rich perceptual environment is needed for such learning, and experiential deprivation prevents it. This kind of learning is seen to be a kind of continuous-feedback evaluation process by which children learn to guide their own development by internalizing a program for perceiving, cognizing, ordering, and manipulating their environments.

We have seen that this process of internalization depends upon interaction with others and has its basis in a need to develop corresponding categories and conceptions for communal action. We must conclude, therefore, that it is misleading to view the course of the human developmental process independently from the experiential and educational opportunities which make that development possible. It is clearly evident that the opportunity for verbalization, and the kind of language training available to the child in his family setting will have a significant impact on his intellectual development. The intellectual model that he develops of the world around him will serve to guide the child's general patterns of cognition and perception. In keeping with this interpersonal approach to human development, let us next turn to the consideration of how the interpersonal environment of the child may foster or hinder his development in other ways as well.

THE ROLE OF SIGNIFICANT OTHERS
IN THE DEVELOPMENTAL PROCESS

Our over-all theoretical interest is that of the impact of the social system on personality. This sociologically oriented social psychology of human development assumes that the basic learning processes involved in general over-all personality development, including the development of a conception of self, affective responses, internalization of socially prescribed and proscribed behavior expectations, and cognitive learning, are all dependent on the individual's ordering of his experience in keeping with rewards and cues from significant others. Thus, social learning (socialization) is the major factor in both intellectual development and in more general personality development, which also includes such dimensions as internalization of role expectations, conscience formation, and the development of a self-concept. Cooley (1902) and Mead (1934) speak of the "other" and "taking the role of the other" as important to the socialization process and the development of personality. Sullivan has introduced the idea of "significant" other in order to refine the concept and add a dimension of selectivity. Individuals are not affected by, influenced by, or even aware of all of those other persons in their interpersonal environment. It is only the responses of *selected* others that are of major importance in personality development. Thus, significant others are defined as those persons whose opinions, values, judgments, sentiments, and attitudes are important in shaping the direction of the developing personality. "Reference group" refers to the multiple version of a significant other. Hyman (1942) has introduced the term reference group and has argued, along with others, that the term is not necessarily synonymous with "membership" group. That is, the individual may be influenced by the values, beliefs, opinions, and attitudes of a group of which he is not a member but with whom he identifies. Significant others and reference groups are seen to serve two functions for the individual. In the first instance, they set the normative standards that the individual adopts as his own, and secondly, they serve as the models for comparative evaluation of self and of others. For the young child, with a limited range of social contacts, these significant others are most certainly found among the members of his family.

The family attempts to exert influence over the child's development in most cases. That is, the socialization process that occurs within the family setting is usually a direct attempt to exert social influence. Kelman (1960) has formulated a useful distinction between types of responses to social influence attempts that points up the kind of power required and the likelihood of long-range success. He delineates three distinct consequents: compliance, identification, and internalization. Compliance refers to a surface level of obedience to the demands of the interpersonal environment, in keeping with a fairly direct surveillance by the influencing agent whose source of power is means control. Identification refers to a somewhat deeper level of conformity to social expectations, in keeping with a need to maintain a rewarding relationship with the influencing agent whose source of power is attractiveness. Internalization refers to a deep-seated level of value orientation in personality developed in keeping with the relevance of these values to maintaining cognitive and affective congruency. At this level the conditions for performance of responses no longer require the presence of an influencing agent, but are mediated through the individual's own cognitive structure.

We are suggesting that this kind of distinction demonstrates the successive development of personality as it is socially influenced. That is, first the child complies with the demands of those in his interpersonal environment because they deliberately maintain a close surveillance over his behavior and place restrictions on his chosen behavior. In addition, the persons in his interpersonal environment, usually his mother during early childhood, have direct power to control the means of satisfying his personal needs for food, warmth, tactile stimulation, and so on. Secondly, if his social relationships are perceived as satisfying to him, the child comes to view those in his interpersonal environment as attractive and compliance with their demands as rewarding. He becomes aware of their expectations of him and concerned that he fulfill these expectations, in order to maintain the rewarding relationship. At this point, identification, in the sense of associating his own behavior and self-conception with the demands and evaluations of significant others, has occurred. As the next step in the development of personality, the child comes to assume those values, beliefs, evaluations, and role expectations of his significant others as his own. These are incorporated into his world view and direct his future activities even in the absence of the significant others who have been instrumental in shaping his personality. At this point, internalization of social expectations, values, conceptions, and beliefs occurs and the conscience (morality guide), the conceptual structure (cognitive guide), the role expectations (behavioral guide), and the self-concept have begun to develop.

Two cautionary notes must be made. First, we have spoken of "successive development" as though the developmental process occurs in some specifiable time sequence—this is *not* intended. It is assumed that internalization is the goal of all influence attempts, but it is quite clearly the case that this goal is not always successfully reached by all those who might attempt to influence the direction of a child's development. It is postulated that compliance is always the starting point and that identification must precede internalization, but nothing is said of when, or even *if*, each of these levels will be reached. Furthermore, it is possible for the child to return to a previous level, if for some reason the object of his identification loses its attractiveness or the values he has internalized are brought into question.

Secondly, we have spoken of the end products of influence attempts as though some developmental limit is reached, at which point no further changes occur. Again this is not the implication intended. It is agreed that the early years of childhood are of great importance to the development of personality. However, socialization is viewed as an ongoing process that does not stop at age five, or at puberty, or at adulthood, or at any other specific chronological point, but continues as long as new experiences do. As social learning continues, continual personality adjustments must be made in response to new perceptions and experiences. Personalities change in response to new experiences or reinterpretations of old ones, in light of changed perceptions which demand a reorganization of beliefs, values, and attitudes. Thus, neither do we postulate that adult personality is wholly dependent upon early experiences, nor do we postulate that early experiences are unimportant. We argue only that personality is also modifiable, at least to some extent, by experiences that occur after the period of early childhood.

Nevertheless, certain aspects of personality remain stable enough to permit investigations with personality as an independent variable. It is assumed, in keeping with Rokeach's (1960) formulation of personality systems, that the various components of a personality system are organized along a centrality-peripherality continuum and, thus, some aspects are more salient and more stable to the individual than others. When we speak of the child's personality development in this chapter, we are specifically addressing attention to those aspects of personality that are normally developed by early experiences in the family. We have used the term "normal" in several instances—a term many writers have found objectionable on the grounds that it represents a value judgment. That is not our intention. Normal, for our purposes, is defined as in conformity with the appropriate socially consensual evaluative standard found in whatever social system is under consideration.

The work of Bandura and Walters exemplifies the social-learning approach to personality development that has been described here. They discuss both intentional instruction and incidental learning as methods of social learning. That is, social learning is achieved through two broadly defined interactional processes, which operate jointly in actual situations. The first of these, intentional instruction, refers to formal institutionalized ways of socialization to value orientations and behavioral expectations. The second, incidental learning, refers to processes of identification with, or emulation of, role models in the imitator's behavioral field. Bandura and Walters place strong emphasis on the concept of "vicarious reinforcement" as it influences social learning, that is, learning from observation of behavioral models without direct personal participation.

> New responses may be learned or the characteristics of existing responses may be changed as a function of observing the behavior of others or its response consequences without the observer's performing any overt responses himself or receiving any direct reinforcement during the acquisition period.[2]

They cite research evidence to confirm the idea that social response patterns, both normal and deviant, can readily be transmitted through the influence of a model, and that imitation of that model's behavior is

[2]Reprinted from A. Bandura and R. H. Walters, *Social Learning and Personality Development* (New York: Holt, Rinehart and Winston, Inc., 1963), p. 47.

facilitated if the model receives rewards. On the other hand, if the model is observed to receive punishments, the observer may refrain from making new deviant responses or even be restrained from making deviant responses he has already learned.

Bandura and Walters employ the single term "imitation" to cover concepts that have been called variously "imitation," "identification," and "role practice." They note that attempts have been made in the literature to differentiate these concepts, but they conclude that any or all of these terms may be defined as behavior that observably reproduces the actions, attitudes, or emotional responses of some real or symbolic model without any formal instructions being given as to how the observer should behave. Accordingly, for our purposes, these terms will be used interchangeably and with the assumption that they are synonymous. The content of this behavior depends, of course, on what is taught and who is selected as the model for identification. In our contemporary society there is a broad range of cultural, subcultural, and individual-family differences in normal socialization practices. In the next section we will consider briefly some fairly typical differences in child-training techniques and some generalizations based on research concerning personality development in response to them.

THE FAMILY AND CHILD-REARING TECHNIQUES
AS THEY INFLUENCE
PERSONALITY DEVELOPMENT

Watson notes that for the infant, considered in relation to a matrix of other persons, the mother, who serves as the first agent of socialization, is the most significant other in the development of the child's personality. He cites research evidence, however, to support the contention that:

> specific practices in maternal behavior have *not* been found to show invariant relationships with consequent personality development. . . . [Generalized] maternal attitudes were found to be much more closely related to behavior in children. Both attitudes and patterns. . . . [of maternal behavior] . . . allow one to see maternal propensities to behave in *general ways* which are then related to later adjustment in their children. . . . Maternal attitudes and patterns of behavior were found to be interrelated.[3]

This conclusion has been borne out by other researchers.

[3]Reprinted from R. I. Watson, *Psychology of the Child; Personal, Social and Disturbed Child Development* (New York: John Wiley & Sons, Inc., 1960), pp. 277–278. (Emphasis author's.)

Sewell (1952) empirically has tested the relationship between mothers' reports of their specific child-rearing practices and subsequent personality adjustment on the part of their children. A child's personality adjustment was measured in terms of scores obtained on a battery of standard paper-and-pencil and projective personality tests, from ratings by teachers, and from behavioral information gained from interviews with the mothers. Sewell's general hypothesis (stated in the null form), that "the personality adjustment and traits of children who have undergone varying specific infant-training experiences do not differ significantly from each other," cannot be rejected. Of the 460 possible interrelations that he examined, between specific infant-training practices and theoretically derived hypotheses concerning their effect on subsequent character and personality development, only eighteen are statistically significant at or beyond the 5 percent level. Of these eighteen, eleven are in the expected direction and seven are contrary to the relationship expected on the basis of theory. This kind of evidence seems to rule out any direct link between certain specific child-rearing practices, such as breast versus bottle feeding, age and abruptness of weaning, age and severity of toilet training, and subsequent specific personality adjustments. However, children *do* differ measurably on standard personality tests, and their experiences in early childhood do seem to be linked with general personality development. Sewell follows the theoretical position noted previously as espoused by Watson, that:

> it is entirely possible that the significant and crucial matter is not the practices themselves but the whole personal-social situation in which they find their expression, including the attitudes and behavior of the mother.[4]

One of the sources of differences in maternal attitudes appears to be social class. Social-class differences in child-rearing practices have been the subject of a number of empirical studies. Perhaps the best known of these is the work by Sears, Maccoby, and Levin (1957). Sears and his associates have investigated patterns of child rearing and have found reported differences among mothers of differing socioeconomic strata and differing levels of formal education. They draw some general conclusions regarding the differences in socialization practices as employed by working-class and middle-class parents. The subjects range from scores of 1 to 5 on Warner's 7-point scale of occupational status, with the two lowest categories entirely missing from the sample.

[4]Reprinted from W. H. Sewell, "Infant Training and the Personality of the Child," *American Journal of Sociology*, **58** (September), 159. Copyright 1952 by The University of Chicago Press.

Generally they find that working-class mothers report themselves to be less permissive and more rejective of dependency behavior than middle-class mothers. Children of working-class parents are reported to experience more severe sex training; their mothers are more strict in the areas of modesty training, masturbation, and social sex play. Working-class mothers report that they are more punitive about aggression directed toward parents, whereas they are less punitive than middle-class mothers regarding aggression toward neighborhood children. Sears *et al.* find no class differences among mothers' attitudes toward sibling aggression.

Working-class mothers report that their attitudes are more restrictive and demanding about noise in the house, care of clothing, table manners, and so forth. These mothers, as opposed to middle-class mothers, also give their preschool children less freedom to cross streets or leave the immediate neighborhood in order to play. (The authors note, in connection with this point, that the area of residence for working-class children is apt to be less safe physically for such freedom than middle-class neighborhoods—suggesting that this particular attitude may be a reasonably objective function of the area of residence.) Working-class mothers also report that they place more pressure on their children to achieve in school than do middle-class mothers while, at the same time, they hold fewer aspirations toward higher education for their children.

Since effective socialization is seen as the result of its reward value for the child, a concern with parental attitudes toward rewards and punishments is an important consideration. Rewards and punishments are not always easily distinguishable. Bandura and Walters point out that punishment may have very diverse effects depending on its timing and intensity, its nature, and on the perceived status of the punitive agent. They also note that nonreward following reward is perceived typically as punishment, while nonreward following punishment is seen as positive reinforcement. Sears *et al.* find that there are some important differences among mothers' general attitudes toward punishment. They discuss two categories of reward-punishment techniques—love-oriented and object-oriented. Love-oriented techniques involve verbal praise as a means of rewarding desired behavior, social isolation as a punishment, and withdrawal of love as the principle punishing technique. The effectiveness of this technique depends on a close, personal and warm relationship between parent and child; a relationship that is perceived as rewarding by the child who will, then, feel punished at the threat of a disruption in the relationship. The parent's source of power in this case is the attractiveness of the relationship. Object-oriented techniques, on the other hand, involve dispensing tangible objects as incentives and rewards, with deprivation of privileges and physical punishment as the primary punitive techniques. The effectiveness of this technique is largely limited to the parents' ability to maintain control of the child by wielding means and ends power or by physical force.

Sears *et al.* find that working-class mothers relate that in general they punish more than middle-class mothers and, at the same time, that their punishment techniques are more often object-oriented. Working-class mothers report that they punish mainly by physical means and deprivation of privileges. The researchers find no class differences in the use of isolation and withdrawal of love as punishment techniques; these would appear to be individual-family differences. However, they do find that working-class mothers more frequently employ ridicule as a punishment technique. There are no reported class differences in the kind of reward technique most frequently used, although working-class mothers report being slightly less demonstrative toward their children in general.

The family setting experienced by the child of working-class parents generally appears to be less stable than that of middle-class children, insofar as working-class mothers report more open quarreling between themselves and their husbands and typically are more critical of their husbands than middle-class wives. In a number of cases it is found that the mother's educational level alone, regardless of socioeconomic status, age, size of the family, and so on, is the determining factor in her attitudes toward socializing her child. After an extensive factor analysis, it is found that the two social classes studied can be significantly differentiated only on the general attitudinal factors of permissiveness versus strictness; general family adjustment; warmth of the mother-child relationship; and aggressiveness and punitiveness.

This particular study by Sears and his associates, being fairly typical in design, exemplifies some problems related to our concern with disadvantaged children. In the first instance, the data was gathered by means of retrospective interviews with the mothers only—all data on fathers' attitudes included—who were asked to recall how they had treated their children from early infancy and their current attitudes toward the child who was entering kindergarten at the time of the investigation. The authors do note that "the interviewing of mothers about their child-rearing practices and attitudes provides a limited description of those phenomena." (Sears *et al.* 1957, p. 448) It is at least possible that such studies do not document actual behavior as much as the middle-class mother's superior knowledge of socially acceptable responses to questions about their child-rearing practices. Quite apart from any suggestion of intentional misrepresentation of her attitudes, there is also the reasonable possibility that the mother may simply fail to accurately recall her prior behavior and attitudes toward the child, especially if she has had other children.

Secondly, the sample of mothers interviewed was drawn from a fairly narrow subsegment of the population. Criteria of selection demanded that the child be living with both natural parents, that neither parent be foreign born, that the child must not be a twin, physically handicapped in any way, mentally handicapped, a Negro, or a pupil in attendance at anything other than a public school. Each of these criteria effectively eliminated from study a fairly wide segment of those children who reasonably might be expected to be most severely disadvantaged. Even with these rigid requirements, another 10 percent of the original 481 target families were eliminated because they refused to participate in the investigation. Apparently nothing is known of the reasons for their refusal.

Bronfenbrenner (1958, 1961) has given serious and scholarly attention to reports of differences in specific child-rearing practices among parents of varying socioeconomic status. His extensive review and analysis of a wide range of studies has led him to some conclusions that are relevant here. He notes, among other things, that for methodologically sound interpretation of reports of child-rearing practices, it is essential to distinguish between the time the data is gathered and the actual period to which this information refers. This is important because it is a well-known phenomenon that child-rearing practices change over a period of time. By comparing generalized changes in trends with the specific information gathered in the various empirical studies (reinterpreted according to the actual period of time they refer to), Bronfenbrenner concludes that these changes in general trends in socialization of the child occur over a time irrespective of the social-class level of the parents. Evidence of changing trends in child-rearing are found in standard infant-care manuals as they are offered in continuously revised editions. Bronfenbrenner's analysis points to the fact that mothers not only read these manuals and take them seriously, but that their behavior toward their children is affected accordingly.

Bronfenbrenner's own general hypothesis about changes in specific child-rearing practices extends beyond the confines of social class.

> Child-rearing practices are likely to change most quickly in those segments of society which have closest access and are most receptive to the agencies or agents of change, for example, public media, clinics, physicians, and counselors.[5]

In this connection he reports that middle-class urban mothers, in general, are more apt to be in a position to read and hear advice than are lower-class or rural mothers. He also notes that the data supports the conclusion that lower-class parents, as a function of increasing income, education, and exposure to the body of child-rearing literature, are gradually reducing

---

[5]Reprinted from p. 411 from U. Bronfenbrenner, "Socialization and Social Class Through Time and Space" from *Readings in Social Psychology* by E. E. Maccoby, T. M. Newcomb, and E. L. Hartley. Copyright 1947, 1952, © 1958 by Holt, Rinehart and Winston, Inc., Publishers.

their "cultural lag." For our concerns this suggests that training programs designed to acquaint the parents of disadvantaged children with effective child-rearing practices are indicated and should prove helpful.

Bronfenbrenner's extensive analysis of child-rearing studies does support much of the same types of general attitudinal conclusions about socialization and social class that Sears *et al.* have suggested. The data depicts the middle-class parent as being more permissive in general, as having a higher level of achievement expectations, and as being less apt to use physical punishment as a disciplinary technique but more apt to resort to reasoning, isolation, and love-oriented techniques. These differences appear to remain constant as a description of the attitudinal polarity of socialization differences among social classes.

In his later work, Bronfenbrenner (1961) examines the data as it applies to the effects on children of the consistencies and changes in patterns of child rearing. He draws several generalizations from the literature, including the fact that increased movement away from techniques of physical punishment, toward reliance on psychological techniques of discipline, is shown to be a powerful and positive force for bringing about desired changes in the child's behavior. He finds that girls are more likely to be disciplined by love-oriented techniques than boys and, as a result, are found to be more obedient, more cooperative, and generally better socialized than boys. Girls, however, tend to become "oversocialized" and susceptible to the detrimental influences of overprotection, whereas boys are more subject to the detrimental effects of insufficient parental discipline and support. Boys are more apt to receive inadequate discipline in the lower socioeconomic strata than boys in the upper classes.

Other indications of class differences are found in studies that report that in the higher socioeconomic levels, girls excel boys in acceptance of responsibility and social acceptance while, in the lower classes, boys excel girls in assuming leadership, in level of aspiration, and in competitiveness. For all socioeconomic levels, it is found that mothers primarily employ love-oriented disciplinary techniques regardless of the sex of the child. This is true, across class levels, for father's disciplinary techniques toward girls. However, all fathers tend to use more direct kinds of discipline toward their male children, with fathers in the lower socioeconomic classes generally employing more physical punishment as a disciplinary technique regardless of the sex of the child. Bronfenbrenner points out that evidence indicates boys tend to be better socialized when the father is the principal disciplinarian and girls profit most when the mother is the primary authority figure. He notes that boys from father-absent homes tend to be more highly dependent and concludes that the absence of the father is especially critical for male children. This is a point that we will discuss more completely in the next section. Bandura and Walters point out, in this connection, that the normative developmental process requires a gradual modification of dependency responses for boys, which is a more marked developmental change than is required of girls. For this reason, the presence in the home of atypical parental sex-role models, or the absence of a male model, during early socialization experiences may make subsequent emotional adjustment outside the home situation particularly difficult for boys.

Bronfenbrenner suggests that emphasis on intellectual achievement is becoming the dominant force in redirecting the aims and practices of socializing the child in the contemporary United States. He also notes that, while specific practices and general attitudes toward achievement training may well successfully produce high achievement motivation in children, this same training may also give rise to such normatively undesirable personality characteristics as extreme aggressiveness, cruelty, domineering attitudes, and anxiety. For our concerns this suggests that in planning practical programs designed to foster achievement motivation, the planners must be willing to accept the full responsibility for undesirable consequences.

The obvious conclusion that can be drawn is that it is wise to be cautious about predicting the effects of specific child-rearing practices on children's subsequent personality development. However, insofar as socialization is defined as the process by which personalities are influenced by the experience of living—and especially by early experiences in family living—the general parental attitudes toward warmth and dependency, permissiveness and strictness, reward and punishment, and achievement training do seem to have a far-reaching impact on personality development. Furthermore, these attitudes are, at least in part, differentially distributed among the various social classes as they are distinguishable in our contemporary society. It should be equally obvious that not all the families within a given socioeconomic status subscribe to the typical pattern.

Several of the works we have considered have noted sex differences in both parental attitudes and in children's responses to them. Most developmental studies treat the mother's role extensively. In the next section we will consider the influence of the mother and the father specifically, giving special attention to the often neglected role of the father in the developmental process.

THE ROLES OF THE MOTHER AND FATHER IN THE SOCIALIZATION PROCESS

Bronfenbrenner's analyses indicate something of the importance of family structure in the child's personality development. The particular problems created by observing the differential effects of varying child-rearing practices and their general ineffectiveness as a predictor of long-range personality development, raise the issue of the relative influence of such efforts at intentional instruction, as opposed to incidental learning from parental attitudes and behavior. In this section we will be interested particularly in the effects of incidental learning accomplished through identification with the parents as role models. The concept of "identification" is employed here to describe the process that accounts for the selection of one role model rather than another. Mussen, Conger, and Kagan (1963) define identification as a belief that some of the attributes of a role model belong to the self. They postulate that the motivation for identification is provided by the child's desire to command the attractive goals possessed by the chosen model. Many other possible motivating influences on identification have been postulated in the literature, including observation reinforced vicariously (secondary reinforcement as exemplified by the thinking of Bandura and Walters), dependency as the primary motivating mechanism (as exemplified by Sears *et al.*), status-envy, social power, similarity to self, and others. There seems to be general agreement that children learn many things by copying the behavior of models, and each of the various theories of the underlying motives that induce identification finds some experimental support. It is most probably the case that several or all of these mechanisms may operate simultaneously or at different times in different situations to produce identification with a chosen model. We will take the position that identification is multidetermined and go on to consider its effects rather than its causes.

In current child development literature, incidental learning through identification is most often cited as influential in the areas of achievement motivation, aggressive behavior, and in the area of adult role modeling, especially sex-role identification. There is, in the majority of the developmental literature, a strong and consistent emphasis on the importance for personality development of a warm and satisfying relationship between mother and child in the early years of socialization. We do not deny that the mother is assuredly a most important figure in the child's interpersonal matrix, especially during infancy and very early childhood. However, only recently has the role of the father in the developmental process been given much attention. Kohn and Carroll (1960) reflect this fairly new emphasis in their study of social-class differences in the perception of the proper allocation of parental responsibilities in child rearing. Their purpose is to examine the effects of varying socioeconomic class attitudes toward the division, between mother and father, of responsibilities for training and disciplining their children. Their sample consisted of 200 white middle-class and 200 white working-class families of fifth-grade children. The data were obtained by interviews with all of the mothers and slightly over a fourth of the fathers and children. The findings indicate that middle-class mothers emphasize the equality of the mother-father roles in training the child, while the fathers' role as disciplinarian is given only secondary importance. Middle-class fathers generally agree with this assessment of their responsibility, though they are stronger in their agreement as to their proper role in relation to sons than to daughters. Working-class mothers expect their husbands to be firm disciplinarians, but expect little from them in terms of supportive training. Working-class fathers are found to feel that child-rearing, in all its aspects, is properly the mother's responsibility. It seems reasonable to assume that the parents' perception of their role responsibilities has an important influence on the development process in children.

Earlier references to the father's role have been made largely in terms of his influence as a sex-role model for boys. In more recent works, considerably more emphasis on the general role of the father has appeared. Sears, Rau, and Alpert (1965) have tested a series of hypotheses derived from a theory of identification motivated by dependency, which concerns child-rearing antecedents of certain behaviors in children, for example, attention seeking, prosocial aggression, sex typing, and emotional upset, which are presumed to be learned through this process of identification. Little theoretical support is found, perhaps because of Sears *et al.* unidimensional approach to identification motivation, but some general conclusions, particularly concerning the father's role, are of interest to us. They find, among other things, that the level of permissiveness of *both* parents is an important factor in the socialization of boys and girls. The father is seen to be important, not only as a male sex-role model, but as the source of power in the family, an agent of morality training, and the one who sets high achievement standards. Studies have been done that specifically deal with the parental role in the development of achievement motivation.

Rosen and D'Andrade (1959) have examined the origins of achievement motivation among ten-year-old boys in light of their training in the family setting. Forty white boys, matched by group on the factor of measured intelligence (IQ), were assigned to "high need achievement" and "low need achievement" groups each consisting of twenty boys on the basis of Thematic Apperception Test (TAT) procedures. The subject groups were further controlled so that there were ten middle-class and ten lower-class boys in each of the two "need achievement" groups. However, no differences by social class were found, so it is possible to disregard this division. The parents of the forty boys also participated in the experiment.

Each boy, in the presence of his mother and father, was given a series of tasks to complete, which allowed his parents the opportunity to interact with the child while the child was observed by the experimenters. From these observations it is concluded that parents do provide achievement and independence training, but that fathers contribute more toward training boys than do mothers. However, it is found that mothers of boys with high achievement motivation give more emphasis to achievement training, are more dominant, and reward their sons with approval and punish them with hostility more often than do mothers of boys with low achievement motivation. In short, these mothers behave more typically like fathers than like love-oriented mothers. The study concludes that for high need achievement to develop, the boy needs both more autonomy from his father than from his mother and, at the same time, a strong model for achievement motivation—usually his father. Thus, we suggest that parental pressures for, and reward of, early achievement, when coupled with a high ratio of successes to failures for the child, result in high need for achievement in the school situation—provided the child identifies with his supportive parents.

In the Sears *et al.* (1965) study, the size and direction of the correlations among their findings do not allow for many specific conclusions about the effects of parental influence, but a general indication is that in the socialization process, the mother's influence is more significant for girls, whereas the father's influence has the greatest impact on boys. They state the general principle that "when the parent of the opposite sex rewards dependency, the child develops behavior qualities characteristic of that sex." (Sears, Rau, and Alpert, 1965, p. 255) They add, however, that the converse of this principle is not so clearly supported. They also find that there is little support for a dependency-motivated theory of identification to account for the development of masculinity in boys, though such a theory does appear to account for the development of sex-appropriate roles for girls and sex-inappropriate behavior among boys who have not had a strong masculine role model.

Kagan (1964) has suggested that sex-role identity plays a central role in directing the child's personality development, because this identity sets boundaries on subsequent behavioral choices. He notes that sex-role influences are felt in several behavioral areas, including general stability of behavioral responses and differential mastery of academic skills, in addition to sexual behavior toward love objects. He cites research evidence to support the position that boys typically have higher levels than girls of academic achievement with respect to tasks involving spatial and mechanical reasoning, science, and mathematics. Furthermore, boys are typically more autonomous and persistent than girls in their orientation to problem-solving tasks—in response to differential sex-role socialization. These pervasive aspects of sex-role identity on personality development make concern with sex-role identification an important one in the consideration of the causes of the Leftout's maladjustment to school.

Kagan defines a sex-role standard as a learned association between selected characteristics, behaviors, and attitudes with concepts of male and female. Early sex-role discrimination by the child is in response to a desire to make his behavior and attitudes conform to his perception of the sex-role standard. Kagan points out that the sex-role standard applies to two distinct kinds of response in the child: (1) as an internalized part of his self-concept, and (2) as knowledge of a set of culturally consensual behavioral expectations. Sears has made an important distinction between sex-role "preference" and "identification." Sex-role preference refers to sex-linked behavior, which the individual would like to adopt or which he perceives as the preferred or more desirable behavior. This preference may differ from his sex-role identification, which refers to sex-linked behavioral proscriptions and prescriptions that the individual internalizes as appropriate for those of his biological sex. It is interesting to note that psychoanalytic theory postulates that the girl is expected to experience greater difficulties in assuming her feminine role than is the boy in assuming his masculine role because of "penis envy," that is, masculine sex-role preference. This is diametrically opposed to the social-learning theory offered here, which assumes *less* difficulty in learning the feminine sex-role, since girls typically have more and closer contacts with their mothers, who act as role models, than do boys with their fathers. We assume that sex-role preferences, which differ from the appropriate sex-role identification of the child, are abnormalities produced by inadequate socialization.

For adequate socialization and subsequent personality adjustment, the child needs to acquire a sex-role identity that matches his biological sex. This learned identity is acquired by differential identification (whatever its motivating force) with the parent of the same sex, parental surrogates, older siblings, and significant others. Unfortunately, for the children who are the center of our concern, abnormal family structures and inadequate sex-role models, for example, father-absent or mother-dominated, both parents absent, and so forth, are an all too typical occurrence.

Lynn and Sawrey (1959) examined the effects on both boys and girls reared in father-absent families. They selected forty father-absent and forty father-present Norwegian families of equal socioeconomic levels. The absent fathers were sailors—away for an average of nine months each year. Their data were gathered on the basis of interviews and doll-play situations with the early elementary-school age children of these families. It is found that more father-absent boys than father-present boys show signs of immaturity, stronger striving toward masculine identification, and have poorer peer adjustments. Father-absent girls are better able to make peer adjustments than father-absent boys, though their problems in this area are more pronounced than those for father-present children, regardless of sex. Father-absent girls also evidence more dependency on their mothers than do father-present girls. This suggests that an important part of developing sex-role identities includes the opportunity to observe and interact with complementary-sex models as well as same-sex models.

Lynn and Sawrey conclude that the absence of the father affects the personality development of both boys and girls, although boys seem to be more severely disadvantaged by their father's absence. They also suggest that other factors may also have influence, for example, the personality and attitudinal orientation of a woman who would marry a sailor.

Others have suggested, as we have seen, that mothers' attitudes toward the father's role responsibilities differ. Thus, presumably, if the mother is content with the family structure—whatever it may be—there is less apt to be strain associated with a situation that demands that she fulfill the typical aspects of both parental roles. However, this assumption does raise the question that if developmental inadequacies can be found among children of father-absent families when the mother willingly accepts the situation, what more severe problems might lie in wait for the child of a father-absent family when the mother is more apt to resent the situation, such as a case in which the father is in jail or has deserted the mother?

The U.S. Department of Labor Report (1965), reviewed in the previous chapter, concerns itself with this kind of situation among Negro families in our society. In this report to the President it is emphasized that the fundamental problem among Negroes in general is that of a disorganized family structure. The report points out that for vast numbers of the unskilled, poorly educated, urban Negro working-class, the fabric of conventional family relationships is all but absent. The Report notes that nearly a quarter of urban Negro marriages are dissolved, a large and growing number of births are illegitimate, and that more than a quarter of Negro families are dominated by females. Whether or not the male is actually absent, he frequently is a socially emasculated, inadequate sex-role model. We have discussed in the preceding chapter the special case of Negroes in the contemporary social structure; the point we wish to make here is that Negro families are not the *only* families that suffer from structural disorganization, and Negro children are not the only victims of the effect of personality development that this kind of disorganization spawns. While the specific role of the father in influencing developing personality is far from crystal clear, it is clearly an important role and deserves the attention that is slowly becoming focused on it.

Nash (1965) has recently reviewed the literature relating to the father's role in personality development; he notes the literature to be meagre compared to that directed toward the mother's role. It is not entirely incidental that we point out that he specifically criticizes the common but methodologically unsound practice of investigating father attitudes indirectly by way of his wife's reports concerning them. He cites evidence that independent interviews with both mother and father yield only small agreement between them on either their perceptions of their children's behavior, or on their own statements about attitudes toward and interactions with their children. Independent outside criteria tend to support the father's reports as being more accurate than the mother's.

Nash concludes from his review and analysis of the literature that the general opinion among sociologists today is that American society in particular, and Western industrial society in general, is "mother-centered" in its philosophy of child care. The development of this philosophy can be traced to the economic history of industrial civilization, in which the traditional family cooperative economy has been supplanted by an economic pattern in which the father is typically engaged in economic activity away from the home. This pattern, in turn, forces him to delegate his child-rearing responsibilities to his wife. Some psychologists have accepted this generalized cultural phenomenon so uncritically as to come to the assumption, as evidenced by their theoretical writings, that the rearing of children is an exclusively feminine responsibility. However, Nash cites research evidence from clinical studies and investigations of delinquents, which suggests that father-child relationships, especially those between fathers and sons, may be of considerable etiological importance to both social and psychological maladjustments. He points out that psychosexual problems apparently result from a child's major identification with the opposite-sexed parent. Thus, a mother-centered family structure—as is reasonably common for the children with whom we are particularly concerned—is peculiarly unsuited to the needs of boys. Nash concludes that evidence supports the view that identification of the child with his same-sex parent is not only significant in sex-role development but in general personality development as well. He notes that this identification can be understood in terms of social-learning theory, that is, warm, affectionate relationships and prolonged associations (in contrast to the hostility assumed in the oedipal theory), and that these kinds of relationships are essential requirements for successful identification, adequate socialization, and well-adjusted personality development.

Since we are interested in children who are apt to suffer disruptions of one sort or another in family relationships, it becomes important to look at the body of literature specifically relating to deprivation in the area of these relationships. Nearly all such studies are found classified under the rubric of "maternal deprivation." While we do not wish to be accused of underestimating the mother's role, we do suggest that the evidence strongly indicates that deprivation of one parent has different effects for boys and girls, depending upon which parent is absent or inadequate. Furthermore, for boys at least, paternal deprivation may be as serious as maternal deprivation. In all fairness, it should be pointed out that many of the studies of maternal deprivation have been, in reality, concerned with the effects on children who are deprived of *both* parents. Since few, if any, of the authors of these studies have made any attempt to separate the differential effects of maternal versus paternal deprivation, Nash has suggested that the term "parental deprivation" would be more accurate. Consequently, we will treat the findings of this body of literature as relating to a more general disruption in the social structure of the family, rather than to the specific loss of a close personal relationship with the mother alone.

LIMITATIONS OF PARENTAL INFLUENCE ON THE DEVELOPMENTAL PROCESS

The general over-all conclusion that can be drawn from our examination of the developmental process is the hardly surprising one that a verbally-oriented, close, warm, supportive, and continuous relationship with both parents is the best possible family setting in which both boys and girls may develop. Concomitantly, any disorganization in this family pattern will deprive the child to some extent of a chance for adequate socialization, or, at least, it will limit the influence that the family has over the developmental process.

Although these basic premises are acceptable, Yarrow (1964), among others, has pointed out that the differential impact on personality development between good parental care and the adverse effects generated by parental deprivation is not a simple and straightforward problem. He suggests that the terms "deprivation" and "separation" need to be distinguished, despite the fact that they are employed synonymously in the literature. Furthermore, he notes that there are several possible varieties of separation experiences: single brief separation with reunion, single permanent separation, repeated permanent separation (such as when the child is shuttled about among relatives or a series of foster homes), and others. He suggests the need for examining the effects of these various types of separation. He also postulates that the age of the child at separation, before or after the development of a meaningful focused relationship with specific significant others, has an important influence on the consequences of separation.

Yarrow suggests the need for considering several other factors as well. Among these is the quality of the relationship between the child and his parents prior to separation. For example, if the family setting is such that there are distortions in the parental attitudes, separation may be preferable to highly deviant conditions. In short, it is assumed that separation will have different meanings for the child depending upon whether it represents a break in a meaningful, satisfying, intimate, protective relationship or simply is the culmination of parental indifference or overt rejection.

Other factors such as the nature of the relationship with the parents during temporary separation, the duration of the separation experience, the nature of subsequent parental care following separation with reunion, and reinforcing experiences outside the family setting must also be considered. Yarrow concludes that accumulated evidence supports the view that the effects of deprivation in the areas of sensory, social, and emotional stimulation, which are frequently concurrent with parental separation, are more harmful than parental separation per se. This kind of *stimulus deprivation* would appear to be clearly linked with inadequate intellectual development and to more general inadequacies of personality development.

Casler (1961) has also undertaken to summarize the major findings of the maternal deprivation literature. He has reviewed a wide variety of studies that employ the institutional, cultural, animal-experimental, and neuro-anatomical approaches to the problem. His central proposition is that many kinds of sensory reinforcement bridge the gap between physiology and social learning for the child. Such sensory stimulation may be tactile, visual, or auditory. He concludes, as does Yarrow, that there is no real proof that the absence of the mother (or parents) per se accounts for the observed problems of deprived children, but that stimulus deprivation in general is a more useful and precise concept for accounting for their problems. He argues that deprivation of maternal love can have ill effects only after specific affective responsiveness has been achieved by the child. This normally occurs in the last six months of the first year of life. However, it can be postulated that this affective bond may occur much later, or not at all, in a child-parent relationship characterized by hostility, rejection, or severe structural disorganization. Ill effects found among children who have not established this affective bond probably has some other cause than that of separation from one or both parents. This other cause may be perceptual deprivation, that is, the absolute or relative absence of tactile, verbal, visual, or emotional stimulation.

Evidence indicates that this kind of stimulus deprivation may be produced by either social isolation, environmental sameness, or both. In this connection, Casler points out that "it is not the stimulus itself, but rather the *response* to the stimulus which provides the perceptual or sensory stimulation." In short, stimulation without benefit of contrast may not be perceived, and stimulation that does not fit the socially learned cognitive structure may be ignored.

Casler postulates a causal relationship between perceptual stimulation and intellectual, emotional, and physical functioning. In light of the earlier discussion of the importance of language acquisition for intellectual development, it is interesting to note that Casler cites studies by Brodbeck and Irwin of the verbal behavior of institutionalized children, who are found to be consistently less vocal than those raised in families. He points out, however, that those forms of social stimulation necessary for proper language development *can* be provided in an institutional setting if the need for doing so is recognized. In addition, he notes that:

> recent evidence indicates that there is no relation between the relative extent of early vocalization and later verbal facility if sensory reinforcement later occurs. . . . Perhaps the most conclusive support for the contention that social reinforcement, not mother love, plays a dominant role in the development of vocalization comes from a study by Rheingold, Gewitz, and Ross. Three-month-old babies showed increased vocalization after visual, auditory, and tactile reinforcements; and extinction was demonstrated when the reinforcement was withdrawn.[6]

For our purposes, these kinds of findings, along with others we have discussed, suggest the feasibility of programs in the school designed to compensate for early stimulus deprivation.

In addition to the limitations of parental influence on the developmental process among children which we have already discussed, for example, separation and role-model inadequacies, other factors are particularly relevant to the culturally and socioeconomically disadvantaged children with whom we are primarily concerned. In the first instance, we are centrally focusing on the school-age child: Mussen, Conger, and Kagan propose that development during middle childhood, that is, elementary-school age of approximately five to twelve, is normally characterized by an expansion of the social environment. Bandura and Walters point out that innovations in social behavior may occur, as the child gets older, because of increased opportunity for contact with role models provided by peers and adults other than his parents. They suggest, however, that the *degree* of innovation is likely to be a function of the diversity of available models. They cite Schachter's (1951) conclusion that in homogeneous groups, individual deviant behavioral patterns are likely to elicit social rejection from other members of the group. Bandura and Walters suggest that in a heterogeneous group, behavior and values acquired in the family situation will govern the choice of role models outside the home. In this connection, it is suggested that this selection may be made either on the basis of similarity, if family relationships have been satisfactory, or dissimilarity (rejection of familial values), if the child's relationship with his family has been unsatisfactory.

In any case, the influence of the social subsystem represented by the school is an important one for any school-age child. Watson points out that in general children of this age group are in a great deal of contact with

---

[6]Reprinted from L. Casler, "Maternal Deprivation: A Critical Review of the Literature," *Monographs of the Society for Research in Child Development,* 26 (2), 6 and 28. Copyright © 1961 by The Society for Research in Child Development, Inc. Reprinted with permission.

adult role models outside the home. These adults, for example, teachers, recreation leaders, religious instructors, and so forth, are as intent upon bringing about in the child those behaviors, attitudes, and values that they consider proper as the child's parents. He quotes Havinghurst's view that the school systems in our contemporary United States go far beyond minimal instruction in academic subjects—and that it is necessary for them to do so. It is suggested that there is no area of the developmental process in children that the school may safely ignore and still accomplish its goals. In the social subsystem of the school, teachers are required to perform a wide variety of socializing tasks and, in successfully doing so, employ much the same methods that are effective for parents in the subsystem of the family.

It is important to note again, in this context, the fact that the child is usually in school for seven to nine hours a day, five days a week, nine months a year. Of the remaining time available to him daily, he spends eight to twelve hours in sleep, and from one to several hours outside the home engaging in a variety of recreational activities. The parents are fortunate to have personal contact with the child for more than three to six hours a day during the normal school year—and often have little more during vacation periods. Hence, the direct influence of the parents over the developmental process in *any* child is severely limited in time for this age group.

It is also worthwhile to consider briefly the influence that peers and older siblings may have on the socialization of the child. The role of peers will be examined in more detail in Chapter 4, but by way of an example of their importance to the developmental process, consider Sutton's (1962) findings. Using the scores of ninety fifth-grade children on the Syracuse Scale of Social Relations, in addition to socializing records kept by their teachers, Sutton concludes that school-age children select their same-sex peers as sources for both academic and social help more frequently than they select either teachers or family. For the school-age child at least, the peer group is a significant influencing agent for personality development.

There is some research evidence to support the viewpoint that for socioeconomically disadvantaged school-age children particularly, parental influence is quite drastically limited. Lewis (1961) finds evidence to support the hypothesis that among low income families, unguided, unplanned influences outside the family are relatively more important and affect the socialization of the child relatively earlier than among higher income families. An effect of this outside influence is the early appearance (at ages five or six) of the point at which the parents cannot or will not attempt to control their children.

One reason for this limitation of parental influence among low income families is the fact that the mother and the father (if there is one) are often both employed outside the home. A reasonably typical pattern among low income families leaves much of the responsibility for child-rearing to older siblings. In the case of actual separation from the parents, in which the child is raised by a married (or at least considerably older) sibling, the sibling's influence on the developmental process probably differs little from that of the parents. However, Rosenbaum (1963) has suggested that the psychological effects on a child who is reared largely by a sibling only slightly older than himself may be extreme and severely maladjustive. He postulates that this is the case because the older sibling who is not biologically or psychologically prepared to cope with child-rearing is apt to have negative attitudes toward his premature responsibility, which will, in turn, have negative consequences for the personality development of the younger sibling left in his care. Rosenbaum also points out that such codeterminants as parental illness, separation or rejection, social and economic deprivation, and physical abuse often accompany the situation in which an older sibling becomes responsible for the rearing of younger members of his family.

We may conclude that parental influence on the developmental process, particularly among disadvantaged school-age children, may be limited by several factors. Some of these are a normal part of the developmental process for this age group, for example, wider social contacts, which allow for diversity of identification with nonfamily adult role models, and the increased influence of the peer group. Other factors are more directly related to socioeconomic disadvantage and parental inadequacies. Disruptions or dysfunctional relationships in the family structure create intellectual and general personality maladjustments in the developing child. Families of low socioeconomic status, in addition to exhibiting a greater tendency toward broken homes and inadequate financial means or educational skills for offering a rich and stimulating environment, may also place their children in the position of being the object of social discrimination and possible rejection. This discrimination reduces the child's chances of developing satisfactory extrafamilial social relationships with other adults or peers.

Families of low socioeconomic status are often characterized by a high rate of residential migration in a search for opportunities for economic and social betterment or to escape liabilities. This frequent moving from one neighborhood or community to another also tends to limit the child's potential for developing long-term, satisfying interpersonal relationships outside the family setting. If these social structural factors of poverty, discrimination, and residential mobility are coupled with a broken home or inadequate parental relationships, then the chances that the child will be adequately socialized or will develop normally are slim indeed. Even if one of the many dysfunctional factors considered in these chapters is present during the developmental process, it is reasonable to conclude that the child will be disadvantaged to some extent and that compensatory measures are required for fully adequate intellectual and emotional development.

Although the school is not regarded as a panacea for either the personality maladjustments of individual children or the social ills of society in general, the school is regarded as a powerful influencing agent in the learning of attitudes and values. The schools do, therefore, have a socializing responsibility not unlike that of the parents—and the learning environment the school provides must allow *all* children to learn under as nearly ideal conditions as possible. This means that school personnel must be aware of the background and developmental experiences to which the children in their care have been exposed, and some compensatory adjustments must be made in curricula, social climate, and teaching techniques when this background has inadequately prepared the child for the demands of the school situation. Some suggestions concerning directions the school might take to help compensate for children's disadvantage will be, in part, the subject of the final chapter.

SUMMARY

Each child enters school with an already partially developed set of behavioral expectations and value orientations derived in large part from his experiences in the family. The family serves as the first and very important agent of socialization. Personality and intellectual development are heavily influenced by the child's interpersonal relationships with his parents and his siblings.

This chapter has dealt with the role of the family in the general developmental process, the consequences of deprivation in early family affiliations, and the limitations on familial influence. A review of social-learning theories helps to pinpoint the elements of the family environment that appear to be most significant in influencing the general social learning of the child, as well as such more specific factors as measured intelligence, school achievement, social acceptance, and so on. In very general terms these elements may be identified as: (1) providing the tools, stimulation, opportunity, and reinforcement for general learning; (2) providing role models for social learning; (3) providing help and guidance in language development; and (4) providing stimulation, concern, and support for achievement and learning outside the home, especially at school. If the family fails to provide these experiences, or does so inadequately, the child is indeed disadvantaged.

Language acquisition and the development of conceptual thinking have been shown to be interdependent: language is the primary tool for intellectual development. For the normal child, measured intelligence (on the basis of verbally-oriented tests) seems clearly more dependent on experience than on hereditary factors. In addition, "proper" language usage is one basis for achieving status with teachers and more advantaged age-mates. If the child is deficient in his experience with language skills, or has had inadequate training in using his language, he is apt to be severely disadvantaged, both academically and socially in the heterogeneous school situation. Thus, another possible cause of the Leftout's academic, social, and emotional disadvantage and potential for failure to adjust to the school situation is a relative lack of language facility.

The evidence suggests that there are generalized social class-linked differences in child-rearing practices but that emphasis on intellectual achievement is a dominant force in directing parents' efforts to socialize their children. It is clear that while there is little or no evidence that various specific child-rearing practices subsequently have a direct influence on the child's personality, generalized patterns of warm-permissive-rewarding versus cold-strict-punishing relationships have a significant impact. In general, girls tend to be more adequately socialized than boys.

The father's role in personality development is an important one. He serves as an authority figure and a sex-role model. He influences achievement motivation and acts as an agent of morality training. His influence is great with both boys and girls, but his absence or inadequacy has the most serious consequences for boys.

It is concluded that a verbally-oriented, close, warm, supportive, and continuous relationship with both parents is the best possible family setting in which both boys and girls may develop. On the other hand, any disorganization in this type of family pattern will deprive the child to some extent of a chance for adequate socialization. Thus, it is suggested that a third possible kind of disadvantage a Leftout may experience is a lack of stimulating, close, and supportive affiliations with his family, particularly with his father. The general pattern of a Leftout's interpersonal relationship with his family is seen as another crucial variable in efforts to understand how he comes to be left out in the heterogeneous school situation.

There is some evidence to suggest that for children in the lowest socioeconomic strata, parental influence on the developmental process is quite drastically limited. For any school-age child, the social subsystem of his peer group and of the school itself become important influences on academic, social, and emotional adjustment potential. Thus, whatever the adequacies or inadequacies of familial training and relationships, these, taken alone, are also poor criteria for predicting who will be a Leftout and who will not. However, an understanding of the developmental process and knowledge about a particular Leftout's language skills and family background can help us understand the basis for his deviant variations in attitudes, values, and behavior and can point the way to compensatory measures.

4

Social and
Emotional Adjustment
in School:
the Role of Peers
and Self-Concept

The opinions, values, beliefs, and attitudes of the particular significant others who are our peers are of great importance to all of us, and children especially are apt to be influenced by social pressures from peers. The child is simultaneously pressured by adults and his age-mates, and these pressures may be directed toward opposing value orientations and behavioral expectations. The child is automatically excluded from certain kinds of rewarding associations with adults because of his age and immaturity. It is only from his age-mates that he may derive such things as prestige and hierarchical status, and with whom he may develop friendships based on equality. An acceptable social status is an important requisite for satisfactory social and emotional adjustment at any age. Our view of man as inherently a social being implies a strong need to form significant and meaningful relationships with others. Thus, social isolation, real or threatened, is a powerful motivating force for producing behavioral changes in keeping with the perceived requirements of social acceptance.

The means for initiating and maintaining close personal relationships are learned during the developmental process. This learning is, in part, based on perceptual awareness of others' emotional needs, value orientations, and behavioral expectations. Horrocks and Buker (1951) have shown that the capacity for enduring friendships is gradually acquired during childhood and adolescence, and that the social skills necessary for

developing satisfying friendships are teachable. For learning children's social skills the "teachers" are other children. That the peer group is the
most common social reference group for school-age youngsters is a well
documented fact. Only one study, conducted by Sutton, will be cited here
for illustrative purposes, because its findings are typical of many such studies. Much of the research on the impact of the peer group has been done
with adolescent subjects; this study has been chosen specifically because it
deals with preadolescent youth. Sutton (1962) has conducted research
with ninety fifth-grade children using the Syracuse Scale of Social Relations, supplemented by socializing records kept by teachers. His results
show that children tend to select their peers as sources of help, for both social and academic goals, more frequently than either teachers or parents.
A good deal of what children learn, then, is taught by other children. Thus,
one critical dimension in the study of adjustment to school is the impact of
the peer group.

The impact of peers is, to some extent, inherent in the structural
system of the school in which large numbers of children are brought into
daily contact with one another in a setting which has both a social group
orientation and a task group orientation. A general principle of our
theoretical perspective is that the more individuals associate with one
another under conditions of equality, the more they come to share value
orientations and behavioral norms, and the more they come to like one
another. For the Leftout, the problem centers on the fact that the "conditions of equality" portion of that principle may not prevail in the actual situation. There is an indisputable difference between physical and social
propinquity—the first does not necessarily result in the second. The child
in the group is part of a complex network of relations with other children.
Each child observes and evaluates the events around him, responds with
feelings of like or dislike, acts in the situation, and is the recipient of actions of others. Through such processes, the role and status of each child
becomes established, and the particular nature of his relationship to the
peer group emerges. Homans (1950, 1961), among many others, notes
that the closer individuals' normative orientations are, the more frequently
they will interact. Further, when people are forced into physical proximity, from which they cannot withdraw, for example, a work group or a
schoolroom, maximal general interaction will result from positive sentiments, whereas neutral or negative sentiments will tend to restrict interaction to minimal, formal, or problem-solving situations. Homans proposes
that interaction, the communication of sentiment in the form of rewarding
activity, must be *mutually* rewarding or it will cease. Schachter supplies
some evidence that when a deviant is present in the group, there is an initial upsurge of communication in his direction, probably aimed at bringing
him into line, but, if these efforts go unrewarded, communication dimin-

ishes. The deviant is still present in the group but is ignored. This is effective social isolation.

An important factor, very much related to peer group influence, is that of the quality of the interpersonal communication among individuals in the same behavior field. McClosky and Schaar (1965) point out the importance of communication for the development of anomic, that is, left out, responses to social situations.

> One does not learn values and norms in precisely the way one learns facts: one is "socialized" into them through numerous interactions—living, working, and talking to others—repeated over time and in a variety of contexts. . . . [One's] opinions and values have a considerable effect on the way [one] is received by a community or group. . . . Partial acceptance of the rules will get one into the club; once inside, the processes of indoctrination and absorption can be carried much farther. . . . On the other hand, persons who fail to learn the dominant values of a group, or who hold beliefs and opinions not widely shared, are not likely to be well received by group members. This in turn reduces communication and makes socialization into the group even more difficult. A deviant lacks the intimate, vital experience of participation which is essential to full appreciation of the group's norms and values. His knowledge of those norms may be abstract and "theoretical," insensitive to subtle shadings of mood and meaning—a caricature rather than an accurate portrait.[1]

This, in essence, is the problem of the Leftout, because he has not had the prior training or experience to allow him to develop the appropriate value orientation, internalize the proper behavioral expectations, or learn the accepted means of communication, which would allow him easy access to the more advantaged peer group and gain for him acceptance as an equal.

The broad environmental contexts of culture, subculture, and family examined in the earlier chapters need to be viewed as an integral part of peer relationships, since these variables have important consequences for the impact of children's associations with age-mates. These environmental variables help determine the nature of the peer relationship by providing, or failing to provide, adequate training in requisite social skills and by setting the parameters for the sphere of peer group influence. General cultural, subcultural, and family influences serve to establish the framework within which peer relations operate, and within which the peer group becomes yet another agent of the socialization process. Thus, we may view the peer group as a determinant of stability and acceptance in social rela-

---

[1]Reprinted from H. McClosky and J. H. Schaar, "Psychological Dimensions of Anomy," *American Sociological Review*, 30 (1) (1965), 14–40. Reprinted with permission of the authors and the American Sociological Association.

tionships, as a contributor to the child's developing self-concept, and as another force contributing to the form and substance of the child's value orientation toward the world around him. The extent of the peer group's influence is delimited by such factors as the characteristics of the situation itself, individual variations in susceptibility to influence, the characteristics of the children doing the influencing, and the impact of adults (such as teachers) on children's peer groups.

One of the most important and enduring functions of peer relationships is their influence on the development of the child's self-concept. This notion of "self" is a key concept in sociology for the interpretation of personality. Mead regards the development of "self" as dependent on language and arising "in the process of social experience and activity. . . . The self, as that which can be an object to itself, is essentially a social structure, and it arises in social experience. . . ." (pp. 135–140) Self-concept has been used in sociology as the equivalent of the self; that is, one's self is the way one conceives of himself, or one's self-concept. Central to an individual's self-concept is his identity, his perceived generalized position in society derived from his status in each group of which he is a member, the role that attends each status, and the social categories that he comes to accept as "his," for example, age, sex, race, social class, and so on. Thus, self-concept is defined as the individual's view of himself, derived from taking the role of significant others in social interaction, by means of which he organizes his personality and directs his action to reciprocate the perceived expectations of others. The self-concept consists of: a view of identity, attitudes that express personal interests and aversions, a "world view" frame of reference, knowledge of goals and degree of past success in achieving prior goals, and some kind of self-evaluation on the basis of comparison of self with others and their perceived evaluation.

Early in his group experiences a child becomes aware that his peers evaluate him along particular lines and, as the developmental process continues, he learns proficiency in interpreting his own status in the eyes of other children. High status in the group is a source of a positive self-concept; lack of status and social acceptance becomes a source of dissatisfaction with himself which produces either a rejection of the group and status seeking elsewhere, high motivation to change in the direction of the group's expectations, or a lowering of his self-concept.

It is clearly an oversimplification to suggest that acceptance by peers directly determines the nature of the child's self-evaluation. Family influences, success or failure in nonsocial experiences (for example, academic tasks), perceptions of teacher's and other adults' evaluation, and so on, also play important roles in shaping the self-concept. Nevertheless, the peer group remains an extremely important source of self-evaluation. It is perfectly possible, of course, that an adequate self-concept leads to social acceptance, while an inadequate self-concept leads to social rejection. It is probable that the causal relationship between self-acceptance and social acceptance works both ways. In other words, an adequate self-concept is a prerequisite for social acceptance, and social acceptance increases the likelihood of positive self-evaluation, which, in turn, raises the level of the self-concept. And, conversely, an inadequate self-concept leads to social rejection, which, then, increases the likelihood of negative self-evaluation and tends to lower the self-concept even more. It is being postulated that self-acceptance and social acceptance are positively related, regardless of the causal sequence, and that an adequate self-concept is a necessary prerequisite to successful adjustment in school.

In the interrelated threefold criterion of adjustment to school (academic, social, and emotional dimensions), the social acceptance dimension is an important one. It is probably best to regard the affective and cognitive dimensions of learning as interacting aspects of a single process. In certain task-oriented situations, formalized teaching aimed at the perceptual-cognitive dimensions gains ascendancy, and emphasis is directed away from the self-social reference features of the learning experience. In other school situations in which the focal point is the social group, the social-emotional dimensions are predominant, and greater emphasis is given to personality needs, value orientations, motivation, social status, and the conception of self in relation to others. In both types of learning situations, some aspects of all the dimensions of adjustment are present, although primary emphasis may be given to one rather than another. These considerations, and others we have indicated, will be the subject of the remainder of this chapter.

PEER RELATIONSHIPS FOR THE LEFTOUT

For the Leftout peer relationships are apt to be of particular significance. Evidence cited in the last chapter (Lewis, 1961) suggests that by school age the socioculturally disadvantaged child is apt to experience comparatively little concern, attention, or support from his parents. Concomitantly, it is suggested that the peer group takes on added importance for such a child. Campbell (1964), in his comprehensive review of peer relationships in childhood, points out that there are subcultural variations in the relevance of the peer group for children. His data support our view that parents in lower socioeconomic strata show less concern about their children's activities outside the home than do parents of higher socioeconomic levels, and that lower-class parents typically exercise less control and supervision over their school-age children. As we have seen, middle-class child-rearing practices give more emphasis to self-direction and the

development of internal standards of conduct, while lower-class parents
tend to emphasize conformity to external proscriptions. Given such differences in background and training, it seems reasonable to suggest that
one consequence is to allow greater opportunity for the peer group to
assume an important socializing role in the development of the lower-class
child. Ausubel (1958) claims that "it is mostly in heterogeneous urban cultures that values during preadolescence tend to acquire a wider base and
peers tend to replace parents as interpreters and enforcers of the moral
code." (p. 393) From ethnographic comparisons Eisenstadt (1962) concludes that peer group pressures are greatest "in those societies in which
the family or kinship unit cannot ensure . . . the attainment of full social
status on the part of its members." (p. 34) As we have seen, these are the
types of social systems of which the Leftout is most typically a member. It
is also suggested that children's overt dependent behavior on peers increases in the case in which there is parental rejection or lack of cohesion
in the family, or both. The objective structural characteristics of both the
community and the family, such as the degree of integration or
disorganization, the degree of differentiation, and the degree of financial
security, help to shape the unique nature of the child's relations with his
peers and his value orientation to the social world around him. Leftouts
are apt to be disadvantaged in these areas, since they come typically from
the poorer urban areas and from families whose interpersonal processes
are apt to be disorganized. Thus, for the Leftout, the peer group and its acceptance of him becomes extremely important.

At the same time, variations in socioeconomic background have been
found to be associated with differences in children's value orientations and
their aspirations to achieve in school. Such differences in training and experience create for children different world view frames of reference that,
when translated into behavior, have consequences for peer relationships.
Values and aspirations asserted in the home, as well as the quality of interaction within the family, contribute to the nature of peer relationships.
Parents help to provide the child with knowledge of social expectations
and to crystallize his value orientations. Middle-class parents especially
influence peer group relationships by intentionally or unintentionally controlling contacts and by teaching their children discriminatory life-styles.
The middle-class child's relationship to his parents is apt to be far closer
than that of the lower-class child and hence, he is apt to be particularly
influenced by parental views.

There is a well-documented tendency for people to gravitate into
groups or subgroups, and the effect is one of maximizing their shared
values. Children, as well as adults, feel more comfortable when they are
associating with others similar to themselves. For this reason, when the
Leftout comes into contact with his more advantaged age-mates in the sub-

system of the school, he may find that he does not share the values necessary for social acceptance among these children. A child learns quite early in life, usually by his first years in school, what social class he belongs to: not what name to give it, but how his value orientations and behavioral expectations distinguish him from others, who is above and below him, and with whom to be friends. Stendler (1949) found that in a midwestern community, children at the first-grade level were largely unaware of class-status symbols but that by the fourth grade they were partially aware and by the eighth grade they were as aware of the meaning of such symbols as adults and could identify their own class position. Even at the preschool level, children are aware of ethnic and racial differences (Clark and Clark, 1952; Goodman, 1952; Stevenson and Stewart, 1958; and others). The hypothesized age at which these recognized differences are found to be actually reflected in children's social selection ranges from four to ten years on the basis of several studies. The point worth noting here is that subcultural differences *do* play a part in social acceptance among elementary-age school children.

Information on the extent to which friendship ties are related to socioeconomic status criteria is slightly contradictory, but there is reasonable support for the generalization that socioeconomic status criteria are at least partially responsible for friendship choices. Neugarten (1946), using a modified sociometric procedure, has found that both elementary-school children and high school students discriminate along class lines in their selection of friends. In addition, among the younger children, social status is also clearly linked to rejection of peers. Bonney (1946) has reported that socioeconomic status criteria play a small but consistent part in determining children's friendships. Hollingshead has concluded that clique membership tends to be established on the basis of class. Both Neugarten and Elkins (1958) have found significant correlations between sociometric preference and socioeconomic status. Other factors that may counterbalance a low socioeconomic status for the Leftout in his chances for social acceptance by his more advantaged age-mates will be discussed in the next section of this chapter.

The peer group with whom any child associates tends to be of the same socioeconomic strata as his own because of residential proximity, school location, family friendships and preferences, and so forth. Thus, children of the same class are apt to be in close association, which results in identification of the characteristics they hold in common. However, the impact of status differences on peer relationships is not based on such ecological segregation alone. Macdonald, McGurie, and Havighurst (1949) have found that children living in the same heterogeneous urban neighborhood and attending the same schools but having different social-class backgrounds, use leisure time in quantitatively and qualitatively different ways. It has been noted in earlier chapters that this and other differences might be assumed to influence peer relationships. For example, social-class-linked differences in aggressive behavior have been noted. Tuma and Livson (1960) have found that among early adolescent boys there is a strong negative relationship between socioeconomic status and conformity to authority. When children of such diverse socioeconomic strata, experience, and training are brought into contact in the heterogeneous school situation, the mingling of divergent value orientations and behavioral expectations may become a source of disturbance to each group of children. On the positive side, however, such culture contact becomes a source of knowledge about "how the other half lives" for children from each socioeconomic strata and opens a potentially important avenue for social tolerance and understanding on the one hand, and upward social mobility for the lower-class child on the other.

We have postulated that the more eager an individual is to become a member of a group, the more he will conform to its norms of behavior. Unfortunately, although the upwardly aspirant Leftout is eager for social acceptance, he may well be at a loss to know what norms to conform to. He may be subject to pressure toward some norms at home, others from his teachers, and still others from his peers. When the child is caught in cross pressures between the norms of different groups of which he is simultaneously a member, he is apt to suffer some emotional strain; such that, if conflicts are both severe and pervasive, the resultant strain may become incapacitating, and even moderate amounts of strain will create some anxiety. The closer the correspondence between the value orientations and behavioral expectations of socializing agents (parents vis-à-vis teachers, or home vis-à-vis peers, for example), the more adequately and the more rapidly socialization takes place. Conversely, the more conflicts there are between the various agents of socialization, the slower and more inadequate the process.

It is possible, of course, that the child may not be aware of conflicts, because he may not be aware of his more advantaged age-mate's group norms. It has been suggested earlier that individuals are more likely to attend to those aspects of their environment they anticipate than those they do not, and they are more likely to anticipate those things with which they are familiar. It seems clear that frequency of contact, ecological separation, and differences in value orientations and behavioral expectations fostered in the home or subcultural group all play a part in whether or not a child is aware of the socially acceptable norms. The more interaction that occurs, the more similar become norms and values; the less communication or interaction, the greater the likelihood of conflict and, with more conflict, there is less interaction and communication of normative expectations. Thus, it appears obvious that the Leftout's potential social rejection by his more advantaged classmates may be yet another reinforcing aspect of his disadvantage.

The Leftout may have problems of both acculturation and social assimilation. "Acculturation" refers to the process of learning the value orientations and behavioral expectations of a group different from the one in which the individual has been socialized originally. "Social assimilation" refers to the process by which an "outsider" is accepted as a genuine member of a group, with full responsibilities and privileges that are accorded to any member. We are suggesting that the Leftout may be culturally alienated. By this we mean that he has neither been acculturated to, nor socially assimilated by, his more advantaged age-mates. Furthermore, he does not know the appropriate norms; the content of much of what he sees and hears is meaningless to him; he is powerless to make changes in either the system or himself without special help; and as a result of these problems, he is socially isolated from the more advantaged peer group. It is postulated that the more contact the child has with appropriate role models, the faster and more complete his acculturation, and the more complete his acculturation, the more complete his social assimilation. Thus, the Leftout who is brought into daily contact with his more advantaged age-mates has the best chance of learning the norms essential for academic and social success. It is necessary, however, to remember an earlier qualification of this simplistic model: that the *nature* of the contact is extremely important. It is possible for the Leftout to be acculturated without being assimilated, and vice versa. Either one in the absence of the other is more difficult, less frequent, and the process is apt to be more costly, psychologically and socially, to those being influenced than in the case in which acculturation and assimilation go hand in hand.

The Negro in our society, especially the educated urban Negro, is a good example of acculturation without assimilation. The child from a middle-class Negro home may have all or more of the advantages in his family background that contribute to academic and social success than his white age-mates, yet continue to be socially and even academically disadvantaged, because he is not assimilated into the advantaged peer group or because he is the object of discriminatory behavior by teachers. Children of religious or ethnic minorities may serve as the example for assimilation without acculturation. Such children may be fully assimilated members of the peer and student groups, while maintaining widely divergent ideological and normative patterns. It is probably more often the case, however, that the child with a different but strong cultural background is socially tolerated but not fully accepted by all of his peers or his teachers. He too may become the object of academic disadvantage and mere social toleration—a kind of partial assimilation, accepted in some situations but not in others. This is the position in which children of Indian, Jewish,

Puerto Rican, Mexican, Amish, and other families find themselves in certain communities, certain schools or classes, or certain activities.

The kind of disadvantage associated with ethnic or racial discrimination is far more difficult to overcome and differs qualitatively and quantitatively from the kind of disadvantage based on socioeconomic criteria. This author would suggest that the adverse consequences of the various causes of disadvantage are cumulative. Thus, for example, a child raised in a lower-class cultural environment is less disadvantaged than one who also comes from a disorganized family, and the latter, in turn, is less disadvantaged than a lower-class child of a disorganized family who is also a Negro. The more "strikes" there are against the child, the poorer the prognosis for successful adjustment in the school situation. The balance is most favorable when all children meet on personal terms, through a common task, with shared interests, and on terms of social and academic equality. Davis (1957) has summarized the situation in terms of the educational system and ethnic and racial minorities. It does not seem illegitimate to generalize these conclusions to include *any* disadvantaged child or group. In general, both the acculturation of the subordinate group and its social assimilation with the dominant group in public schools are found to be most successful when: (1) the minority group is of approximately the same social-class level as the dominant group; (2) the minority group is relatively small, constituting at the very most not more than 25 percent of the school population; (3) the minority group comes from a middle-class background; (4) the minority group has been in the United States a relatively long time; and (5) the minority group comes from the same kind of community (rural or urban) as that in which it now attends school. (pp. 446–449)

We have suggested that, even in the case in which no barriers are inherent in the social situation itself, the child who is ill prepared to understand and cope with the value orientations and behavioral expectations of his more advantaged age-mates and his teachers will have a slow, difficult, and conflict-ridden time of socialization. Thomas and Znaniecki (1918–1921) have written that, if men define situations as real, they *are* real in the consequences. Thus, whatever the cause of his lack of social success with his more advantaged age-mates—racial, ethnic, or class discrimination, inadequate preparation, personality problems, or some combination of all of these—the Leftout feels rejected, withdraws and becomes more ingrown and isolated, or seeks support and acceptance from others like himself who suffer status deprivation and, as a result, is more left out by the majority group.

However, several things can short-circuit this maladjustive downward spiral. The Leftout may possess some valued talent or special skill; he may be particularly intelligent; he may be highly adaptable to changes in his social environment; he may be fortunate enough to be in a classroom in which the teacher consciously attempts to influence the social integration of *all* the students; or he may simply have fewer strikes against him in terms of his family relationships, his racial and ethnic identity, and his own personality stability. Therefore, in the next section of this chapter we will examine more closely the "how" of the acculturation-assimilation process and the bases on which social status is awarded in children's groups.

PROCESSES OF PEER INFLUENCE

Tuddenham (1952) has pointed out that "the influence of other children constitutes a major component of the social milieu to which the child must adapt." (p. 1) He assumes that a child's reputation *with* his peers is of central importance in assessing his social adjustment *to* his peers. Roles are learned through interaction with others. As a part of this learning process the child acquires expectations of how others in the group will behave, learns to predict what others expect of him, and how they will react to him. Bandura and Huston (1961) have studied the influence of peers on role learning. They hypothesize that identification with a reference person or group is a process of incidental learning and that children will more readily adopt the behavior of others with whom they identify. In their experiment, a reward was hidden in one of two boxes in a playroom. The subject child was allowed to observe the behavior of a role model through a one-way mirror. He was then allowed to go into the playroom with the role model under "model friendly–model cold" conditions. They found that children conformed to the behavior of the friendly model in several task situations, including verbal tasks. There was no conformity to the behavior of the cold model except in aggressive reactions. Since interaction leads to assimilation of roles, and friendly, rewarding social situations produce more interaction, it follows that friendly accepting situations will stimulate incidental role learning. This is, essentially, a restatement of Homans' liking-interaction hypothesis that we have already noted. We will return again to the subject of the relationship between the attractiveness of the agent of influence and the extent of his ability to influence.

Fjeld (1961), in a thesis concerned with the relationship of communication variables to the process of social interaction among freshman women college students, finds that the nature of the interpersonal relationships formed tend to fit the pattern Homans suggests exists between communication and interaction. It is hypothesized that the values that individuals hold are important in determining the success of communication with others and, thus, the subjects' preferences for each other. It is also hypothesized that social preferences are initially based on simple indices of value agreement but that continued interaction necessitates more complex indices of agreement, and if there is failure to establish value agreement, interpersonal relationships will disintegrate. By comparing sociometric choice ratings over an eight month period, Fjeld finds strong support for both hypotheses. It is suggested, in short, that the bases of social acceptance change over a period of time. Later in this section we will examine the criteria by which children establish status with their peers and the sex and age differences among these criteria.

The notion of incidental learning is an important one for considering the process of peer group influence. In Chapter 3 it has been suggested that the learning of new roles, which the culturally disadvantaged child faces in the school situation, is accomplished through two broadly defined, jointly operating, interactional processes: intentional instruction, referring to deliberate and formal role socialization, and incidental learning, referring to processes of identification with or emulation of role models in the imitator's behavior field. It is postulated that different goals will correspond to different socialization processes. Thus, a goal such as academic achievement will be primarily obtained through intentional instruction. Social goals, on the other hand, are more informally achieved. It is logical to suggest that in the school situation, the teacher primarily provides intentional instruction for attaining achievement goals, while peers primarily provide a role model for learning social skills. However, the attitude of the teacher toward the social aspects of the school situation, as well as the attitudes of his peers toward the academic aspects, also influence the Leftout's adjustment potential.

Campbell suggests that at least five different types of situational factors exert some degree of influence over peer group processes of influence. First, the physical setting itself influences the group process. For example, there has been much experimental work done with the relationship between the structure of the environmental setting and communication potential. We have argued that interpersonal communication is a prerequisite to interaction and social influence, but that when children are in a typical classroom setting, that is, seated in chairs or at desks arranged in ordered rows, each child has only limited access to the others in the group and no child can exert much direct influence over any other. On the playground, where physical movement is maximally free, the potential for direct influence is much greater. This kind of consideration leads to another situationally limited factor suggested by Campbell: that different activities lead to differences in behavior and behavioral expectations. Yet another situational factor that has an impact on the influence process is that of group size. Evidence is abundant to support the notion that the smaller the group is, the greater the communication potential, the higher the rate of participation for each individual member, and, therefore, the greater the influence potential.

Campbell points out a fourth situational factor; that of the clarity of the task and associated expectations, which affects the nature of the child's response to influence attempts. The Leftout lacks knowledge of and experience with the behavioral expectations of his more advantaged agemates. Ambiguity is apt to lead to deviance, and the Leftout's deviance, and consequent rejection by the group—especially in a situation such as that of the school in which he cannot physically withdraw—may make him anxious. Parsons (1951) notes that insecurity in social relationships and inadequacy in achievement-oriented performance are the primary foci of anxiety. In an environment in which the value pattern places a special emphasis on achievement in many forms—as in the school—the problem is accentuated. That anxiety may have a crippling effect on the cognitive process is not only established in numerous experiments but is apparent as well from everyday observation. Intense anxiety sometimes leads its victims to withdraw from reality, or at least to retreat from contacts of a social nature. Obviously, this reduces the possibility for communication, which leads in turn to a reduction in socialization and learning potential.

Duffy (1961) gives some insight into the incidental learning process, as it is affected by anxiety, among sixth graders. In his study subjects were chosen on the basis of experimentally induced anxiety extremes (high and low extremes on the Taylor Manifest Anxiety Scale) and assigned randomly to two groups. The experiment involved two situations. The task for both groups was presented as a series of line discriminations, but one group was presented with easy choices and the other group with more difficult choices. During the experiment both groups listened to a taped recording of the names of twelve cities—offered as a "distraction" but really serving as the focus of the study. After completing the line discrimination task, recall scores for the "incidental" material were obtained. Duffy finds that anxiety is increased by perceived status differences, by the ambiguity of instructions given, and by the difficulty of the task. However, regardless of the difficulty of the task, high-anxious children direct their attention to the assigned "relevant" task, that is, intentional instruction, and learn significantly less incidental material than the low-anxious children. It does not seem too far fetched to generalize Duffy's work in order to suggest a negative relationship between high-anxiety levels and incidental role-learning potential. Thus, if the Leftout feels status deprivation and if his academic tasks are both difficult and ambiguous for him, he is apt to experience high levels of anxiety. High levels of anxiety, in turn, hinder the Leftout's ability to profit from incidental role learning. This has negative consequences in terms of his potential for social acceptance among his more advantaged age-mates.

Kitano's (1962) research findings indicate support for such a suggestion. He finds that, in specifically structured situations, in which role expectations are clear, in which there is consensus, and in which role expectations are readily enforceable (such as in the formalized structure of the classroom), there is a relatively high degree of adjustment on the part of *all* children. However, when the situation is such that role expectations are not highly structured and there is ambiguity and a lack of consensual norms (such as in more informal peer group relationships), some children are anxious and fail to adjust.

A fifth situational factor noted by Campbell, the nature of the reward system, relates to the cohesiveness of the group and the degree of influence exerted by peers. It is assumed that the more cohesive the group is, the greater influence it can exert and the greater the reward power it has with any individual member. It is being postulated here that the Leftout minority aspires to academic success, which is typically rewarded by the formalized school system, but has difficulty in achieving that success and, thus, is apt to be left out of the formal reward system. From the child's point of view, teachers distribute approval and disapproval in a consistent but unfair manner. In one illustrative study, deGroat and Thompson (1949) have examined teacher's attitudes, as perceived by sixth-grade children, and have found that "Guess Who" nominations are consistent in showing that a few children receive the bulk of the teacher's approval, and another small group bears the major burden of disapproval. These perceptions remain quite consistent over a time. There is a correlation of .80 between the original test and a retest taken five weeks later. The children receiving the greatest teacher approval are the most intelligent (as measured by standard tests), show the highest academic achievement (as measured by grades), and have the best over-all personality adjustment (as measured by a personality questionnaire administered by the researchers). Whether these results connote cause or effect is of less importance for our purposes here than the fact that rewards are perceived to be differentially distributed with some consistency and that this disparity in the reward system probably has consequences for peer relationships, academic achievement, and such personality factors as the child's self-concept. The Leftout is not likely to be among the better students in terms of either measured intelligence, academic performance, or well-adjusted personality measures and, thus, is not likely to be found among those who are reaping the rewards of the formal system. Hence, the Leftout's social acceptability by his peers takes on added importance to him for its reward value. But he is not likely to receive school-sanctioned rewards until or unless he views his more advantaged age-mates as a reference group, that is, when he seeks to conform to their behavioral expectations. Thus, conformity to his advantaged peers' expectations becomes especially important for the Leftout elementary-age child who is at least initially eager to succeed in school.

Conformity depends on several factors that may create variations in children's susceptibility to influence. No over-all generalizations can be made, but, on the basis of evidence already cited, several factors appear to be associated with susceptibility to influence. Age and sex are two important considerations. Younger children, such as those who are the focus of our concern, are more susceptible to influence than older children; girls are more inclined to yield to social pressure than are boys. Status is another important factor. The Leftout, whose status is apt to be precarious, must rigidly conform to group expectations if he is to be socially accepted. His advantaged age-mates, who are more apt to become, or already are, firmly established as accepted members of the group, are far more free to deviate from group norms to some extent, especially if they are group leaders. Wilson (1960) has discovered that boys with indefinite status, who are neither rated as fully accepted nor are rejected, conform most closely to group norms. Thus, status striving among Leftouts who feel that they can be accepted into the advantaged peer group helps to account for some of that group's influence on conformity behavior. It also has been suggested that dependency needs and moderate (but not high) levels of "functional" anxiety contribute to susceptibility to influence.

Conformity is not a maladjusted response. Conformity to social expectations is a perfectly healthy response for any child and is highly desirable as an element of adjustment to school. Conformity is only maladjustive in the situation in which the child becomes committed to deviant role behavior or value orientations that are dysfunctional for school-oriented success. Conformity to deviant roles most likely is to be found among those Leftouts who have experienced social rejection by their more advantaged age-mates and who feel that they cannot gain acceptance.

Although deviancy and delinquency are not the same thing,[2] some of the research done in the area of delinquency offers some clues for our consideration of the causes and consequences of deviation—which is the other side of the coin of conformity. The work of Gold (1963) is particularly relevant for our interests, since he deals with forces exerted upon deviant behaviors and values that are not necessarily legally delinquent.

[2]Delinquency is a legal term, usually referring to arrests made for behavior that violates some duly constituted law. As noted earlier, deviance is a generic term referring to behavior that is different from some standard. Thus, the delinquent is always a deviant, but a deviant is not necessarily a delinquent. The Leftouts with whom we are concerned are deviants—whether or not they are also delinquents is of no concern for our purposes. Since we are dealing with elementary-age youth who are not usually regarded as responsible under the law, their behavior—whatever it may be—is not apt to be defined as delinquent in any case.

His sample included boys who were merely police "contacts," truants and runaways, in addition to those boys who were actually arrested. His data also compared deviant responses to responses of a matched, control sample of boys who had had no police contacts at all. The latter group will be referred to here as "nondeviants." Gold employed two criteria in order to select the behavioral items on which to compare deviants and nondeviants. First, the items include only the boy's own behavior and attitudes, rather than general sociocultural variables, which is consistent with our theoretical position and Gold's orientation that "the causes of deviancy are to be found in the provocations and social controls created in the boys *themselves* by these and other factors." (Gold, 1963, p. 176) Secondly, the items include only those factors that distinguish deviants from nondeviants. Among his major findings Gold notes that:

1. Data based on self-report of deviant behavior suggest that proportionally more lower status boys exhibit deviant behavior and attitudes than higher status boys (p. 6);
2. When the relationship between quality of neighborhood recreation facilities and boys' attitudes toward aspects of their community is examined, more attitudes toward the neighborhood are negative in those school districts with poorer recreational facilities (p. 112);
3. Deviants tend to regard their community and neighborhood less favorably than matched nondeviants (p. 113);
4. The poorer the quality of recreational facilities in an elementary school district, the higher the deviancy rate is likely to be in that district (p. 114);
5. Teachers are better paid in elementary schools surrounded by neighborhoods with high property values; schools are newer in areas where a greater proportion of people own their homes (p. 116);
6. Newer schools and schools in which teachers are, on the average, earning higher salaries are located in neighborhoods with lower deviancy rates (p. 120);
7. Deviants are more likely to have negative attitudes toward school than matched nondeviants (p. 121);
8. Deviants, especially in the lower socioeconomic strata, less often report doing things with *either* parent than nondeviants (p. 130–131);
9. Fewer deviants than nondeviants feel they can take their personal problems to adults; they are more likely to go to a peer or to no one (p. 132);
10. Deviants report less agreement with their parents concerning standards for their behavior than nondeviants (p. 133);
11. Fewer deviants than nondeviants regard their fathers as ideal-typical adult models (p. 136);

12. Deviants perceive their chosen models to be less disapproving of deviant acts than nondeviants do; the parents of deviants do in fact express less disapproval of these acts than the parents of nondeviants (p. 143);
13. More fathers of deviants than of nondeviants punish physically their sons' misbehaviors or by depriving them of privileges; differences in discipline among mothers tend toward the same direction (p. 145);
14. Compared to the parents of nondeviants, parents of deviants do not believe their sons' chances are as good for eventually getting the kinds of jobs they would like them to get (p. 157);
15. Parents of deviants believe their sons will need less education for their future jobs than parents of nondeviants (p. 158);
16. Both deviants and nondeviants think of schooling mainly as a path to future opportunities (p. 160);
17. Deviants are likely to have earned lower grades in the fifth and seventh grades than their nondeviant matches (p. 163);
18. Boys' attitudes toward school are more positive when their grades are higher and when they think they have better chances to eventually get the jobs they want (p. 169);
19. Deviants less often feel that their teachers take a great deal of interest in their future than do matched nondeviants (p. 170);
20. An index composed of items that distinguish the attitudes and behaviors of deviants from those of nondeviants proves to be related to social status (p. 177).

In one sense, much of Gold's research contributes yet more evidence for the consequences of disadvantage in socioeconomic areas that we have discussed. Proportionately more lower-class boys commit deviant acts than their higher-class age-mates. Disorganized family structure, unfavorable perceptions of community, school, and teachers, and lack of social acceptance by age-mates are some of the provoking factors in deviant behavior. In a second sense, this work is especially valuable because it deals with the value orientation of deviant boys and implies the great importance of conformity to behavioral norms of the peer group, for both deviants and nondeviants. Gold concludes that the controlling forces in behavior:

> consist most importantly of attractions to norm-supporting individuals and organizations. The greatest potential for control is shown to be the family group and within it, the attractiveness of the father is most crucial.[3]

The next greatest source of control lies with the peer group, and if the

[3]Reprinted from Martin Gold, *Status Forces in Delinquent Boys* (Ann Arbor, Mich.: Institute for Social Research, University of Michigan Press, 1963), p. 181.

family fails in its control function, the peer group will assume the most prominent role.

Gold hypothesizes that the provocation force peculiar to deviant behavior is perception of status deprivation, that is, a feeling that there is little or no hope of achieving a position of social acceptance with more advantaged age-mates or of eventually achieving a position of wealth and power that is considered prestigious. This notion of status deprivation, in relation to deviant behavior, is explored more fully in the work of A. K. Cohen. Cohen (1955) argues that deviant behavior is an ideal solution for status deprivation problems, because such behavior repudiates the value orientations of the reference group, which serves as the basis for self-evaluation of failure, and rewards the child with status among any peers who may share his status problems. Children who suffer status deprivation are quite synonymous with those whom we have been calling Leftouts. Children of the lower socioeconomic strata tend to be overrepresented among these Leftouts, because several of the problems often associated with lower-class styles of life that we have mentioned tend to weaken adult controls and the control potential of the more advantaged classmates and, simultaneously, tend to strengthen provocation to deviant behavior. As has been suggested, it is expected that the same conditions can and do appear, but less frequently, among children from the higher socioeconomic strata.

It is important to consider the nondeviants, for many of the children from essentially similar backgrounds are not and do not become deviants. The peer group again comes to the fore as a significant agent of socialization for the Leftout who is successfully acculturated and assimilated by the more advantaged majority. We have assumed that peer group acceptance is a strongly felt goal among all children and that conformity to peer expectations is the primary means of gaining social acceptance. Thus, situations in which conformity is instrumental to social acceptance should have the greatest impact on the child's sensitivity to influence. Walker and Heyns (1962) have examined the relationship of conformity to social acceptance. They have tested Festinger's (1950) principle that the more attractive the group, the more cohesive it is, and the more cohesive the group, the more conformity there exists. Under one experimental condition conformity is instrumental to being liked, while under another condition it is not. Under the condition in which conformity is instrumental to being liked (socially accepted), the degree of conformity is greater in high-cohesive groups than in low-cohesive groups. Under the second condition, in which conformity is not stressed as being instrumental to liking, conformity is slightly greater in the low-cohesive groups. The work of Tiktin and Hartup (1965) provides further substantiation for this latter point. They find that in the case in which conformity refers to task-oriented behavior and social acceptance by peers is not a major consideration, or an instrumental goal, then unpopular or disliked peers may be more effective in eliciting conformity than popular or liked peers.

The apparent discrepancy between these findings and Festinger's theoretical principle may be resolved by considering the factor of instrumentality, as Walker and Heyns suggest, as well as that of time. It must be noted that the empirical findings of both Walker and Heyns and of Tiktin and Hartup were derived from short-term laboratory experiments. Especially under the conditions in which conformity is not instrumental to social acceptance, the fact that the children are not *at that particular time* conforming to popular or liked peers may be more a function of the specific situation than of long-term modes of response. These kinds of findings do suggest several derived hypotheses:

1. Task-oriented conformity and socially-oriented conformity are not necessarily complementary processes in any given situation.
2. In any specific situation, if task-oriented conformity (for example, academic achievement) is the *only* goal, it may be influenced best by reinforcement supplied by unpopular or disliked age-mates.
3. However, in the total school situation, social acceptance by more advantaged age-mates and academic achievement are both initial goals for the individual.
4. In the total school situation, social acceptance is one condition necessary for an adequate self-concept that, in turn, is a prerequisite for over-all adjustment to school—including academic success.
5. Total adjustment may be developed best through conformity to the behavior and value orientations of achievement-oriented age-mates.
6. Such conformity is influenced best by the situation in which it is instrumental to social acceptance by the child's more advantaged age-mates who are achievement oriented.

Thus, it becomes crucial to our consideration to examine those things that are instrumental in offering potential avenues of social acceptance by the advantaged peer group to the Leftout. The theoretical and empirical research literature indicates a number of factors associated with the awarding of status and prestige among children. Among these, sex and age, socioeconomic background, physical skills, personality factors, intelligence, and verbal ability appear to be the most influential criteria for peer group acceptance. Overriding all of these is the general principle that social rejection is primarily associated with lack of knowledge of, or conformity to, the values and expectations of the majority group into which the upwardly aspirant Leftout seeks to be assimilated. Conversely, social acceptance can be attained by learning the socially acceptable values and by subscribing to the appropriate behavioral expectations.

From preschool age until adolescence, sex homogeneity is a principle determining factor in friendships and clique memberships. Next to sex, age is the most important factor in the formation of peer groups. (Tuddenham, 1952) Such segregation by sex and age is associated with differential interests and activities, and serves the function of teaching and strengthening differential sex roles. Children who learn and adopt the behavior prescribed for their sex and age group are rewarded with peer acceptance. White (1948) argues that the crucial arena for the development of self-esteem is to be found among the child's age-mates. He notes that in the home the child must be:

> love-worthy: this may include being competent, but is heavily weighted on the side of being good, obedient, and affectionate. On the play-ground the values are different: he must be respect-worthy, able to command respect because he shows competence and handles himself with ease. . . . He must now show what he has in the way of physical prowess, courage, manipulative skill, outgoing friendliness, all in direct comparison with other children of his age. The penalites for failure are humiliation, ridicule, rejection from the group.[4]

Investigators in this area of social acceptance have referred to "reputation," "popularity," "social success," "social status," and "prestige" in their specific works. In all cases these terms seem to be synonymous with what we have been calling social acceptance. Typically this factor is measured by a variety of sociometric techniques, employing the "Guess Who" and "Who Am I" tests extensively. In the elementary-school situation, the child's degree of social acceptability has been found to remain fairly constant over periods of up to three years between studies, with increasing constancy found among older age groups (Bonney, 1946; Horrocks and Buker, 1951; Singer, 1951). The evidence is clear that, once elementary-age children have been brought together as a group: (1) in general, *group* patterns of relationships are quickly established and remain fairly stable over a time; (2) there is little or no *group* difference in friendship fluctuation between boys and girls at any of the various age and grade levels; (3) there are considerable *individual* variations in the stability of dyadic friendships at all age and grade levels; (4) the criteria by which acceptability is judged is similar within groups but changes between age, sex, and sociocultural groups; thus, the socially acceptable child has as his primary characteristic social adaptability. (Tuddenham, 1952; Watson, 1960)

[4]Robert W. White, *The Abnormal Personality.* Copyright 1948, The Ronald Press Company, New York, pp. 144–145.

These findings are important for the Leftout's social acceptance potential. In the first place, they indicate that the earliest school years are most important in terms of gaining social acceptance by the Leftout's advantaged age-mates. As has been suggested earlier, clique boundaries are less rigid in the earliest years, and thus, the child has the greatest chance of acculturation and assimilation when the group is newly formed, and in general his chances decrease the longer the group has been established, the older his age-mates are, and the more stable existing patterns of acceptance or rejection have become. Secondly, these findings suggest that all is not lost if social adjustment to the expectations of the advantaged peer group is not successful in the earliest years. Since criteria for acceptance change over a period of time, the Leftout may possess or develop skills, talents, or personality characteristics that serve to reduce or overcome his disadvantage at a later date. Compensatory measures that foster his acculturation and eventual assimilation—whether they are the product of intentional instruction or incidental learning—also become important.

Research evidence (Campbell, 1964) indicates that those personal characteristics most important to social acceptance are: (1) social adaptability, (2) high intelligence, (3) well developed motor skills (especially for boys), (4) biologically appropriate sex-role identification, and (5) friendliness and sociability. The criteria associated with differential socioeconomic backgrounds that are most important to social acceptance are: (1) verbal skills; (2) general core-cultural value orientation toward lack of physical aggressiveness, scholastic achievement, cleanliness, and grooming; (3) stylish mode of dress; and (4) time for, or interest in, participating in a variety of organized extracurricular activities.

Pope (1953) has found definite contrasts to exist between children's peer group prestige values among different socioeconomic levels in the same school. In his study of twelve-year-olds, a variation of the "Guess Who" technique yielded a "reputation" score for each child (a combination of twenty-five traits). Cluster analysis of these scores shows characteristic social behavior patterns by social class. For lower-class boys, the most prestige among their peers is awarded on the basis of aggressive, belligerent, domineering leadership; those who are happy, sociable, and "able to take a joke" are socially acceptable, but those who are studious, conform to teacher's expectations, and are "sissies" are rejected by the lower-class peer group. For middle-class boys, those with the most prestige are active and skilled in competitive games, friendly, personable, attractive, but not aggressive; those who are "classroom intellectuals" are acceptable; but those who are "sissies," bossy, unkempt, or physically aggressive are rejected by the middle-class peer group. In other words, middle-class children accept boys who are either athletically or academically competent but they reject aggressive behavior, while lower-class children award prestige to boys' aggressive behavior but they reject academic competence and are not especially concerned with athletic ability (as opposed to sheer physical strength). Both groups value friendly, sociable personality characteristics, but middle-class peers emphasize these as more prestigious than do lower-class peers.

Pope has found that for girls, social acceptance is based mainly on personality characteristics and academic ability. Little or no emphasis is given to motor skills in awarding prestige to girls. For lower-class girls, the most widely accepted traits among the lower-class peer group are friendliness, "goodness," tidiness, and academic ability. The socially accepted lower-class girls are neither leaders, nor do they associate with boys. A second lower-class pattern among girls, less frequently found but most prestigious among lower-class peers, consists of those who are somewhat "rowdy," highly talkative, attention-getting in behavior and dress, aggressive, and who associate with boys. Only one acceptable pattern for middle-class girls is found: those who are attractive, friendly, tidy, vivacious but not "rowdy," good students, and likely to associate with boys in limited but friendly competition. The middle-class peer group rejects those girls who are aggressive, bossy, or "tomboys." In short, prestige among the lower-class peer group tends to follow the general cultural stereotype of dividing girls into those who are "good" and those who are "exciting," and awarding prestige—but of a different kind—for each pattern. The middle-class peer group limits prestige to only one acceptable pattern for girls but allows a wider and more sexually equal range of behavioral norms within that pattern. For both lower-class and middle-class girls, academic ability is a source of prestige.

These findings indicate that the lower-class boy who seeks both academic and social prestige must do so through acceptance by the middle-class peer group, and to gain their acceptance he must give up the rewards offered by the lower-class peer group—a situation apt to be fraught with cross pressures and consequent anxiety. For the lower-class girl whose goals include both academic and social success, the road to successful school adjustment is not likely to be such a difficult one, especially if she subscribes to the good girl pattern acceptable to both her lower-class and middle-class age-mates. For girls, relatively minor factors, such as mode of dress and specific interests, are more apt to be decisive in determining what particular place she will occupy in her peer relationships. And, although such minor factors can have devastating consequences for social acceptance or rejection, these factors are more readily amenable to maturational change or compensatory training than more pervasive characteristics, such as aggressiveness or degree of physical ability, which are important among boys.

Watson (1960) points out that, especially for boys, the social-psychological significance of motor skills is greatest in the early school years. A high premium is placed upon motor skills by age-mates in the early elementary grades. The poorly developed child may be discriminated against, which leads to the possibility of adverse consequences, such as withdrawal, depression, hostility, and so forth. Smith (1950) has found that social indifference, withdrawal, rebelliousness, and hostility are attributes of low-status or rejected children. Thus, one vicious circle that can contribute to the Leftout's disadvantage is rooted in motor skills. If he has had little training in or opportunity for the development of motor skills, for example, bicycle riding or ball playing, because of limited family finances or poor recreational facilities in his neighborhood, or if improper diet or lack of medical care, or both, have restricted his potential for muscular development and control, the prognosis for his early social acceptance is not good. On the other hand, the child adept in motor abilities is not only more accepted by his peers but, because of these skills, is more apt to be chosen as a leader, which may lead to leadership nominations essentially independent of motor skills, and most certainly will aid in the development of a more adequate self-concept. McGraw and Tolbert (1953), in a study of 438 boys, conclude that sociometric status and athletic ability are significantly related. Both athletic skill and willingness to participate in athletic events play an important part in making the child among the best-liked of the peer group. Thus, if the young Leftout boy does possess some degree of motor ability, this may serve as one important avenue for social acceptance.

Schurr (1964) studied 289 children in grades one through six to determine the relationships between objective scores on three motor skills, running, throwing, and jumping, with peers' judgments of their ability in these skills. She finds that judgments are accurate at all grade levels and that teammate choices are made in relation to objective skills. However, Schurr's data tends to refute that of McGraw and Tolbert in that she finds no statistically significant relationship between choice of friends and choice of teammates. While it may be the case that Watson is wrong, and that McGraw and Tolbert's research is merely an idiosyncratic finding, it appears more reasonable to suggest that Schurr's contradictory findings are a result of (1) combining boys and girls, that is, girls may be as accurate as boys in judging motor ability and selecting teammates but girls give such ability less weight in the selection of friends; and, (2) combining age groups, that is, motor abilities are more important as a source of prestige and social acceptance to younger children than to older children. Watson notes that by the sixth grade, research evidence shows that qualities desired in a friend shift in emphasis to personal characteristics such as friendliness, cleanliness, cheerfulness, and tidiness, which point to an increase in socialization to the core-cultural norms. Therefore, it will be postulated here that motor skills are one means available to the Leftout—especially younger males—for overcoming some of his other disadvantages and gaining at least a modicum of social acceptance.

As we have seen, ability to fulfill behavioral expectations may get the child into the club but, once in, he must subsequently learn the appropriate value orientations of his more advantaged peers during his association with them, because the criterion for his initial acceptance will not suffice alone for long-term assimilation. Homans and Watson both have emphasized that in order for friendships to endure, they must be mutually satisfying. If one or the other gets nothing from it, the interaction will cease. Thus, when increasing age brings social development and acceptance away from prestige accorded on the basis of motor skill alone, the child must adapt his social abilities to fit the changed requirements of friendship with his advantaged peers or he will find himself again left out.

There are other sources of potential prestige open to some children who might otherwise be left out in terms of what appears to be similarity in backgrounds. We have seen that lack of physical aggressiveness is one valued characteristic among the members of the more advantaged peer group and in the formal school system. If the Leftout is disadvantaged in many sociocultural areas, but has been reared to devalue or avoid physical aggression, his chance for social acceptance by his more advantaged agemates and for rewarding associations with teachers is enhanced.

THE INFLUENCE OF "INTELLIGENCE" AND THE SITUATION

In the same way, high intelligence may compensate for sociocultural disadvantage among those who usually would be Leftouts. Measured intelligence is statistically related to socioeconomic background. Substantially lower average IQ's are consistently found among members of the lower socioeconomic strata. For example, Cronbach (1960) has found the mean IQ of children from low-income urban or rural areas to be 90, while the mean IQ of children from white-collar and skilled-labor homes to be 115. Siller (1957) also has found that children of the higher socioeconomic strata outscore those of the lower socioeconomic strata on all tests of conceptual ability. However, when his subjects are matched on nonverbal concept tests dealing with the same kind of conceptualization as the verbal tests, lower-class children score more highly than middle-class children. It is important to note that these findings represent averages and that any given child from a particular sociocultural background may deviate widely from these averages. It should also be pointed out that the largest absolute numbers of people with high IQ's are from the numerically larger lower classes.

However, as was noted in the preceding chapter, lack of educational stimulus, as well as poor language training and development, is often associated with lower socioeconomic environments. Both of these things may foster the formation of general modes of perception and problem solving, which, though successful in the home and community situation, may stand in the way in the school situation in which these modes are not appropriate and in which they hinder the child's measured intellectual ability. Thus, while the Leftout is most often a product of this kind of background, not *all* children from the lower socioeconomic strata are Leftouts. Some of them experience more adequate stimulation in their homes; some of them receive more language training, which aids in concept formation and adaptability; and some of them are more secure in their social relationships, which allows for less anxiety, more acceptance of self, and greater ease in learning and which, in turn, is reflected in increased levels of measured intelligence. Wolf (1964) has found that thirteen variables can be employed to describe the background interactions between parents and children, insofar as this interaction concerns the development of measured intelligence. These variables are classified into three major groups: (1) pressure toward achievement motivation, (2) pressure toward language development, and (3) provision for general learning. Wolf has interviewed the mothers of sixty fifth-grade children in a midwestern community. Each family or home is rated on each of the thirteen variables. He finds a multiple correlation of $+.76$ between these ratings and Henmon-Nelson IQ scores. This correlation may be contrasted with correlations of $+.40$ or less between measured intelligence and the variable of socioeconomic status, as measured by parental occupation or parental education.

Watson contends that intelligence is a noun that should be a verb. A child is intelligent insofar as he acts intelligently; stupid insofar as he acts stupidly. For Watson, intelligence is always expressed in some behavior, not an entity but a construct inferred and indirectly measured, and related to cognitive functions and learning. Many research studies concerned with intellectual development of school-age children employ the Stanford-Binet Tests of Intelligence as their basic measuring instrument. Factor analysis of the items in this test show the test to be most heavily weighted on verbal factors. Thus, major intellectual differences between individual children reduce largely to differences in facility in dealing with such conceptual thinking as can be most readily measured by the use of verbally-oriented tests. Experience and training can have a major impact on "intelligence" as it is thus measured. Environmental factors such as prior schooling, socioeconomic status (interpreted in terms of differential reinforcement of verbal learning), and social-emotional factors such as anxiety may significantly influence measured intelligence. Nevertheless, the standardized tests, however "culture bound" and however weighted in favor of the more advantaged child, do reflect efficiency of adjustment to the culture for which they are designed—the formal core culture taught in the public schools. While it is true that children from certain subcultures typically do not do as well on conventional intelligence tests as their more advantaged peers, these tests do predict academic success in the higher grades. (Lavin, 1965) Thus, the otherwise disadvantaged child who is atypical in terms of his verbal experience and language training (and therefore is more "intelligent"), less likely will be left out either academically or socially.

The child of a disadvantaged background who does do well on intellectual performance is socially rewarded, in that his chances of academic success are greatly increased and, thus, he is more acceptable in the eyes of his teachers. In addition, the more intelligent and creative children are generally more accepted by their advantaged age-mates, while the slow learners are less accepted. (Campbell, 1964, p. 305) Comparative ineptness, therefore, in communication skills is related to maladjustment, not only for formally taught academic goals but for informally taught social goals as well. Commoss' (1962) study among second-grade school children who score in the top and bottom quarters in sociometric ranking among their peers substantiates this point. She has found that strong positive relationships exist between social status and (1) certainty of the appropriate values in interpersonal relationships, and (2) ability to communicate verbally. In a sociometric study of three classes in an elementary school, Potashin (1946) set up special discussion sessions for "friends" and "nonfriends," that is, those who had and had not made reciprocal sociometric choices. He finds that for friendly pairs, uninterrupted discussions are significantly longer than among nonfriendly pairs. He also finds that for nonfriendly pairs, there are significant differences among the members in the amount of talking each does and the number of initiations of interaction made by each child. Friendly pairs are much more likely to share equally in the interaction process than are nonfriendly pairs. Taken together, these studies and many others like them indicate the reciprocal process between communication skills and interaction and this interaction and social acceptance. It is being postulated that there is a high correlation between verbal aptitude and other abilities. It is assumed that general intelligence both stems from and contributes to this verbal ability.

In their survey of research, Berelson and Steiner (1964) have shown that communication skills develop earlier and better: (1) the healthier the child, (2) the greater the opportunity to learn (from family, books, peers, and so forth), (3) the higher the socioeconomic level of the family (especially related to parental educational level), (4) in girls than in boys—and this difference increases with age, (5) in financially secure family environments, as opposed to financially insecure or structurally disorganized families, (6) the fewer the number of siblings (each child has a greater chance for individual attention and educational stimulation), (7) if the child is learning only one language. Much of our examination has substantiated these points. We have seen also that the Leftouts characteristically are disadvantaged in all or the majority of these areas, but the more of these favorable factors any child possesses or experiences, the less likely will he be comparatively disadvantaged along a continuum of potential for school adjustment. Thus, when speaking of similarity in background among those who are Leftouts and those who are not, it is essential to consider carefully the way in which similarity corresponds *in fact* to a point by point analysis of family, subcultural, and individual differences.

Another important element that may have a significant influence on the Leftout's potential for successful social adjustment in the school situation is his teacher. The classroom teacher is apt to be a significant other for the elementary-age child, not only because the teacher is in close contact with the child and possesses the power to reward him academically, but because she may also reward him socially. If she herself accepts him, and is neither prejudiced nor discriminatory in her interpersonal relations with him, this has important positive consequences for his self-evaluation. She may also influence and guide peer relationships. Trager and Yarrow (1952) have found that among first- and second-grade children, substantial changes in attitude and behavior toward age-mates who are of ethnic and racial minorities can be brought about through the teacher's influence. Their study covered a period of fourteen training sessions, with before-and-after projective tests and systematic observations as the source of the data. Two groups of children were selected. In the experimental group, the adult leader openly accepted sociocultural differences among the children and worked consciously toward creating an atmosphere of intergroup participation, understanding, and social acceptance. A control group met in a comparable situation but without the specific efforts of the teacher to foster intergroup unity. The data show major changes in the children's responses in the direction of the atmosphere established by the adult leader. Thus, for the Leftout, a warm, receptive teacher who makes conscious efforts to influence acceptance of him by his more advantaged peers is a very valuable asset.

It is not only what the teacher teaches that is important but also the manner in which it is taught. Watson points out that the teacher:

> helps individual children in the school group by a variety of consciously recognized devices—by creating situations in which it would be possible to cast a previously objectionable child in a new role, getting a previously ignored child to contribute a talent which

the other children have not recognized, helping a child accept her by accepting him as a person of worth, hoping this will lead to peer acceptance.[5]

The extent to which an adult can influence sociometric status of specific children is experimentally verified by Flanders and Havumaki (1960). They brought seventeen groups of children together for a single discussion session with a teacher unknown to any of the children. The teacher gave praise only to those seated in odd numbered seats. Subsequently, sociometric data were obtained which indicated that the praised students received the greatest number of choices. The relevance of this finding becomes more important still in light of the evidence previously cited that teachers' responses to perceived high status children differ from their responses to those perceived to have low status. This leads to the possibility of a vicious circle, in which: (1) the child may be negatively evaluated by teacher and peers alike, (2) such negative evaluations mutually reinforce one another, (3) the child may become aware of his own rejected status in the eyes of significant others, and (4) he may respond in such a fashion that his behavior serves to further reinforce his rejection from the group. This kind of vicious circle may lead to a lowered self-concept that, as we will see, has consequences for academic maladjustment as well. While increased awareness of group processes and personal evaluations are not alone sufficient to permit the teacher to circumvent this sort of situation, her awareness can constitute a reasonable step toward the creation of a positive environment for the social, emotional, and academic development of the Leftout.

There is at least one other important situational influence on the Leftout's potential for successful school adjustment, that is, the "value climate" most prevalent in the school he attends. Coleman (1959, 1960) finds that in each school he has investigated there is a similarity in those things for which prestige is awarded by peers, for example, athletic skill and physical attractiveness, irrespective of the size of the community, the type of school, or the socioeconomic backgrounds of the children. However, his investigation also makes it clear that schools do differ in specific value climates, which can alter a child's previous value orientations and behavioral expectations. The peer group social climate in the subsystem of the school not only helps to determine the general behavior pattern of age-mates outside the classroom but has a strong influence on academic achievement as well. It has been suggested that, at least initially, the Leftout is apt to seek social acceptance by his more advantaged agemates. Mobile individuals identify, in norms, values, behavior, and appearance, with the upper level to which they aspire (anticipatory socializa-

[5]Reprinted from R. I. Watson, *Psychology of the Child; Personal, Social and Disturbed Child Development* (New York: John Wiley & Sons, Inc., 1960), p. 565.

tion). The upwardly mobile child is not likely to cling strongly to value orientations and behavior patterns not associated with prestige and achievement among his more advantaged age-mates, except in those cases in which he is clearly socially rejected by them. Thus, if the Leftout finds himself in a value climate in which academic achievement is highly valued by his peers, his chances for successful academic adjustment are enhanced.

According to one extensive study, conducted by Rogoff (1961) among 35,000 high school seniors, regardless of their socioeconomic background, seniors *at least double* their chances of scoring in the top 25 percent in college aptitude tests, if they attend a school in which the majority of their classmates come from the upper socioeconomic strata. In other words, the more advantaged students there are in a high school, the higher the college potential of all students—advantaged and disadvantaged alike. It is suggested that this is true because of differences in value climates prevalent among more or less class-segregated schools. Even considering the measured intelligence of the students, these class-linked differences remain. Kahl (1953) has noted that the higher the social-class background of the student, the more value is placed on formal education as both an end in itself and a means to future goals. He finds that the college plans of boys from different socioeconomic strata indicate that the low IQ sons of upper-class fathers are *twice* as likely to go to college as the high IQ sons of lower-class fathers. Of course, this kind of finding can be interpreted in terms of relative financial ability on the part of upper- and lower-class families to send their sons to college. However, in light of the proliferation of junior colleges and other small schools, particularly in urban areas, the increased pressure for college attendance that has been seen in the last five to ten years, and the relative availability of scholarship aid and loans to financially disadvantaged youth, it appears that much of this difference is still centered in differential value orientations.

We assume that these value climates do not spring up full-blown at the high school level but are representative of value orientations that develop in the elementary-school years with which we are concerned. Thus, we hypothesize that differential value orientations in various school settings also influence a Leftout's potential for school adjustment. These findings, coupled with what has been said about the dynamics of the social-learning process, lend credence to the position that, while the range and scope of social adjustment problems may be greater in heterogeneous schools, the Leftout's achievement potential is also greater, particularly in the kind of school setting in which the socioculturally disadvantaged child is in the statistical minority.

We have seen that the school child's concept of himself and his place among his peers and teachers is influenced by a great many variables: (1) his family's socioeconomic status and type of structural organization; (2) the value orientations and behavioral expectations of the subcultural group with which he identifies; (3) the educational background and language skill of his parents; (4) his ethnic and racial identification; (5) his sex-role identity; (6) his knowledge of the value orientations and behavioral expectations of his age-mates and teachers; (7) his degree of social acceptance and adaptability; and (8) his own experiences with success or failure—socially and academically. In short, an individual's self-evaluation is strongly influenced by the social system's ranking of him and of whatever group he is a member. It seems likely that those children who are upwardly mobile are more subject to emotional disorders and to decreases in self-esteem than those who are stationary, partly because of the cross pressures in value orientation and behavioral expectations to which they are subject.

It is important to distinguish between *perceptions* and *feelings* in this context. Any given child may have extensive and accurate perceptions of differences between himself and others, but feelings and attitudes about these differences may be absent, confused, positive or negative. It is only when he *feels* left out that the Leftout's environmental and situational disadvantage adversely affects his self-concept. However, if he does feel left out, a lowered self-concept is almost surely the consequence. This inadequate self-concept can and does have important ramifications for social adjustment, as well as for academic and emotional adjustment in the school situation. In the next section we will examine some of the adverse consequences of an inadequate self-concept.

SELF-CONCEPT IN RELATION
TO TOTAL SCHOOL ADJUSTMENT

The period of the elementary-school years that is of primary concern to us is one of social and self-discovery. We have assumed that the initial goals of *any* child in the school system involve some degree of personally defined success in academic achievement and social acceptance. Thus, we postulate that failure, particularly repeated failure, in either of these areas will have negative consequences for the child's self-concept, and failure in both of these areas at the same time will foster serious emotional maladjustment. For defining adjustment to the school situation there must be a twofold criterion, analogous to the twofold goals of the child assumed above. In the first sense, failure to adjust to demands for scholastic achievement centers on the restricted background of the culturally alienated and socioeconomically disadvantaged child. The Leftout will have difficulty when he is confronted with a formal communication-oriented curriculum that assumes that he has certain verbal skills and a relatively sophisticated awareness of the world beyond his immediate neighborhood. Our schools operate, for the most part, in terms of norms that specify that the "good" student is not only expected to be capable in learning academic materials, but he is also supposed to possess already a variety of social skills and attributes. Within the first few years of his formal educational training, the Leftout, unless he is exceptionally intelligent or unless there is a concentrated effort on the part of the educational system to broaden his experiences, may fail to adjust academically. Unfortunately, the Leftout is the one who is most likely to experience a lack of adequate compensatory experience from his teachers, and often lacks the support of his parents and more advantaged age-mates as well.

It has been noted that, from the perspective of the social system, symbols emerge as institutionalized patterns in the form of language. The learning of language skills, then, is one of the most important areas of educational achievement for any school child, and especially so for the culturally alienated child whose verbal skills are apt to be severely delimited. However, the very lack of facility in the manipulation of symbols may strongly influence scholastic achievement and trap the Leftout in yet another vicious circle.

The youngster who comes from an impoverished background is no less eager to learn and to discover than are other children. However, whatever his initial motivation and desires, the Leftout will be the first to experience a disenchantment with formal schooling as he falls behind his age-mates who come from more advantaged backgrounds. This disenchantment leads to diminished chances for successful adjustment. Malpass (1953) finds significant correlations between ninety-two disadvantaged eighth-grade students' perception of their school situation and their mean semester grades. He concludes that there is a positive relationship between the attitudes revealed by the Leftouts toward school situations and their academic success. This is true because, over a period of time, as failure to achieve continues and he encounters repeated failures and disappointments, the Leftout is apt to experience a change in his self-concept. He may become convinced that he can do no better and that he is destined to fail in whatever he attempts.

Fink (1962) has investigated the relationship between self-concept and academic achievement among elementary-school pupils. He hypothesizes that an adequate self-concept, as measured by independent analysis of the data by three psychologists, is related to high academic achievement and that, conversely, an inadequate self-concept is related to low achievement. His findings support these twin hypotheses at the .01 level for boys and at the .10 level for girls. (This sex-linked difference will not be treated here but obviously bears investigation.) Of particular interest for our purposes is the *area* of this underachievement. Curry (1962) has discovered that the socioeconomically disadvantaged child is particularly prone to failure to achieve in the area of language skills. In his investigation of 360 randomly selected sixth-grade children, Curry finds that, as intellectual ability decreases from high to low, the effect of social and economic background conditions on scholastic achievement increases greatly—not surprising in light of our discussion of verbal skill influences on measured intelligence—but, importantly, this effect is most severely felt on the subsequent learning of language.

In Curry's study, the California Test of Mental Maturity is used to determine the "intellectual ability level"; the California Achievement Test (Elementary Battery) is used as the measure of "achievement"; and questionnaire responses from the children's parents are the basis for assigning "socioeconomic level." Among his conclusions, Curry notes:

1. Socioeconomic status seems to have no effect upon the scholastic achievement of sixth-grade students when the students have high intellectual ability. High intellectual ability offsets any deficiency that may be created by lower socioeconomic conditions.
2. Social and economic factors have a significant effect upon language achievement in the medium intellectual ability group. The upper and middle socioeconomic groups both achieve a greater amount than the children of lower socioeconomic levels. Likewise, in total achievement, the upper socioeconomic group achieves a greater amount than does the lower group.
3. In the low intellectual ability group, social and economic factors have a negative effect on achievement in reading, language, and total achievement. In language especially, the upper socioeconomic group achieves more than the middle and lower socioeconomic groups.

Thus, as has been suggested, unless the Leftout is highly intelligent, he finds himself caught in a downward spiral from which there is little hope of escape. His initial lack of verbal facility works to his disadvantage in academic achievement efforts; lack of achievement over a time negatively effects his self-concept; a low self-concept is related to continued lack of achievement; and, for the lower socioeconomic child especially, this lack of achievement is felt primarily in the area of language skills. Therefore, the Leftout is indeed apt to be left out in the dimension of academic adjustment to the school situation, which may reduce the level of his self-concept of ability.

Brookover et al. (1965) have studied the relationship of self-concept of ability to school achievement. They define "self-concept of ability" as "those definitions a student holds of his ability to achieve in academic tasks as compared with others." (p. 13) Their longitudinal research, designed to follow a group of students during the six-year period from grades seven through twelve, only recently has been completed. This 1965 interim report details the findings of three experimental efforts to enhance self-concept of ability among low-achieving students. The authors' basic postulate is that, among potentially successful students, academic achievement is artificially limited by the child's self-concept of his ability to achieve. They argue, as we have done, that this inadequate self-concept is a consequence of perceived negative evaluations by significant others. Their initial research (Brookover et al., 1962) clearly indicates that self-concept of ability functions quite independently of measured intelligence in influencing academic adjustment, and is a better predictor of achievement potential. This is in keeping with our theoretical position, but a later work of Brookover also supplies evidence that positive changes in significant others' evaluations will raise the child's self-concept of ability and positively influence academic achievement.

In this study, three groups of low-achieving students were selected, and each group was treated with a different experimental method in an effort to raise the student's self-concept of ability. For one group, the significant others were their parents (who actively cooperated in the experiment); for a second group, the effort was made by the school counselor; and for the third group, an outside "expert" from a university made conscious efforts to enhance the student's self-concept of ability. Only in the parent-centered group were found any significant positive changes in self-concept of academic ability and achievement. Neither frequent sessions with the counselor, nor efforts by the expert were successful, although the authors note that some long-range effects may yet appear. While Brookover et al. have successfully induced changes in the expected direction through cooperative parental efforts, they find that simply "involving" parents is not enough. The parents' attention must be directed toward their responsibility for raising the evaluations and expectations of their children.

Obviously, supportive parents are an extremely helpful asset to the Leftout. However, as we have suggested in Chapter 3, the parents of at least some of the Leftouts who might be expected to have inadequate self-concepts of ability are apt to be somewhat less than wholeheartedly interested and fully cooperative in attempts to effect positive changes. In these instances, the classroom teacher might be a quite reasonable source of conscious efforts to raise the Leftout's self-concept of academic ability. The experimental work of Brookover et al. does not include the cooperative participation of regular teachers. There are complex difficulties inherent in designing an experimental situation in which the teacher's directed efforts to raise a student's self-concept of ability do not contaminate the results of such efforts. If a workable program can be designed, it is suggested that in the elementary-school situation the teacher is apt to be a significant other for the child's self-concept of academic ability, and her early help in efforts to raise an inadequate concept can be most influential. We have also cited evidence to show that the role of peers can be significantly influential in determining over-all self-concept and, therefore, that they might be expected to be extremely helpful in raising a child's self-concept of academic ability if their support is properly elicited by the teacher's efforts.

We have cited evidence to show that failure to achieve academically may result in a lowered self-concept, and that an inadequate self-concept of academic ability places functional restrictions on achievement. A second criterion of school adjustment relates to the Leftout's goal of social acceptance. We have suggested that social failure also results in lowered self-concept. Research evidence supports this viewpoint (Wilson, 1960; Horowitz, 1962). While school adjustment is thus seen to be strongly influenced by self-concept of academic ability, total self-concept is dependent upon several other interrelated variables. We are suggesting that these variables include: (1) the importance to the individual of the specific area of focus of others' evaluations; (2) the individual's knowledge of others' expectations and evaluations; (3) his perceptions of the quality of these evaluations; and (4) his attraction to those doing the evaluating. When the area of evaluation is in interpersonal relationships, and the child accurately perceives what is expected of him by the age-mates to which he is attracted, but he perceives that he has failed to gain social acceptance among them, he may come to evaluate himself in a less favorable way.

Berelson and Steiner cite evidence to show that, as a result of prejudice and discrimination, members of ethnic and racial minority groups particularly tend to suffer some deterioration of personality, especially self-doubt, self-hate, impulsive and superstitious behavior, resigned exploitation of their inferior status, deviant behavior, and even mental illness.

It has been noted that, from the perspective of the individual, systems of shared symbols also serve as objects of orientation for personality systems. It is postulated that social learning is vital to the formation of personality and that some degree of social acceptance is crucial to a healthy personality adjustment. Prejudice and discrimination against minority groups (racial, ethnic, or socioeconomic) are maintained by a reinforcing spiral of cause and effect: those who are disapproved of are deprived of social contacts with approved others and, as a result, fail to learn the acceptable values and behavioral expectations and are further disapproved of. It is clearly an oversimplification to suggest that acceptance by the Leftout's more advantaged peers directly determines the extent of his self-esteem. Nevertheless, the likelihood is that a Leftout's more advantaged age-mates may make major contributions to his developing identity and, if they reject him because he deviates from their value orientations and behavioral expectations, his low social status and isolation from the majority group can adversely affect his emotional adjustment. The problem of social deviance and isolation from the advantaged majority is also circular: social isolation leads to a lack of knowledge of acceptable norms, which leads to probable deviation from those norms, which reduces the likelihood of communication and interaction with the majority group, which restricts the opportunity for learning the acceptable norms, which leads to social isolation.

Lest this author be accused of placing too much emphasis on peer group interrelationships and their impact on the Leftout's personality, consider the evidence that has already been cited concerning the influence of peers, especially their influence among disadvantaged children. Carlson (1963) has also examined the relative role of identification with parents and peers in the development of the child's self-concept among forty-three sixth-grade children. Children who identify with supportive parents are consistently more self-accepting, less dependent upon current social relationships, and more accepted by peers. However, Carlson also finds that, for the children in this sample, self-ideals are closer to modal peer group ideals than to those of either parent—suggesting that for *all* children models outside the family may be important as sources of self-ideals at this developmental level. When self-esteem is defined as the amount of agreement between the child's self-description and his description of an ideal self, this kind of finding places crucial significance on the relationship of peers to the development of an adequate self-concept. Especially so for Leftouts who are often disadvantaged in that they do not identify with supportive parents.

In a consensus of several studies, Hovland and Janis (1959) find evidence to support the contention that individuals low in self-esteem are more persuasible, more field dependent, and more conforming than those with a high level of self-esteem. This relationship between self-esteem and orientation toward the social environment has implications for behavioral change under social pressure—implying that predispositions to social influence are built into the self-concept structure of an individual with low self-esteem. For the Leftout, whose self-esteem is apt to be low, this means that he is likely to be especially susceptible to social pressures, which may, of course, be adjustive or maladjustive in content. On the positive side, it means that pressures toward conformity by his advantaged peers may be very effective in influencing his adjustment to the demands of the school situation. On the negative side, it means that he is also highly susceptible to social pressures from other status-deprived children and to any cross pressures that may exist. As has been noted, it is postulated that, if these pressures are both severe and pervasive, the Leftout may experience emotional maladjustment.

That social acceptance in the school situation may be a significant influence on emotional adjustment and mental health is indicated by the findings of Bedoian (1953). He tested 743 "socially over-accepted" (on the basis of a multicriteria sociometric test) and "socially under-accepted" sixth-grade pupils, using Thorpe, Clark, and Tieg's Mental Health

Analysis (Elementary Series, Form A). He finds that the socially over-accepted children have a significantly better average mental health score than do socially under-accepted children. However, it must be noted that what is defined as emotional maladjustment ranges considerably from one social system to another and even from one subsegment of the same system to another. Trained professionals in the field of mental health disagree on the symptoms, the classification, and the appropriate treatment of emotional problems. We will not be concerned here with an effort to rectify these difficulties. For our purposes, "emotionally maladjusted" is defined as any case in which the individual concerned seeks or is referred for special help to a professional outside the regular classroom, for example, school counselors, visiting teachers, child guidance clinicians and so forth. Also included is any child placed in a special school class designed to specifically serve disturbed children (as opposed to retarded children). In addition, this includes any child who would be classified as emotionally maladjusted by psychologists or psychiatrists if they were to be tested by them.

Between teachers in the public schools and professional clinicians, there is apt to be disagreement on the characteristics rated most maladjustive. Schrupp and Gjerde (1953) find that teachers rate as most serious: (1) impertinence and defiance, (2) impudence and rudeness, (3) writing obscene notes, (4) disobedience, (5) disorderliness, (6) heterosexual activity, (7) masturbation, and (8) untruthfulness—in that order. On the other hand, professional clinicians rate as most seriously maladjusted: (1) shyness, (2) suspiciousness, (3) dreaminess, (4) fearfulness, (5) sensitiveness, (6) excessive criticism of others, (7) imaginative lying, and (8) nervousness—in *that* order. Two obvious conclusions can be drawn from these findings. First, teachers are apparently primarily concerned with behavior that is disruptive in the classroom and tend to overlook the emotional maladjustment of the quiet, withdrawn child. Secondly, there is no agreement whatsoever between teachers and clinicians about the symptoms of serious emotional disturbance. It may be hypothesized that the practical consequence of this difference in opinion may be that, from the viewpoint of the professional clinician, the children who are most in need of help are least apt to be referred to sources of outside aid by school personnel. Conversely, those most often referred are least in need of professional help. This is particularly important in considering the Leftouts, because their behavior is not apt to fully meet the demands of the core-cultural norms expected in the classroom, and they are especially likely to behave in a way that can be described by the teacher as rude, impertinent, disorderly, and so on.

It is important to note that the perceptions of teachers and counselors who are responsible for evaluating school children's emotional adjustment may be unintentionally influenced by the child's socioeconomic level. McDermott *et al.* (1965) present the data obtained from psychiatric evaluations of 263 children of "blue-collar" families who were referred to the University of Michigan's Childrens Psychiatric Hospital during the year of July 1961 to July 1962. These children were further divided into two groups on the basis of their father's occupational status and were referred to in the report as "skilled" (n = 115) and "unskilled" (n = 148).[6] McDermott *et al.* give special emphasis to the clinical and social questions that are raised as the result of differential diagnoses between the two groups. They find that significantly more often (p < .05 in each case) the unskilled group is seen to exhibit overt hostility, impulsiveness, paranoid reactions, affective disturbances, and withdrawal, while the skilled group is seen to exhibit anxiety, obsessive compulsive behavior, and somatic complaints. Unskilled children are characterized as coming from unstable, conflict-ridden homes significantly more often than skilled children (p < .005). Nevertheless, families of both groups rate their children alike with respect to adjustment at home — 30 percent of both groups claim their children are "doing well at home." However, marked differences in the children's adjustment to the academic standards of the school are noted. The upper end of the scale, that is, "doing very well in school," is assigned to the skilled group significantly more often (p < .02), and the lower end of the scale, that is, "doing very poorly in school," is assigned to the unskilled group (p < .025). In fact, general school maladjustment among children in the unskilled group most frequently is considered the primary reason for referral to the clinic. It is also found that there is a significantly longer delay in referral of the unskilled children to the clinic from the time their problems first become apparent (p < .01).

As we have seen, it is hardly surprising that children with backgrounds typically found among the lower socioeconomic strata should have difficulty with the academic demands of the school, with affective relationships, and with conflicts created by a disorganized home life. However, McDermott *et al.* observe that the heterogeneity of the blue-collar group makes class distinctions difficult to identify and follow. They also suggest that unskilled people, in our complex and rapidly changing social system that is based on technical competence, are increasingly more socially and culturally isolated and, therefore, less able to help their children adjust to the demands of the core culture taught in the schools. They contend that teachers and counselors who appraise behavior as normal or abnormal unwittingly view the unskilled group differently because of their

[6]The "skilled" group are chosen on the basis of occupations such as machinist or self-employed farmer. The "unskilled" group is comprised of children whose father's occupations are such things as janitor or assembly-line worker.

own values. The authors point out that paranoid thinking, withdrawal, hostility, and impulsiveness are, at least in part, the reaction of a perfectly normal child who is uncomfortable and totally foreign to the setting; a child who simply does not know how to communicate and interact with teachers and more advantaged peers. Again we see the significance for adjustment of communication skills and of the tremendous advantage the verbally and socially facile child has over one who is inept in these areas.

There is evidence to suggest that some of the emotional difficulties of Leftouts may center in self-concepts of sex-role identity, especially among boys. The family life of Leftouts is prone to disorganization. This disorganization often takes the form of father-absence or of inadequate male-role models. However, the total blame cannot be put on the structure of the boy's family. Lynn (1959) finds that the identification process differs for boys and girls in that the girl identifies with a particular feminine model, while the boy identifies with a general cultural or subcultural stereotype of a masculine model. Hartley (1959) offers impressive bibliographic and empirical evidence to show that stereotyped male-role demands contribute to serious adjustment problems for boys. He notes that the higher rates of referral of boys over girls to child guidance centers indicates the markedly greater incidence of failure in social functioning in boys, as compared to girls. In addition, males are more apt to engage in deviant behavior, and, among the intellectually gifted, boys are more apt to be underachievers than girls. Through a sifting of this kind of evidence and through interviews with forty-one eight to eleven-year-old boys, Hartley concludes that there are at least five major adjustment problems associated with the demands of the male sex-role: (1) lack of adequate models, (2) extensive supervision by women, (3) the conflicting nature of multiple demands within the male role, (4) lack of clear positive definition of the male sex-role during socialization, and (5) the rigidity of role demands.

Teachers, especially women, may compound the difficulty for Leftout boys. The quality of the interpersonal relationship between a teacher and student is significantly important in determining the effects of the school situation on a child's psychological development and adjustment. The teacher, because of her position of authority, possesses a great deal of reward power. Her judgment of what constitutes good or bad, proper or improper behavior determines which behaviors will elicit her approval and to whom she will dispense rewards; even though she may not be aware of the basis for her evaluations. Davis and Havighurst (1947) have discussed at length the divergence of cultural normative expectations between lower-class children and middle-class teachers. Their work may be summarized in the assertion that the goals defined by the middle-class teacher do not receive reinforcement from the lower-class child's peer group or from his family. Subcultural definitions of acceptable male and female behavior are particularly divergent—especially with respect to physical aggression among boys. Several investigators have suggested a sex-typing hypothesis in connection with teacher-student interrelationships; that is, that the behavioral tendencies of girls (irrespective of social-class background) is in closer agreement with teachers expectations than is that of boys—especially lower-class boys who are more apt to be aggressive. These more "masculine" boys are the ones who receive the greater share of the teacher's disapproval. This teacher disapproval, in turn, is likely to generate anxiety and have an adverse affect on the general personality adjustment of boys—especially, again, on boys reared in a lower sociocultural milieu. Although some degree of aggressiveness is a normal part of the masculine sex-role, the Leftout who typically lacks a strong sex-role model and who is the subject of consistent disapproval from his teachers, may find that the conflict only increases his own anxiety and has negative consequences for his self-esteem.

This author is postulating that such factors as anxiety, inadequate sex-role identity, social rejection, cross pressures on upwardly mobile children, and repeated academic failures will certainly tend to create emotional maladjustment of some kind for Leftouts in the school situation. However, there is a paucity of evidence concerning the nature and extent of this maladjustment, and the little evidence that does exist is clouded by such issues as the nature of the developmental antecedents of various specific symptoms, as well as their proper identification and classification. The whole difficulty is even further compounded by the influence that socioeconomic and subcultural variables might have on the recognition, diagnosis, and appropriate treatment of emotional maladjustment among school children. This is obviously an area that demands and deserves some immediate theoretical and experimental attention.

In the next chapter we will briefly review a few of the major works intended to give an over-all picture of the causes and consequences of disadvantaged children's maladjustment to the social subsystem of the school. We will then proceed to the task of putting together the various interrelated findings and suggestions we have discussed and of building an analytical framework with them, designed to illuminate the particular consequences of sociocultural disadvantage for children in heterogeneous schools.

SUMMARY

The avoidance of social isolation, real or threatened, is a powerful force motivating any child's behavior. It is especially rewarding to a child to be accepted by his peers. An acceptable social status is an important requisite for satisfactory emotional adjustment. Thus, children are heavily influenced by their peers' expectations, values, behavior, and evaluation of them. In general, the people in the social subsystem of the school—age-mates and teachers—are very important agents of socialization. Associations with this group are one determinant of stability and acceptance in social relationships, are a contributor to the child's developing self-concept, and are a force contributing to the form and substance of the child's value orientation toward the world around him, including the demands of the academic world.

This chapter has dealt with the powers and limitations of the peer group in influencing children, the basis of social status among children, the influence of "intelligence" in compensating for other disadvantages, the role of peers in the development of a child's self-concept, and the special importance that peer relationships may have for the Leftout. It has been suggested that social acceptance and emotional adjustment are positively related. It has been argued that status deprivation by teachers and age-mates may be another cause of the Leftout's potential for academic and emotional maladjustment. Thus, the quantity and quality of a child's interaction with his age-mates and his teachers is another crucial variable for efforts to understand how he came to be left out in the heterogeneous school situation, and for pointing the direction toward compensatory efforts.

For the child whose background includes socioeconomic deprivations or a lack of warm, close affiliations with his family, or both, the peer group is apt to assume an especially important socializing role. However, a child from such a background is apt to deviate widely from his more advantaged age-mates in value orientations and behavioral expectations. In his need for social acceptance under these circumstances, he may either change his own behavior and values or change his reference group, seeking out others like himself with whom to coalesce.

It has been suggested that potentially the heterogeneous school situation is an important avenue for social tolerance and understanding on the part of more advantaged children, in addition to serving to facilitate upward social mobility for disadvantaged children—but both have to be *worked at*. It is clear that a disadvantaged child in a heterogeneous school may have problems with academic acculturation or social assimilation, or both. If these problems are severe, in either or both areas, his self-concept is apt to suffer. However, evidence also strongly suggests that a heterogeneous school situation, with a value climate of achievement orientation, is the best one for fostering acculturation and social assimilation.

Measured intelligence is statistically related positively to socioeconomic background, but any given child may deviate widely from these averages. Thus, high intelligence may compensate for other sociocultural disadvantages among those children we typically expect to be Leftouts. On the other hand, the more usual failure to do well on standardized intelligence tests may prejudice teachers and age-mates against him and convince the Leftout that he is stupid.

Self-concept develops through many experiences, but perceptions of evaluation by age-mates and teachers is one important source. Intense anxiety over inadequate social relationships and perceptions of inadequacy in achievement-oriented performance, may have a crippling effect on the cognitive process. Thus, it is suggested that a low level of self-esteem may be yet another possible cause of the Leftout's disadvantage and potential for academic as well as social and emotional maladjustment. At the same time, it seems clear that the Leftout's dependency needs and moderate (if not too high) levels of "functional" anxiety contribute to a particular susceptibility to influence that can, at least potentially, help him to overcome his disadvantage.

The adverse consequences of the various causes of disadvantage seem to be cumulative. For example, a child raised in a lower-class cultural environment is probably less disadvantaged than one who also comes from a disorganized family. If other factors such as racial or ethnic group discrimination, lack of social acceptance by peers and teachers, and low level of self-esteem are added, the child's potential for successful school adjustment is severely impaired. In short, the more strikes there are against the child, the poorer the prognosis for successful academic, social, and emotional adjustment in the heterogeneous school situation, unless the social subsystem of the school offers real compensatory experiences.

5

Analysis:
Causes,
Consequences
and "Cures"

There have been several recent major works directed at a comprehensive overview of the causes of socioculturally disadvantaged children's maladjustment to the school system. Riessman (1962) has sought to describe the general characteristics of disadvantaged school children and to suggest specific remedial approaches to their education on the basis of general principles derived from current knowledge. He postulates that disadvantaged children often do not have experience with and do not accept such school-centered things as books, formal language, and many other aspects of the educational system. He suggests that the "culturally deprived" are ambivalent toward education, that is, they value education as an abstraction but are often antagonistic towards the goals and practices of teachers and schools. The basis of this ambivalence is proposed by Riessman to be a strong negative attitude toward intellectualism, coupled with an equally strong positive attitude toward vocational training.

Riessman points out that the contemporary school system lacks transitional techniques for assimilating the socioculturally disadvantaged child into the existing academic mainstream. He notes in the manner of teachers and counselors a "discrimination without prejudice,"[1] a devastating al-

[1]President Mary Bunting of Radcliffe has termed such people "the hidden dissuaders."

beit inadvertent lack of respect for the disadvantaged child based on failure to recognize and accept differences in value orientations. He argues that the "underprivileged" not only possess a culture, but possess one that has some values that are both utilitarian and worthy of emulation. This may well be the case, although the subject is surely a controversial one. Certainly some subcultural, ethnic, and religious groups among those who can be defined as underprivileged in our social system do have fully developed cultural heritages that simply are different from the core culture taught in the school system. At the same time, it has been suggested that a number of the children with whom we are principally concerned lack such a clear and unambiguous religious or ethnic heritage and develop instead in a "culture of poverty," in which a sense of low status, lack of power, cultural alienation, economic deprivation, and limited opportunity are its principle characteristics (Lewis, 1966; Will and Vatter, 1965). In any case, one should not confuse lack of "conformity" per se with school maladjustment. Conformity to certain norms is a prerequisite for successful school adjustment, but total conformity to an ideal-typical core-cultural pattern is both irrelevant to our concerns and probably impossible in practice.

Riessman points out specific aspects of the socioculturally disadvantaged child's value orientation that makes him deficient in school know-how. The normative culture of the socioculturally disadvantaged is, typically, strongly masculine in value orientation, whereas the school system is seen as strongly feminine in orientation. Furthermore, Riessman argues, families in the lower socioeconomic levels typically employ physical discipline, which conditions the child to expect physical violence for infractions of rules and to react with physical violence when he feels wronged. The tendency is for teachers to use the same bland control measures, irrespective of the severity of the misbehavior. When mild and severe problems are handled in the same way, it is difficult for any child to distinguish between what is a grave trespass against the person or rights of others and what is a relatively harmless infraction. For the child who anticipates physical punishment for severe infractions, the disciplinary measures he encounters in the school situation may be meaningless to him, and, hence, he continues to break rules until he is in grave difficulty, at which time he feels wronged and is apt to react with what is interpreted by his teachers and counselors as unwarranted and unacceptable violence. Riessman contends that the family background of the disadvantaged child is also significant in that the lower class tends to discourage individualism and self-concern in the child's development of self. He argues that far more emphasis is given to compulsive conformity to external demands and cooperation in such families, while the school expects individual achievement striving in competition with others and injects fear of personal failure as a motivating device.

Riessman's major argument centers on the disadvantaged child's "Achille's heel" of ineptness in formal communication skills. This relative lack of skill appears in intelligence testing and in an unfamiliarity with core-cultural speech and is often translated into a designation of the child as a "slow-learner." He notes that it is often contended that the disadvantaged child is nonverbal and cannot conceptualize, but he argues that this is not true; the disadvantaged child is seen by Riessman as merely unfamiliar with formal English as it is used in the school system. He argues that the disadvantaged child usually possesses a well developed symbolic communication system, but this system fails to correlate highly with the system he is expected to employ at school. No data are supplied to substantiate this position, which disagrees with several works we have cited (Luria and Yudovitch, 1961; Bruner, 1961; John, 1963; Deutsch, 1964), which offer ample empirical evidence that communication skills are not merely equivalent to speech patterns. For example, Gussow (1965) points out that socioculturally disadvantaged children watch TV as much or more than their advantaged age-mates, and are able to reproduce whole units of formal language that they have heard. Nevertheless, this rote reproduction is nonfunctional in that such standard speech is not subsequently employed as a language variant in situations unrelated to TV. It is not argued that the disadvantaged child is nonverbal in the sense that he does not possess speech patterns (although he may suppress these in the school situation if he is ridiculed or criticized). It *is* suggested that he lacks knowledge of and experience with broad communication skills, including abstractions and formal language, which is maladjustive for the development of complex conceptualizations required in the school situation. We agree with Riessman insofar as it is possible to say that every mentally and physically normal child acquires speech. What we question, in opposition to Riessman, is the adequacy of speech among disadvantaged children for full *intellectual* development. Communication skills are functional for the disadvantaged child in his interpersonal environment in those situations in which they are applicable and needed, but we argue that these situations are fewer, more monotonous, and hence, less educationally stimulating for the disadvantaged child. Language skill is not only related to the way a child *speaks* but also to the way he *thinks*. A low status dialect may hamper social mobility, but a restricted language development places limits on intellectual potential. Thus, socioculturally disadvantaged children may begin school with a deficit, not only in using formal language but in conceptualizing as well.

We have seen evidence that this deficit is cumulative and that it has negative consequences for the Leftout's ability to adjust to the academic and social demands of the integrated school system. The need to develop curricula aimed specifically at fostering formal verbal skills among children who lack training and experience in this area is a very clear one.

Whatever nonformal verbal skills the disadvantaged child may have, they are largely irrelevant for his school adjustment (which correlates highly with future occupational potential and his adult social status), unless he also develops communication skills in keeping with the expectations and requirements of the school system. The speech patterns, the symbols, and the conceptual ability a disadvantaged child spontaneously acquires may be a major barrier to his potential for achievement of intellectual and social equality in the school system.

Riessman has been criticized for his lack of a consistent educational theory or any over-all conceptual framework with which to unite his diagnosis and his proposals for treatment. His syncretism of "educationally deprived," "disadvantaged," "underprivileged," "lower socioeconomic group," "lower class" and just about anyone else who is not defined as middle class allows for sweeping generalizations that are simply not true of all children from such backgrounds. We can sympathize with his problem because these are the global terms employed in the literature, but we cannot condone his lack of probing into the specific variables of lower class, underprivileged, and other backgrounds in more detail to point out those that provoke social and academic deviancy among some lower-class children but not among others. For example, while much of his discussion concerns racial and ethnic minorities, he fails to consider the import of social acceptance and rejection of such children. His work is an oversimplification of the problem and is not adequate alone to give insight into the causes of school maladjustment among socioculturally disadvantaged children. He does suggest that differences in subcultural and family value orientations play a part, and he gives emphasis to the importance of ineptness in communication skills as a significant variable in school maladjustment. In doing this much, Riessman offers at least two keys to understanding the Leftout's problem of social and academic maladjustment in the school system.

Passow (1963) has edited a compendium of contemporary research and theory bearing on the problems of the disadvantaged. His volume contains articles relating to five different though interrelated, aspects of school disadvantage: (1) the schools themselves as they are found in depressed areas, (2) the psychological aspects of education in depressed areas, (3) the sociological aspects of education in depressed areas, (4) the quality of teachers in depressed areas, and (5) school programs in depressed areas. Much of the material to be found in this volume relates to more or less class-segregated schools, in which the disadvantaged are the majority group. Because our concern is aimed at understanding the problems of the disadvantaged child who attends school with advantaged age-mates, we will not review it in any detail here. However, Deutsch has contributed an article to this work that emphasizes the interaction of social and developmental factors that have an impact on the intellectual growth and school performance of the Leftout. He offers the theoretical framework surrounding language deficiency and its consequences that Riessman failed to supply.

Deutsch's thesis is that the child lacking in language facility enters the school situation so poorly prepared to produce what the school demands that initial failures are almost inevitable and the school experience becomes negatively rather than positively reinforced over a time. These children are seen to have a qualitatively different preparation for school arising from a background of stimulus deprivation. Deutsch centers his discussion on the causes and consequences of stimulus deprivation. He argues in terms of Piaget's developmental theory, that the disadvantaged child has had access only to a limited segment of the spectrum of stimulation potentially available and that the segments that have been made available to him tend to have poorer and less systematic ordering of stimulation sequences, and thereby prove less useful to the developmental growth and activation of cognitive potential. This deprivation does not, necessarily, limit eventual cognitive capacity, provided the initial handicaps can be overcome. Deutsch postulates that the culturally disadvantaged home is not verbally oriented, which implies a restriction on the opportunity for the development of auditory discrimination skills. He argues that in order for the disadvantaged child to successfully adjust to school he must have special help. Further, the community, family, and school share the blame for the child's disadvantage, but the school, as the institutionalized receptacle for and purveyor of social values, must accept the major responsibility for correcting the situation. He contends that the school must be willing to engage in productive experimentation and innovation.

Deutsch notes that stimulus deprivation does *not* necessarily imply a restriction in quantity but, rather, a restriction on quality and variety. When a child is placed in a position of competition with other children who have had broader and constructively stimulating experiences, the child whose language training has been inadequate has a greater potential for failures and frustrations. As we have seen, repeated failures have consequences for the child's evaluation of his own ability. Brookover's notion of "self-concept of ability" has been reviewed and shown to offer yet another key to understanding the Leftout's problem.

Riessman's work suggests something of the complexity of the antecedents of school maladjustment among socioculturally disadvantaged children. Deutsch helps by offering a theoretical cause and effect explanation of one of those areas of disadvantage. Brookover explains how an inadequate self-concept of ability can, in and of itself, place functional limits on the child's academic potential in later years if it is not overcome by compensatory measures. We have argued that the appropriate time to begin compensatory measures is during the child's earliest school years, when his cumulative academic deficit is not so large and when, for the Leftout, he is most likely to be accepted by his more advantaged age-mates and most amenable to their influence and that of his teachers.

We are particularly concerned with this elementary-age group, because many of the most severely maladjusted leave school at the earliest possible opportunity and, thus, become difficult to reach, if not entirely lost, for later compensatory programs. Lambert (1964), reporting the results of an intensive five-year follow-up study of children rated in elementary school as potential dropouts, finds that those children who experience the most difficulty in academic and social school adjustment in the elementary years are the ones who become delinquent earlier and drop out of secondary schools sooner. Her data reveal that academic and social vulnerability and failure in the early school years is a significant predictor of greater vulnerability and likelihood of failure in the child's later years. "The path of the vulnerable student from elementary school on is not a level one; it is nearly always downhill." (p. 63)

The Leftout is a vulnerable student. On the one hand, he is open to criticism and attack in the school system and in interpersonal relationships with his more advantaged age-mates, because he lacks social and academic skills derived from prior knowledge, experience, training, and motivation. On the other hand, this very vulnerability also makes him potentially very responsive to pressures exerted toward conformity to expectations of teachers and more advantaged age-mates. Most of the literature we have examined has dealt specifically with the socioculturally disadvantaged child—as defined in one way or another. Whatever the definition employed in each work, the clearly common element these children share is vulnerability to a situation with which they are unfamiliar and for which they are inadequately prepared. We argue that for the Leftouts, that is, those disadvantaged children who must attend classes with children who are prepared and for whom the school situation has many elements of familiarity, the adjustment problem is apt to be more severe while, at the same time, their potential for successful adjustment is also greater.

Title VI of the U.S. Civil Rights Act of 1964 provides that Federal aid shall not be available for programs involving racial discrimination. Federal aid to educational programs is an important source of financial support for public schools. Francis Keppel, U.S. Commissioner of Education, has interpreted Title VI to mean that not only racially segregated schools in the southern United States but schools in the North that evidence de facto racial or social-class segregation because of the way in which school-districting lines are drawn, are not eligible for federal monies. For example, in October of 1965 the government suspended payment of a $30 million aid program for Chicago public schools under this ruling. This payment was eventually made, despite a lack of appreciable change in the system, but the challenge has been issued and may well indicate the direction of future interpretations of civil rights legislation. In Massachusetts a 1965 state law requires schools to correct any discriminatory practices or to forfeit the state funds that supply a major source of income for operation. The city of Boston has an "open enrollment" policy that permits any child to transfer to any school of his choice as long as there is room. These are but a few examples of the kind of legal changes that are occurring, which will most certainly have repercussions on what are now largely segregated schools—segregated either racially or in terms of social class and area of residence. Add to this the number of separate rural schools that are closing their doors in favor of consolidation with the nearest urban center or largest semirural school and the likelihood of bringing together numbers of children who are ill prepared for the academic and social demands of an integrated school system with those who are adequately prepared increases. Thus, the problem of the Leftout is very large in scope and is growing larger.

In our exploration of some of the relevant theoretical and empirical literature, we have discovered and discussed a large number of antecedent and consequent variables that have been shown to have a significant impact on the disadvantaged children's maladjustment to school. No one of them is sufficient alone. Some are unique to maladjusted children; most are not. These variables must *all* be taken into account in a comprehensive analysis of the Leftout and his special problems. Even for understanding disadvantaged children in general, singular concepts such as "stimulus deprivation," "language deficiency," "low self-concept of ability," "delayed gratification pattern versus immediate gratification pattern," and so on, are insufficient alone. So too are such glittering generalities as "sociocultural disadvantage" or "status deprivation." It is necessary, for example, to specify the theoretical consequences of stimulus deprivation or status deprivation and how both relate to low self-concept of ability. Other considerations are also important. For example, given an apparently similar background of socioeconomic deprivation, all children do not fail to adjust to the contemporary school system. Lower-class children can and do successfully adjust to the school system—academically, socially, and emotionally. This variation, and others, suggests a multidimensional cause of school maladjustment.

Disadvantaged children have a wide variety of socioeconomic, cultural, and personal experiences both prior to school and in the classroom. This variation suggests a continuum of disadvantage in school adjustment potential, ranging from very little trouble to severe maladjustment problems. We would suggest that the greater the number of areas of disadvantage any disadvantaged child experiences, the more severe is his maladjustment to the school system likely to be.

The unique thing that separates Leftouts from other disadvantaged children is the nature of the particular social situation in the heterogeneous school and the impact this has on the consequences of his general disadvantage. We have argued that these consequences are in some ways similar to those experienced by any disadvantaged child in any school. We have also suggested that for Leftouts the consequences may, at the same time, be more severe and yet offer a more favorable setting for overcoming his disadvantage.

We have discussed a number of vicious circles. Taken in the broad sense, the entire problem of sociocultural disadvantage is a vicious circle. Disadvantaged backgrounds produce children who are disadvantaged in relation to others when they begin school; comparative disadvantage portends early school maladjustment that tends to become cumulative over a period of time; school maladjustment is reflected in limitations of potential and restrictions on future adult status; low status and comparative lack of education produces disadvantaged parents whose children suffer comparative disadvantage in background knowledge, experience, training, and motivation, and thus it continues from generation to generation.

The problem is to break into this vicious cycle and stop its downward spiral. The Leftout must be recognized and compensatory measures must be taken to influence positive changes in his academic, social, and emotional adjustment to school. To do this, it is necessary that a theoretically-oriented analysis be available that allows for an understanding of the interplay of socioeconomic, cultural, social-interactional, and personal forces and how they combine to influence the Leftout's potential for school maladjustment. An analysis that improves the power to understand human behavior also makes it possible to more effectively plan compensatory programs for behavioral change. The next section is devoted to seeing how the variables explored in our earlier discussion may be synthesized into a coherent picture of the causes and consequences of the Leftout's problems.

THE ANALYSIS

Let us begin with a brief restatement of some of the more important concepts that influence the analysis. We have defined the Leftouts as socioculturally disadvantaged elementary-school children who attend a heterogeneous school, in which the majority of their age-mates are significantly better prepared than they are to meet the academic and social demands of the school situation. Their general disadvantage, shared with all disadvantaged children, centers on cultural alienation and economic disadvantage—a combination that increases the Leftout's specific potential for maladjustment to the socially approved academic and interpersonal demands of a heterogeneous school system, because of the resultant deviation from the normative expectations of the majority group.

Cultural alienation is defined as foreign to or outside of the core culture of the majority group, neither acculturated to nor assimilated by the majority group and, therefore: (1) knowledge of appropriate norms is lacking; (2) the content of the norms, if known, seem meaningless; and (3) power to make changes in the norms or his own behavior is lacking. The *core culture* represents the "official" culture taught in the public schools. It's major features are: (1) an emphasis on "success" in the form of upward social mobility, which is seen to be achieved by (a) ambition (as opposed to aggression), (b) honesty, (c) thrift, (d) hard work; (2) an emphasis on "propriety" in the form of conformity to both overt and covert normative guides to behavior, which demands (a) courtesy to all people, (b) loyalty to friends and family, (c) obedience to legitimate authority, (d) avoidance of overt aggression, especially physical aggression, (e) cleanliness in thoughts as well as in body; (3) an emphasis on delayed gratification of needs and desires, which requires (a) impulse renunciation, (b) patient hard work toward future goals, (c) aspirations toward future goals and rewards; (4) an emphasis on the ownership of material goods; (5) an emphasis on active citizenship, which demands (a) participation in organizations, (b) exercising the right and responsibility to vote; (6) an ideological belief in the "American creed," which demands subscription to the principles of (a) freedom, equality, and justice as the right of all citizens, (b) democracy as the ideal-typical form of government, and (c) free enterprise as the basis of the economy.

Adjustment refers to continual adaptive learning in the face of new experiences or modifications in the environment. *Academic adjustment* is exemplified by the successful performance of required academic tasks in the school situation, as measured by age-group placement, grade-point averages, and scores on standardized tests. *Social adjustment* is exemplified by social assimilation and acceptance by teachers and more advantaged age-mates, as measured by sociometric techniques. *Emotional adjustment* is exemplified by over-all personality stability, as measured by standardized personality tests or as defined by teachers and counselors in the school situation.

The Leftout's failure to adjust, or *maladjustment,* refers to a lack of ability to cope with new experiences or modifications in the environment and to learn from them. *Academic maladjustment* is exemplified by repeated difficulty or failure to achieve at a level or rate commensurate with his age-mates. *Social maladjustment* is exemplified by the Leftout's discriminatory exclusion from the social activities of his more advantaged age-mates on the basis of prejudice, an unreasonable bias founded on unfavorable preconceptions, and by his teachers' prejudicially discriminatory behavior toward him. *Emotional maladjustment* is exemplified by undue anxiety or other symptoms, especially (a) rigidity, (b) antisocial behavior, (c) depression, or (d) withdrawal. *Maladjustive* refers to any value orientation, belief, or behavior that for the Leftout contributes to maladjustment in the school situation.

The Leftout's *deviation* simply refers to his being different from some standard, and when this standard is taken to be his more advantaged age-mates, who are familiar with and conform to the core-cultural norms of the school system, the Leftout is, by definition, a *deviant*.

We have suggested that the Leftout's potential for successful adjustment to school is equally dependent on (1) academic success, (2) social acceptance, and (3) emotional adjustment. These factors are seen to be interdependent, and failure in these dimensions of school adjustment are seen as the consequences of the Leftout's disadvantage. Our examination of the literature suggests that the Leftout's lack of general knowledge of and conformity to the value orientations and behavioral expectations of the core culture represented in the heterogeneous school situation results in maladjustment to the academic demands of the school situation, and maladjustment to the social demands of the school situation, since deviation from core-cultural means of achieving academic and social success is maladjustive. We have argued that at least the *initial* goals of any child, including the Leftout, in the school situation are to have some degree of personally defined success in academic achievement and social acceptance. Failure, particularly repeated failure, in either of these areas will have frustrating and anxiety-provoking consequences; and failure in both of these areas at the same time will foster emotional maladjustment.

Our examination of the literature has suggested at least five interrelated, specific causes of the Leftout's academic, social, and emotional disadvantage and potential for failure to adjust to the heterogeneous school situation. These stem in part from his sociocultural background and in part from his position in the school situation. The Leftout's disadvantage, then, is typically based on some or all of the following interrelated problems:

1. relatively low socioeconomic background, with attendant learned deviant values and behavioral expectations;

2. relative lack of language facility;
3. relative deprivation in early interpersonal affiliations;
4. relative status deprivation among teachers and age-mates;
5. relatively low level of self-esteem.

The adverse consequences of these various causes of disadvantage are suggested to be cumulative, such that the more *kinds* of disadvantage any particular Leftout experiences, the poorer his prognosis for successful adjustment to the heterogeneous school situation.

It is the task in this chapter to examine, within a social-psychologically-oriented frame of reference, the processes that connect the causes of the Leftout's disadvantage to their maladjustive consequences in the heterogeneous school situation.

Relatively Low Socioeconomic Background

Theoretical Framework. A fundamental attribute of any social system *qua* system is that it is normative. People who are in prolonged interactional relationships because of relatively similar socioeconomic positions develop characteristic consensual *value orientations*[2] and *subcultural*[3] normative expectations that serve to guide perception, cognition, affective relationships, and general behavior. There are definable sets of system-wide beliefs, values, and behavioral norms that are idealistically defined and known to the members. These sets vary between subcultures, and conformity to these sets of normative ideals varies within subcultures. However, the majority of what any individual thinks and feels, and a great deal of how he acts and reacts, is the direct result of his interaction with others in his subcultural environment.

Behavioral expectations, value orientations, and symbolic systems are learned in social interaction. The more individuals associate with one another under conditions of equality, the more they come to share value orientations and behavioral expectations. The more individuals associate with one another under conditions of equality, the more they come to like one another.

[2] *Value orientation*—the generalized theme of attitudes, represented by the entire complex of the individual's expressions regarding that which is to be valued and the means by which evaluations are to be made; value orientation finds observational expression in each of the behavioral and cognitive choices an individual makes.

[3] *Subcultural*—those behavioral norms and value orientations that are reflected in more or less distinct ways of life among some subsegment within the total population of a social system.

Internalized sanctions (conscience formation), an individual's *self-concept*,[4] sex-role identity, generalized conceptual schema, and other intraindividual factors such as *achievement motivation*[5] are also developed in social interaction. The characteristic value orientations and behavioral expectations of various socioeconomic strata are hierarchically evaluated and differentially rewarded on a system-wide basis.

Synthesis. The Leftout is disadvantaged in his potential for school adjustment in that he often has a lower *social-class*[6] background, which is less likely to have socialized him adequately to the social and academic demands of the heterogeneous school situation. Social classes vary in the extent to which their characteristic socializing influences, that is, intrafamily relationships, child-rearing practices, language patterns, intellectual and leisure time pursuits, behavioral norms, and value orientations equip a child to adjust successfully to the core-cultural expectations of the school situation. However, there appear to be a number of relatively stable social-class differences in the statistical probability of certain generalized attitudes and behaviors affecting child rearing.

Parents in the lower socioeconomic strata (in relation to middle-class parents): (1) more often employ object-oriented rewards and punishments; (2) are more apt to punish the child physically; (3) are more rejecting of dependency behavior; (4) are apt to be less able to provide the bases of achievement motivation; (5) are less apt to have the educational or experiential background to offer specific help in attaining school success; (6) are less likely to provide a verbally-oriented environment; (7) are less likely to place a value on intellectual accomplishment per se (as opposed

[4]*Self-concept*—the individual's view of himself, derived from taking the role of *significant others* [those selected persons whose opinions, values, judgments, sentiments, and attitudes are influential in shaping the direction of the individual's self-concept, behavioral expectations, and value orientation] in social interaction, by means of which he organizes his personality and directs his actions to reciprocate the perceived expectations of others. An individual's self-concept consists of: (1) a view of identity, (2) attitudes that express personal interests and aversions, (3) a generalized conceptual schema for viewing the environment, (4) knowledge of personal goals and degree of success in achieving prior goals, and (5) a self-evaluation on the basis of comparison with others and their perceived evaluations.

[5]*Achievement motivation*—an internalized personality need that gives impetus to actual achievement-oriented behavior; it implies active, goal-directed efforts (as opposed to achievement-oriented values, which merely define and give high evaluation to achievement). Motivation and value ideally occur together, but high evaluation on achievement may occur without the motivation, which is the basis of actual achievement.

[6]*Social class*—(socioeconomic class) the hierarchical ranking of persons in a social system into groups with relatively clear, stable, and definable subcultural differences in life-styles, including value orientations and behavioral expectations. Most usually it is measured on the basis of criteria such as: (1) prestige of one's own or parental occupation, (2) family income level, (3) level of one's own or parents' educational attainment, (4) area of residence or type of dwelling, and so on.

to valuing occupational training); and (8) are more likely to be separated or to be inadequate sex-role models. Thus, one of the sources of difference in school adjustment potential among children is that of the differential backgrounds they bring into the school situation as a result of membership in various subcultural socioeconomic strata.

The programs and teaching methods in contemporary public schools are typically geared to the aims, ambitions, moral and ethical standards of the core culture represented by the white, prosperous middle-class, Protestant, Anglo-Saxon population. Thus, heterogeneous schools often enhance the discrepancies in children's backgrounds, to the increased detriment of the lower-class Leftout, by: (1) discriminatory practices of teachers; (2) inflexible teaching and testing methods; (3) inadequate counseling, especially at the elementary-school level; (4) such school policies as separate classes for slow learners; (5) rejection of deviants by the majority group of age-mates; and (6) allowing for coalition of deviant peer groups.

The Leftout from a lower socioeconomic background may also be disadvantaged in that he statistically more often lacks: (1) achievement motivation, (2) functional anxiety, and (3) a future-time orientation. Thus, socioeconomic background differences may account for some of the Leftout's disadvantage in the heterogeneous school situation. Social classes, by definition, differ in the behavioral expectations and value orientations typical to their members. However, the intensity and extensity of the interaction of social systemic and individual personality variables is delimited to the extent that the social unit is able to control against conflicts created by new experiences and situations.

No individual is wholly a product of the social class of which he is a member, because a social class does not constitute an integrated, structured social system that can specifically define norms, control behavior, and serve as a *reference group*.[7] A social class can have only a generalized or statistically representative influence on individual value orientation and behavior. Thus, the same social class may be experienced in different ways by different individuals who are nominally members. Social-class background may be, for any individual, profoundly altered by subsequent experience with other subcultural groups, or shifts in reference group identification. Thus, Leftouts do not invariably reflect the value orientations and behavioral expectations of "their" social class and, therefore, knowledge of social-class background alone will not allow for prediction about the adjustment potential of specific Leftouts.

----

[7]*Reference group*—a selected group of persons in the interpersonal environment to whose beliefs, value orientations, and behavioral expectations the individual elects to attend and with whom he identifies or seeks to be identified. (The multiple version of significant other.)

Social class is useful as a concept when exploring gross between-group differences, but must be modified to include within-group differences, if we are to fully understand the nature of the Leftout's potential for maladjustment in the heterogeneous school situation. Thus, when concern lies with explaining why some lower-class (or Negro, or immigrant, or Indian, or . . . .) children adjust to the school situation and some from apparently similar backgrounds do not adjust, it is necessary to consider within-group differences.

It is suggested that within the lower socioeconomic strata, family differences have differential effects on the child's potential for school adjustment, such that: (1) if the family structure and economy are both stable, the child is more likely to be upwardly mobile and adjust more readily to the school situation; (2) if the family structure is unstable but the family economy is stable, the child is apt to evidence some personal insecurity in family affiliations that is maladjustive for the school situation, especially as this insecurity relates to interpersonal experiences; (3) if the family structure is stable but the economy is insecure, the child is apt to experience difficulty in academic adjustment because of frequent moves, absences, and so on; (4) if the family structure and economy are both unstable, the child is least likely to adjust successfully to the academic and social demands of the heterogeneous school situation. Upper- and middle-class children, in general, adjust well to the social and academic demands of the school situation, while lower-class children *in varying degrees* tend toward maladjustment and failure.

Academic Consequences
of Low Socioeconomic Background

Subcultural value orientations include differences in specific attitudes toward education, and concern with academic achievement and upward social mobility. These differences affect the adjustment potential of the child in the school situation. In general, the lower the social-class background of the student, the less value he places on formal education as an end in itself and as a means to future goals.

The middle-class child statistically more often is better prepared in motivation to achieve than the lower-class Leftout because: (1) the middle-class subculture approves of adjustive competition, while the lower-class subculture approves of maladjustive aggression; (2) middle-class parents are better able to serve as role models for ambition and achievement; and (3) middle-class parents foster independence and internal controls, while lower-class parents tend to foster obedience to external authority. Obedience to authority is, of course, not maladjustive in the school situation, except insofar as normative expectations are not internalized and this obedience requires direct surveillance by the agent of authority.

The successful adjustment of the lower-class Leftout to the demands of the heterogeneous social situation depends, in part, upon the degree of "functional anxiety" to which he has been socialized. Functional anxiety ("socialized anxiety for education," "adaptive anxiety") is an internalized state related to a need for academic achievement, as a means of upward social mobility, which generates sufficient motivation for the child to seek to overcome any existing cultural, social, economic, or intellectual handicaps. Lower-class subcultures are less likely to socialize the Leftout to the kind of anxiety that leads to ambition and socially approved competition for rewards, and concern lest these rewards are not obtained. Functional anxiety is opposed to both a lack of anxiety and extreme anxiety, both of which are maladjustive in the heterogeneous school situation.

For the lower-class Leftout, much of school learning represents meaningless content, incomprehensible goals, and conflicting value orientations and behavioral expectations. Insofar as he is not motivated to achieve and he does not understand what is expected of him (or the expectations conflict with what *he* expects), then his lower socioeconomic background is maladjustive for the academic demands of the heterogeneous school situation.

A great deal of what goes into the adjustment demands of the school system requires a future-time orientation (delayed gratification pattern). For lower-class children a present-time orientation (immediate gratification pattern) is statistically more often central in their conceptual schema. This is maladjustive for the academic demands of the school situation.

It has been shown that *measured intelligence*[8] is statistically related to socioeconomic background, such that substantially lower average IQ's are consistently found among children from the lower socioeconomic strata. Children of higher social classes outscore those from the lower classes on all verbally-oriented tests of intellectual ability. The lower-class child's lack of verbal skill and motivation produces low scores on standard achievement and intelligence tests. Very low socioeconomic status, low intelligence ranking, low educational aspirations, and low levels of academic achievement tend to vary together statistically. Thus, a low

---

[8] *Measured intelligence*—the comparatively measured overt aspects of intellect. *Intellect* refers to the observable aspects of internal cognitive ordering hypothesized as resulting from the individual's mental operations upon raw stimuli from internal and external sources, to change these into productive thinking aimed at problem solving, analytical and logical inductions and deductions, as well as creative cognition.

socioeconomic class background is maladjustive for the academic demands of the school situation. However, for any individual this tendency may be mitigated by: (1) an unusually stimulating background, (2) a financially secure and structurally stable supportive family, (3) high need for achieve- ment, (4) association with achievement-oriented peers, or (5) compensatory training at school.

Children from the lowest socioeconomic strata are apt to be found as a large proportion of those who lack facility with formal language, come from broken or inadequate homes, and suffer status deprivation among their teachers and age-mates. However, not all lower-class children share these problems, and these problems are not necessarily the product of low socioeconomic status. Thus, these specific factors will be discussed separately in the next sections.

Social Consequences
of Low Socioeconomic Background

Again, insofar as a low socioeconomic class background fosters problems of language facility, inadequate affiliations with parents, and status deprivation, the social consequences will also be numerous. Let us consider here those elements statistically related to socioeconomic background that have adverse consequences for the lower-class Leftout's potential for social adjustment in the school situation.

General socioeconomic, subcultural, and family influences on the developing child's personality serve to establish the framework within which peer relations operate and within which the peer group becomes yet another agent of socialization. Status deprivation problems are statistically more likely to occur among children of the lower socioeconomic strata, because social failure in the heterogeneous school situation is presaged by the lower-class Leftout's lack of background training and experience with core-cultural value orientations and behavioral expectations. The lower-class Leftout is apt to be disadvantaged in social relationships with teachers and his more advantaged age-mates, as a consequence of his lack of the social skills that are a prerequisite to their acceptance of him.

Subcultural differences are one basis for determining social acceptance potential among elementary-age school children. Socioeconomic status criteria are at least partially responsible for friendship choices, such that lower-class children tend to be rejected by middle-class age-mates—and the division increases with age.

Status and prestige is awarded among children's peer groups on the basis of: (1) similarity of age, (2) similarity of sex, (3) similarity of socioeconomic background, (4) physical skills, (5) adaptive, pleasing personality, (6) verbal ability, and (7) intelligence. The lower-class Leftout may be disadvantaged in all of these areas, including those of age, which can differ if he has failed often, and sex, which can present adjustment problems for him if he has failed to develop an appropriate sex-role identity. The socioeconomic status criteria that have the most influence on peer group selection and relationships in the heterogeneous school situation have been shown to be: (1) use of leisure time (which differs quantitatively and qualitatively by social class), (2) social-class-linked differences in attitudes toward education, (3) social-class-linked differences in physically aggressive behavior, and (4) social-class-linked differences in speech patterns, grooming, mode of dress, and other readily identifiable variables. Thus, a lower-class background may be maladjustive for the social demands of the heterogeneous school situation.

Leftouts who fail to learn the dominant values of their teachers and more advantaged age-mates, or who cling to beliefs and values not widely shared, are not likely to be well received in the heterogeneous school situation. This lack of acceptance, in turn, reduces communication potential and makes acculturation and social assimilation more difficult for the Leftout.

If there is a conflict between parental-class culture and the core culture prevalent in the school, moderate anxiety, which is adjustive for social mobility, may result. So too, extreme anxiety, antagonism and rejection, withdrawal, or rigid and dependent clinging to established modes of behavior may result. These latter consequences are all maladjustive for the social demands of the school situation.

Lack of academic and social skill is apt to be anxiety producing for the lower-class Leftout. It has been shown that a sense of shame often accompanies limited opportunity for skill development. Taken together, these maladjustive factors are likely to produce: (1) hostile aggressiveness, (2) lack of trust in others, (3) feelings of inadequacy and a lowered self-concept, (4) withdrawal, and (5) generally suspicious and negative attitudes toward the social environment in the school situation. This is maladjustive for the academic, social, and emotional adjustment demands of the school situation.

As a result of prejudice and discrimination, lower-class Leftouts of ethnic and racial minority groups particularly tend to suffer some deterioration of personality, especially: (1) self-doubt, (2) self-hate, (3) impulsive and superstitious behavior, (4) resigned exploitation of their inferior status, and even (5) mental illness.

Love-oriented techniques of discipline have been found to be a more powerful and positive force for bringing about desired changes in children's behavior than object-oriented techniques of reward and punishment. Thus, children in the upper socioeconomic strata are apt to be more adequately socialized than children with lower-class backgrounds. Lower-class boys especially are more apt to receive inadequate discipline and parental support. These inadequacies are maladjustive for the social demands of the school situation because: (1) inadequate discipline allows for deviant behavior, which may serve as the basis for discrimination; and (2) inadequate support from family affiliations may increase the Leftout's dependency on supportive relationships outside the family.

"Cures" for a Lower Socioeconomic Class Background

When children are given the opportunity to proceed at their own speed, individual differences in academic achievement increase. In such an environment, those who lag behind soon drop out with feelings of failure. On the other hand, when classes are regimented, the well prepared, bright children get bored and lose out from lack of interest or come to feel that they do not like school. The way to maximize both achievement potential and the freedom of the environment is to individualize the encounters each child has with the school situation. In order to individualize the educational experience, at least three things are required: (1) a very thorough knowledge of the child, (2) adequate facilities, and (3) an appropriate method of approach.

To know as much as possible of any child's unique prior experiences and training, knowledge of social-class background is only a beginning point. Since intraclass differences have been shown, there needs to be extensive research conducted for each child in order to explore thoroughly within-group differences, with particular attention given to those variables that have been suggested to have maladjustive consequences for the lower-class Leftout's academic, social, and emotional adjustment potential. Thus, each child's school record, in addition to the typical collection of test results and teacher comments, ought to include accurate information on his family relationships, any problems he may have outside the school situation (for example, he is regularly called upon to babysit with younger siblings; he lives in inadequate housing, and so on), and his level of language skill with formal English. The record should also include some statement of his nonacademic abilities (athletic, musical, or other talents), his general health (both physical and emotional), and his personal goals and ambitions. Other kinds of idiosyncratic information would also be useful.

This kind of record keeping raises several issues. First, it is clear that classroom teachers and existing administrative personnel are not apt to have either the time or the training required to collect the necessary information, record it, keep it up to date, and interpret it to others. Second, resistance to gathering such information would come from several sources, including large numbers of parents. Third, this mass of data should probably be open to only a very few persons and some competent, responsible efforts at communication and public relations would be required. Fourth, such a record would be of little value unless its contents were regularly updated and reinterpreted and unless it led to innovative changes in dealing with the Leftout. All of this strongly indicates the need for a new addition to the staff of elementary schools in the form of a team of professional counselors.

The duties of this team should include data gathering, analysis, and interpretation; serving as liaison between the school and children's homes, other public agencies, and the community in general; and serving as equal members of a larger team responsible for the Leftout, which would include his teacher and school administrators. While this suggestion may appear too costly and idealistic, the other extreme of continuing, as most schools presently do, with a far too limited and often haphazard knowledge of the children they deal with daily, is also costly in loss of human resources, costly in wasted time and money, and unrealistic.

A good beginning point would be to release one or two particularly perceptive and responsive classroom teachers from their teaching tasks for advanced training in the establishment of such a functional record system. The personality of those chosen may be far more important than considerations of tenure, prior training, or available time. Real communication among all concerned is essential, both to facilitate the development of a really useful student record and to assure that its value is reflected in innovative practices in the classroom. Communication efforts should begin with those who would potentially be the severest critics of such a record system, to show them how it would help to overcome existent inadequacies in and aid efforts to individualize, the educational system.

Adequate facilities and an appropriate method of approach are also extremely important to individualized education. Obviously, the method will depend to some extent on available facilities. However, the electronic age has wrought major changes in traditional methods of approach to education. Much routine teaching can be delegated to a wide variety of machines: computers, closed circuit and educational television, audio and visual tape recorders, continuous-loop film projectors and the like. Programmed learning systems and an array of scanning devices can free teachers from detailed, time-consuming, routine, or repetitive instruction; free the teacher to give special help to individual children, prepare better course materials, and concentrate more time on the Leftout's social and emotional development.

The supportive role of the teacher may be fully as important as the managerial one, especially for Leftouts. Traditionally, debate on the value of various facilities has centered on the cost per student taught (input), rather than on the cost per student learned (output). At the same time, educators have invested heavily in the development of new methods—which has paid off handsomely—but far less in substance, and virtually nothing in defining the purposes of education. Certainly the perpetuation of the culture and the dissemination of knowledge are central tasks of the school. But the rapid technological and social changes occuring in our society demand that the school perform other tasks as well.

To serve as an agent of progress is one of these tasks of the school. To foster the advancement of knowledge; to cultivate intellect; to train in the use of reason; to help the child learn to distinguish the meaningful from the meaningless; to teach respect for evidence and logical discourse; to develop powers of insight, analysis, and generalization; to teach understanding of cause and effect, order and theory—these are also purposes to which education ought to direct its efforts.

Another task of the contemporary educational system is that of sensitizing the moral conscience and giving the child a sense of social responsibility. Thus, other purposes of education ought to be to foster social understanding, to teach appreciation of individual, subcultural, and cross-cultural differences, to discern similarities, to analyze changes in values and behavioral expectations, to cultivate effective interpersonal communication, and to seek solutions to interpersonal conflicts.

These tasks are all time consuming and their multiplicity would suggest that a single classroom teacher, even one helped by electronic teaching machines, could hardly be expected to cope alone in a heterogeneous school. Many of these goals imply the need for dividing the class into small groups, some of which could work independently but others would require the presence of the teacher or teacher's aide to guide, suggest, encourage, and reward.

Achieving an effective balance between the conservative and creative purposes of education is surely a difficult and costly task, but one which, if it is not undertaken now, will prove only more difficult and costly when it inevitably is forced. A redefinition of the role of teachers and the goals of education seems to be necessary for overcoming the Leftout's potential for academic, social, and emotional maladjustment. A "recentering" is called for in heterogeneous schools: classes centered not on the teacher but on the child. Mechanical facilities are one tool available that allows for the freeing and remaking of the traditional teacher role. Another alternative, in the form of teachers' assistants—retirees, housewives, college and high school students, and even other elementary-school students—could also help free the professional teacher from routine duties.

It has been suggested that warm and supportive affiliations with other persons can foster intellectual, social, and emotional growth. This would indicate that simply having several friendly persons in the classroom, irrespective of their professional training, would be helpful to the Leftout. It has also been suggested that children learn a great deal from each other. Under the proper circumstances this would indicate that groups of children could be allowed to work far more independently than they do in most classrooms. It would also suggest that other children may be a good source of assistance to the teacher in acculturating Leftouts.

Most teachers could learn to make effective use of two or more assistants, and find it to their advantage to do so for a number of reasons. It is doubtful that most schools could afford fully qualified teachers for the small group and individual contacts required to fulfill the educational purposes that have been outlined. This is especially true when dealing with Leftouts. Teaching assistants at several levels of professional competency and training would offer a real possibility for reaching these goals by serving as another means for freeing the professional teacher from routine, repetitive tasks. At the same time, the presence of teaching assistants in the classroom would encourage role differentiation, such that the professional teacher's status should profit and morale, recruitment potential, and income should go up with it.

Innovations of these kinds, in facilities and methods of approach, take time and may meet with resistance. It is necessary to maximize the planning participation of all who would be concerned with such changes. It is also necessary to minimize compulsion, so that no teacher feels forced to adopt a new teaching technique. Innovations of this kind are often best introduced by allowing one teacher to illustrate to others how it operates through observation of the ongoing process.

Taken as a whole, our examination is provocative and suggests that many, if not all, Leftouts can and should be offered much more cognitive stimulation than they are receiving. The advantages of utilizing the now relatively untapped preschool years for compensatory education are manifest. The crucial probability exists that conceptual learning, interest areas, value orientations, and behavioral patterns are more favorably established during the early years of the developmental process.

The Educational Policies Commission, which is sponsored jointly by the National Education Association and the American Association of School Administrators (but is autonomous), in June of 1966 proposed that free public schooling should be available to and mandatory for every four- and five-year-old child in the United States. This kind of major-change in the structure of the educational system is supported by our analysis of the Leftout's problems. It also reinforces the urgency of cooperative research among social scientists and educators, aimed at the development of programs effectively designed to overcome the lower-class Leftout's social-psychological problems.

For example, qualitatively we know almost nothing about language among lower-class populations. Only a very few studies have attempted to analyze dialectal patterns in the urban United States. We know little of the influence of the peer group on language development, although this influence is likely to be considerable among the early independent lower-class Leftouts. Further research is required to identify those particular aspects of language development and dialectal speech patterns that are maladjustive to the academic and social demands of the heterogeneous school situation. This research would subsequently serve as the basis for designing effective compensatory programs. Meanwhile, compensatory programs of the kind especially designed to foster verbal facility and abstract conceptual reasoning, and to foster early acculturation and social assimilation with teachers and more advantaged peers, should also aid in overcoming the Leftout's social-class-linked disadvantage.

Preschool compensatory education is not sufficient alone to overcome the lower-class Leftout's academic and social disadvantage potential. The school environment must continually offer appropriate role models, compensatory training, and chances for positive evaluation, rewards, and affiliations with teachers and more advantaged age-mates. Both preschool and ongoing compensatory programs should consider the interrelationships of academic, social, and emotional adjustment. There is a need for research designed to integrate social and academic programs in the school situation.

Revising the preparatory education of teachers to include intensive training in group dynamics and extensive objective exploration of sociocultural differences among children should also help to overcome the Leftout's class-linked maladjustment potential in the school situation.

Relative Lack of Language Facility

Theoretical Framework. Man is inherently a social animal, and complementarity of expectations and perceived reactions is necessary for social interaction. *Socialization*[9] is a prerequisite to complementarity of

[9]*Socialization*—a complex social-learning process in which culturally approved value orientations and behavioral expectations are inculcated in the neophyte, including: (1) the acquisition of language; (2) learning a vast body of empirical facts relating to the physical and social environment; (3) developing a variety of specialized skills; (4) the acquisition of moral values, beliefs, and standards of evaluation of self and others; and (5) learning the normative "rules" concerning the appropriate ways and means of relating to other people.

expectations, and interpersonal communication in the form of symbolic systems is a prerequisite to socialization. Symbolic systems provide the basis for the maintenance and elaboration of human interaction. Both egocentric and socially-oriented functions are served by symbolic systems. From the perspective of the individual, systems of symbols serve as objects of orientation for, and as internalized components of, *personality*[10] systems. From the perspective of the social system, systems of symbols appear as institutionalized patterns in the form of consensual language and serve as the vehicle for the transmission of shared value orientations and behavioral expectations. The acquisition of language for any individual occurs within a probabilistic metric, which includes the set of environmentally possible stimulating states that might occur and the degree of bias in the environmental likelihood of their occurrence. As we have seen, the Leftout is apt to be disadvantaged in this area of language skills, because he is less likely than his *age-mates*[11] to experience *constructive (educational) stimulation*.[12]

Synthesis.   This dimension of disadvantage has academic and social consequences that are maladjustive in the heterogeneous school situation. Language acquisition is the primary technique employed in intellectual development—for abstracting, isolating, representing, integrating, organizing, and perceiving relationships among objects, events, and ideas—for the general systematization of experience.

A background that affords little heterogenity of experience, little opportunity for situational manipulation, and lacks diversity of discrimination experience produces a child with: (1) reduced abilities to discriminate, (2) little interest in exploratory or creative behavior, (3) maladjustive modes of coping with problems requiring complex or future-oriented solutions, and (4) a notably reduced tendency toward conceptual organization. However, it is not the stimulus itself, but rather the response to the stimulus, that provides the perceptual or sensory stimulation. Thus, stimulation without contrast may not be perceived, and stimulation which does not fit the socially learned cognitive structure may be ignored.

[10]*Personality*—an analytical construct, based on the observation of overt behavior (including test-taking behavior), which suggests that internal, systematically (but not necessarily logically) organized cognitions and affective relationships influence many overt behaviors in a relatively stable manner.

[11]*Age-mates*—refers to all those children of approximately equivalent age with whom the child is in contact in the school situation—as opposed to peers. *Peers* refers to the subsegment of age-mates who serve as significant others and as a reference group for the child, and with whom he elects to interact when he is free to make a choice.

[12]*Constructive (educational) stimulation*—visual and auditory stimuli, which is ordered, goal directed, allows for interactional feedback, and which aids learning either with or without intentional instruction.

For the socioculturally disadvantaged child, early experiential deprivation prevents the formation of adequate cognitive models and the learning of normative means of coping with the unfamiliar environment of the school. The Leftout's problem in this area centers on the nonspecific transfer of experiential learning, in that he has not established the generalized models, constructs, or concepts that allow him to cognitively represent the school environment in such a way that, when new academic tasks or social situations are encountered, it is possible for him to cope with them as exemplars of familiar concepts that are already associated with normatively appropriate responses.

One of the primary sources of maladjustive anxiety for any individual seems to lie in his being placed in a state in which his conception and perception of environmental demands do not fit into his previously learned conceptual model. He has no basis for prediction of the environment in a manner that makes reasoned action possible.

This author has argued that extreme anxiety may have a crippling effect on the cognitive process, which is maladjustive for academic and social learning. Anxiety is based on lack of knowledge, experience, training, skill, or ability. Anxiety has been found to be increased by: (1) perceived status differences, (2) ambiguity of expectations, (3) the difficulty of the task, and (4) lack of skill to cope with the task at hand. Extreme anxiety can be incapacitating for *any* learning, including both intentional and incidental learning.

A lack of language facility greatly reduces cognitive, perceptual, and learning potential. In the school situation in which communication, basically through language, is a central part of both academic and social learning, a lack of language facility may create extreme anxiety. Anxiety, in turn, may reduce learning even further or preclude it altogether. Thus, comparative lack of experience with symbolic systems, especially lack of language skill, is directly and positively related to difficulties in ability to learn both formally taught academic skills, and more informally taught social skills.

Academic Consequences
of Inadequate Language Facility

The bases of academic achievement include tested intelligence and motivation. Individuals are more likely to be motivated to attend to those aspects of their environment they anticipate than those they do not. Individuals are more likely to anticipate those things with which they are familiar. If the Leftout's background has afforded little constructive stimulation, in such circumstances he learns to be skillful in the art of inattention developed in an effort to drown out indiscriminate *noise*,[13] and thus he may subsequently have difficulty in focusing his attention. This is maladjustive for the academic demands of the school situation.

Experience with the environment is the major influence on the development of measured intelligence and conceptual thinking. Only rarely, if ever, is the experiential environment so rich and stimulating that hereditary limits on intellectual ability are reached for the organically normal individual. Thus, in effect, heredity is not considered to be an influence in fixing the level of the Leftout's intellectual potential.

The learning of concepts and the development of conceptual thinking involves basic processes of perception, discrimination, transposition, and generalization. Standard achievement and intelligence tests are based on such conceptual thinking. They are verbally oriented and assume motivation on the part of the child to do his best. Thus, the Leftout lacking verbal facility is apt to score significantly lower than his more advantaged age-mates on intelligence and achievement tests.

Standardized tests, however "culture bound" and weighted in favor of the child with an advantageous background, do reflect an efficiency of adjustment to the culture for which they are designed and do predict the child's potential for academic success in the higher grades with a reasonable degree of accuracy. The typical public school program is not organized to capitalize on nonverbal types of intelligence. Therefore, any nonverbal skills the Leftout may have are of little value for adjustment to the academic demands of the school situation.

The Leftout who is inept in core-cultural communication skills is faced with learning what is tantamount to a "foreign" language—with the difference that he lacks solid grounding in a comparable "native" language. This is maladjustive for the academic demands of the heterogeneous school situation, which assumes a certain degree of initial facility with formal English.

Initial lack of verbal facility works to the Leftout's disadvantage in academic achievement efforts. As we have seen, this lack of achievement is primarily felt in the area of developing language skills and verbal facility. Thus, the Leftout is apt to become *more* disadvantaged in this dimension of academic adjustment over a time. Lack of achievement over a time negatively effects his *self-concept of ability*.[14] A low self-concept of ability has been shown to place functional limits on academic achievement potential.

[13]*Noise*—a potpourri of visual and auditory stimuli lacking in order, goal, feedback opportunities, and educational intent or value.

[14]*Self-concept of ability*—"those definitions a student holds of his ability to achieve in academic tasks as compared with others." (Brookover *et al.*, 1965.)

Social Consequences
of Inadequate Language Facility

As we have seen, children who are perceived as intelligent and creative are generally more accepted by their advantaged age-mates, while slow learners are less well accepted. Thus, the Leftout's relatively low level of measured intelligence is maladjustive for the social demands of the heterogeneous school situation.

The Leftout may be discriminated against by teachers and age-mates alike because of his general lack of communication skill and his particular dialect, not on linguistic grounds but in terms of status considerations. Thus, the specific language pattern used by the Leftout may be maladjustive for the social demands of the heterogeneous school situation.

Ineptness in communication skill and anxiety induced by lack of language facility may preclude the learning that would allow for social acculturation and assimilation. Thus, lack of language facility and resultant anxiety is maladjustive for the social demands of the Leftout's school situation as well.

"Cures" for Inadequate
Language Facility

Continuous and progressive changes take place in the structures of behavior and thought, but the nature of this *accommodation*[15] implies that the rate of development is largely a function of the diversity the individual encounters in his environment. The more new things a child has seen or heard, the more he is interested in seeing or hearing. The more variation in environment with which he has had to cope, the greater his capacity for coping—to the limit that he is able to make requisite *assimilations*[16] and accommodations without developing extreme anxiety. New experiences are seen as inherently rewarding, because new accommodative modifications and new assimilative cognitive combinations are sources of pleasure to the child. Therefore, special compensatory programs designed to offer educationally stimulating new experiences, which necessitates the child's employing language, coupled with intensive training in language development without the assumption of prior ade-

[15]*Accommodation*—corresponds to external behavioral adaptation, occurring whenever the existing cognitive structure must be modified to meet the demands of variations in environmental circumstances.

[16]*Assimilation*—corresponds to internal cognitive organization, occurring whenever the individual incorporates any stimulus from his environment into his cognitive framework. (Both accommodation and assimilation are explored and explained in Piaget's work.)

quate native experience, should help to overcome the Leftout's maladjustment in the area of communication skills.

Electronic teaching devices have been particularly successful in language instruction. What is missing, for the needs of the Leftout, is an appropriate body of substantive materials designed to teach formal English as a foreign language. A limited number of people are working at developing such materials, but far more time and money needs to be invested in this element of the substance of education. Again, a good beginning point would be freeing a particularly creative teacher from regular classroom duties for the purpose of developing instructional materials (not remedial materials but primary ones), in order to foster language skill among socioculturally disadvantaged children.

Hunt argues that compensatory schooling for young children has been repeatedly shown to have a positive effect on tested intelligence. Even those children rated as retarded have shown rates of intellectual growth ranging from ten to thirty IQ points after special nursery-school experience. Moreover, he points out, children retain their accelerated rate of growth during experimental follow-up periods of from three to five years. This, taken with what we have said of the predictive efficiency of how standardized tests are related to potential for future academic achievement, suggests that compensatory experiences designed to raise the Leftout's IQ level should aid in overcoming part of his disadvantage based on lack of language facility.

However, measures of norms of cognitive development that fail to take into account differences in the lower-class Leftouts' life histories are meaningless as valid measures of their cognitive functioning. The need for research to develop new tests or modify old ones to probe the cumulative limits of cognitive learning is clear. So far nobody has devised a "culture free" intelligence test that is particularly useful. And, of course, such a test might be pointless unless the present aim of testing changes. It should be realized that if the socioculturally disadvantaged child does poorly on the tests, it isn't the test that is unfair, the social circumstances that make him disadvantaged are unfair.

The notion of ordinal scales of intelligence implies a homogeneous level of intellectual functioning, which belies research evidence on the side of asymmetries or heterogenity in talent, that is, intraindividual differences. Compensatory programs can force accommodative modifications only when there is an appropriate match between the environmental circumstances and the prior experiences the child has already assimilated into his cognitive repertoire. Discrepancies between present programs and past experiences that are too large constitute a source of maladjustive anxiety and negative motivation for the Leftout. On the other hand, discrepancies of a lesser order are a source of adjustive curiosity and positive interest. Thus, research designed to answer the question, "how much is too much?", is urgently needed and is essential to effective compensatory programs.

Concomitantly, new techniques for measuring nonverbal types of intelligence and school programs designed to capitalize on this type of intellectual development should be developed and employed—if only as the basis for the subsequent teaching of core-cultural verbal skills.

Conscious efforts by the Leftout's significant others, such as parents and teachers, directed at attempts to preclude or raise a low self-concept of ability, should help in overcoming academic maladjustment. In order to reduce the Leftout's anxiety and help him learn social skills, he should spend as much time as possible in small group sessions. At least three-fourths of the members in any group should be his more advantaged classmates. The groups should be task-oriented, although the tasks may not be necessarily academic ones. Tasks should be planned carefully so that status differences are reduced to a minimum or eliminated entirely, and behavioral expectations should be made clear. With Leftouts especially, the teacher cannot assume that the child ought to or will know how to approach a task or how to behave. Early tasks should be simple. As the Leftout's anxiety decreases and he becomes more confident in dealing with his more advantaged age-mates, tasks should get more complex, although still clear and within his ability to develop the necessary skills.

Leftouts should especially profit from experiences that teach skills of attention: listening closely, perhaps to music or the sounds of the city, and observing carefully, perhaps a detailed picture or a microscope slide. They should be encouraged to be imaginative. The Leftout should be required to use language, but with a minimum of correction, to explain what he sees and hears, in order to help develop his verbal skills. Such training should be interesting, exciting, and, above all, rewarding to him. Leftouts require more than merely ample praise.

In addition, active efforts to foster understanding and social acceptance among the majority group of dialectal differences should aid in overcoming the Leftout's social maladjustment, based on ineptness in core-cultural communication skills. By finding social acceptance, despite his lack of verbal facility, he will be brought into contact with his more advantaged age-mates who are verbally facile and, freed of anxiety over his shortcomings, he can then learn from them.

Relative Deprivations
in Early Interpersonal Affiliations

Theoretical Framework.   All individuals have the need to affiliate. Affiliation with parents or parental surrogates is a prerequisite for early personality development. Affiliation with accepting others is rewarding. An acceptable social status is a requisite for satisfactory social and emotional adjustment at any age. Social isolation or rejection, real or threatened, is a powerful motivating force for producing behavioral changes, in keeping with the perceived requirements of social acceptance. The Leftout may be disadvantaged in the area of personality development, because he is more likely than his advantaged age-mates to experience disorganized family affiliations during the early developmental periods.

Synthesis. The family is the most significant agent for influencing the general socialization of the child, and influences such specific factors as measured intelligence, school achievement, and social acceptance, by: (1) providing the tools, stimulation, opportunity, and reinforcement necessary for general learning, (2) providing role models for social learning, (3) providing help and guidance in language development, and (4) providing stimulation, concern, and support for achievement and learning outside the home, especially at school.

A verbally-oriented, close, warm, supportive, and continuous relationship with both parents is the best possible family setting in which both boys and girls may be reared. Concomitantly, any disorganization in this ideal family pattern will be maladjustive. The greater is the degree of disorganization, the more maladjustive the consequences for subsequent academic, social, and emotional adjustment in the heterogeneous school situation.

The depth and relative permanence of the maladjustive consequences of affiliative deprivations in the Leftout's family experience will vary in terms of: (1) duration, (2) frequency, (3) degree of disruption to established affiliative ties, and (4) compensatory opportunities that are available to him. In general, as we have seen, the effects of deprivation in the areas of sensory stimulation, social training, and emotional support, which are concurrent with family disorganization or parental separation, are more maladjustive than disorganization or separation per se. Thus, a disorganized family structure is more likely than a stable family structure to fail as as a socializing institution.

Both parents are an important source of affiliative support for both boys and girls. The father is especially influential: (1) as a sex-role model, (2) as a source of disciplinary control, (3) as an agent of morality training, (4) in the setting of achievement standards, and (5) as a guide to the development of achievement motivation.

A disorganized family is characterized by: (1) a lack of family traditions and kinship ties, which would lend support to the child in his extrafamilial environment; (2) a lack of socialization to a strong, adequate, and specific value orientation, as opposed to generalized admonitions to be "good," "honest," and so on; and (3) a failure of the father to serve as an adequate sex-role model.

Academic Consequences of Deprivations in Family Affiliations

As we have seen, the specific child-rearing practices of parents have not been found to show invariant relationships with subsequent specific aspects of the child's personality development. Generalized patterns of parental attitudes and behavior, such as strictness or permissiveness and warmth and support of the affiliative relationships, are found to be much more closely related to personality development and behavior of children. Under the condition that the child identify with supportive parents, parental pressure for and reward of early achievement, when coupled with a high ratio of successes to failures for the child, results in high achievement motivation in the heterogeneous school situation. The typical Leftout may not have supportive parents, and his parents' interest, ability, and desire to socialize him to achievement motivation is apt to be inadequate. When the family does not support the child and fails to socialize him adequately, there is less chance of his developing high achievement motivation. This is maladjustive for the academic demands of the heterogeneous school situation.

Pressures toward achievement may have maladjustive repercussions, unless they are accompanied by specific training to the socially approved means for attaining success. In the absence of clearly articulated means-training, the child may: (1) employ normatively disapproved of avenues to success, or (2) develop extreme anxiety because of his lack of knowledge of the appropriate means to his ends. Either of these modes of achievement motivation is maladjustive.

Upward social mobility[17] through academic achievement is contingent upon achievement striving under conditions of observance of normative prescriptions and proscriptions, designed to prevent this striving from having socially harmful consequences. Thus, achievement striving involves a considerable amount of discriminative learning and self-control. The Leftout, whose parental affiliations are not as likely to provide him with clearly articulated value training, may be disadvantaged in his learned ways of maintaining self-control. One means of self-control is

---

[17]*Upward social mobility*—those changes in behavior and value orientation that allow the individual to raise his status evaluation; any behavioral change made for or required of such status reevaluation. It may be: (1) intergenerational, that is, between the individual's rank and that of his family, or (2) intragenerational, that is, between the individual's present or future rank and his own previous or present rank.

devaluation of goals that are not readily attainable. This means is more prevalent among Leftouts but is maladjustive for the academic demands of the school situation. A second means of self-control is high evaluation of sometimes unpleasant means to a desired future goal. This means is less prevalent among Leftouts but is adjustive in the school situation.

Those children who receive the least social stimulation, poorest training, and least support in the family setting will also be those who are in the lowest groups in school on the basis of measured intelligence. The affiliative interaction of parents and children affects the development of measured intelligence in three major ways: (1) parental provision for general learning, (2) parental press for language development, and (3) parental press for achievement motivation. Low levels of measured intelligence are maladjustive for the academic demands of the school situation.

Teachers typically define emotional maladjustment in terms of children's disruptive behavior. The behavior of affiliatively deprived Leftouts is not apt to fully meet the expectations of the classroom. Leftout boys are especially likely to behave in ways that could be interpreted as disruptive, particularly by female teachers. Thus, the Leftout is more apt to be defined as emotionally maladjusted (whether or not he is so in fact). The definition of emotional maladjustment often results in separation of the Leftout from the regular classroom and his more advantaged age-mates and placement in "special" classes. This is apt to have maladjustive consequences for the normal academic demands of the school situation.

Social Consequences of Deprivations in Family Affiliations

Sex-role identity is learned by differential identification within the family. An important part of developing sex-role identities includes the opportunity to observe and interact with complementary-sex models as well as same-sex models. Thus, both parents (or parental surrogates) are influential in the sex-role development of boys and girls. Disorganized families are characterized by the absence of the father or, if the father is present, inadequacies in his ability to serve as a culturally appropriate sex-role model. The absence of the father, or any inadequacy in his serving as an appropriate sex-role model, is maladjustive for the social development of both boys and girls, although boys especially are disadvantaged by the lack of a strong male-role model. This is true because the normative developmental process requires a gradual modification of dependency responses for boys, which is a more marked developmental change than is required of girls.

Boys from disorganized families exhibit more immaturity, stronger striving for masculinity (usually in the form of overplaying the masculine role), and poorer peer adjustment than their age-mates. Girls from disorganized families do not have as severe adjustment problems, but their problems are greater than those of either boys or girls who are reared in normal family settings.

Deprivations in early family affiliations have adverse consequences for personality development. Thus, the presence in the home of atypical parental sex-role models, or the absence of a strong male model during early socialization, makes subsequent social and emotional adjustment outside the home more difficult, especially for boys.

Biologically appropriate social conformity to a *sex-role standard*[18] is crucial to social and emotional adjustment because: (1) it serves as an internalized part of the child's self-concept; and (2) it sets boundaries on behavioral choices through knowledge of a set of socially acceptable behavioral alternatives. For boys especially, some of the Leftout's potential social difficulties in the heterogeneous school situation may center in problems of sex-role identity created by the likelihood of inadequate male-role models during his early socialization experiences. This is maladjustive for the social demands of the heterogeneous school because of the: (1) conflicting nature of multiple demands within the stereotyped male role; (2) typically extensive supervision by women teachers, which deprives the disadvantaged child of adequate models in his current situation; and (3) conflicting expectations concerning appropriate male and female sex-roles among the various socioeconomic strata found in a heterogeneous school.

The school-age child regularly spends a large amount of time daily outside his home and away from his parent's direct influence. Thus, any child is engaged in nonfamily affiliative situations. It has been found that self-ideals among elementary-age children are closer to modal peer group ideals than to those of either parent. Thus, for all children, affiliations outside the family are important sources of affiliative support and socialized learning. However, subcultural and individual variations in the relevance of the peer group for children have also been found.

Children who fail to identify with supportive parents are less self-accepting, less readily accepted by peers, and more dependent upon current social relationships. In a heterogeneous group, behavior and values acquired in the family will govern the choice of role-models outside the home, either: (1) on the basis of similarity, if family relationships have been satisfactory; or (2) on the basis of dissimilarity (rejection of familial values), if they have been unsatisfactory or are inadequate for goal attain-

---

[18]*Sex-role standard*—a learned association between selected characteristics, behaviors, and attitudes with concepts of male and female.

ment. As we have seen, peer group affiliations have more importance when parents exhibit less concern for or control over their children's activities outside the home, and in those cases in which the family unit cannot ensure the full attainment of social status on the part of its members. Thus, the Leftout deprived of satisfactory family affiliations is more likely to seek affiliations with his age-mates while, at the same time, he is less likely to be accepted by them. This is maladjustive for the social and emotional dimensions of adjustment in the heterogeneous school situation.

"Cures" for Deprivations in Family Affiliations

Obviously the school cannot become a family to the Leftout who has been deprived of early satisfactory family affiliations. However, the kinds of academic and social problems fostered by the Leftout's inadequate family affiliations suggest that compensatory programs should make every effort to enlist the aid and active participation of parents, especially fathers. Compensatory programs ought to be broadly focused not just on the Leftout, but on his teachers, his classmates and his parents as well. Schools should be able to help foster parental interest and concern in several ways.

At the very least, any school program should include several parental orientation sessions: *informal* open house periods, partially social and recreational in character, which familiarize parents with classroom procedures, subject matter, teaching facilities and format. These should be well publicized and held at hours when parents, particularly fathers, could attend. One function of the counseling team that was suggested earlier would be to seek out and encourage parental enthusiasm and support for orientation sessions such as these.

Better yet would be an open door policy in which the school is kept open on evenings and weekends for supervised study and family recreation—sometimes referred to as "lighted schools." This kind of policy would foster the idea that school is a good place to be, both for children and adults. Ideally, the school building should be a "community building," a place for both formal and informal meetings for all age groups. Community recreation should also center on the school, and the school should serve as a communication center for the neighborhood. This would mean a substantially more efficient use of existing physical plants, in addition to a serving of the obvious end of creating interest in and concern with the school by the Leftouts' parents. The major disadvantage, beyond the interest problem, is the additional personnel required. Here again, this kind of program could best be handled, to a large extent, by nonprofessional aides, with the help of the parents themselves.

Evidence suggests that an important part of compensatory education for Leftouts should consist of employing more male teachers in the early elementary grades. One key function served by male teachers is that of providing a strong sex-role model. Male teachers are also more likely to be accepting of the type of masculine behavior that is often defined as disruptive by female teachers. At present, nearly two-thirds of the nation's teachers are women. At the elementary school level 88 percent are women. Teaching salaries are relatively attractive to women, especially married women, but relatively unattractive to men, especially those with families to support. This fact, coupled with the particular need for men in dealing with affiliatively disadvantaged children, would suggest that it may be necessary to base salary on such factors as family size, other income sources, and sex scarcity, despite strong ideological forces to the contrary.

Compensatory programs aimed at the development of close, warm, personal, and supportive affiliate relationships with selected teachers or teaching assistants should aid in overcoming the affiliatively deprived Leftout's potential for school maladjustment. College students, readily available in most parts of the country, or high school students are a good source of supplemental affiliative relationships.

Compensatory programs should be centered in the classroom. They should foster identification with teachers and more advantaged classmates as significant others. Student programs should aim for integration of efforts. As presently conceived, there is apt to be little cooperation and continuity between college-student volunteer programs and the public schools. Some of these programs have political overtones. For example, the University of Chicago's Student Woodlawn Area Project (SWAP) believes it is a part of their task to press for changes in the operation of the city school system. Nearly all of these tutorial programs are run as after-school projects. The student volunteers dress casually and try to avoid creating the impression that they are teachers, but rather seek to be "friends" with the children with whom they work. While this may be an excellent way to reach children who have suffered status deprivation in school, this kind of philosophy also tends to foster the impression that it is only *outside* of the routine school situation that individualized, supportive attention is available. Michigan State University's Student Education Corps (SEC) is a unique exception. SEC volunteers work directly with the schools, during regular school hours, and in cooperation with the regular classroom teacher. This kind of help allows for individualizing the child's experience while, at the same time, fostering the idea that school is a good, helpful, and rewarding place to be. (Warden, 1964)

Other sources of aid in dealing with the problems of Leftouts are also available. Title I of the Federal Elementary and Secondary Education Act of 1965 allowed for the authorization of more than $1 billion for the fiscal year of 1966 to aid school districts with even *small* numbers of low-income families to supply books and materials, community educational centers, conduct research and teacher training programs. This program is aimed at assisting the educationally deprived, whatever the cause may be, although the majority of children in this classification are also from families regarded as economically disadvantaged. Title I financing has been made available to heterogeneous schools for:

1. increasing the number of counselors in elementary schools;
2. financing field trips;
3. providing enrichment courses in creative writing, art, music, and drama;
4. hiring additional supervisory personnel;
5. hiring additional teachers with special training;
6. providing remedial courses in all subjects;
7. financing additional administrative help required by the program;
8. intensifying instruction;
9. hiring of community-school coordinators;
10. supplementing the Head Start program in regular classes;
11. improving elementary-school libraries; and
12. establishing neighborhood and youth encouragement programs.

This kind of program conducted within the structure of the existing school system, with integrated planning, and special selection and training of teachers would seem to come much closer to fulfilling the needs of the Leftout. At the same time, there is no reason that volunteer help could not be used to supplement this kind of compensatory education effort.

Compensatory programs, aimed at specific means-ends training, and with careful attention given to clearly relating present tasks to desirable future goals, should prove helpful in overcoming the Leftout's maladjustment potential. Our evidence indicates that the Leftout, even if he strives to achieve, may select inappropriate means. An earlier emphasis on team sports, drama, or other such team-disciplined activities could help foster achievement striving under conditions of socially approved self-control. Such activities, emphasizing conditions of equality, should also foster social learning and acceptance among the Leftout's more advantaged age-mates. Conscious efforts to foster understanding and the Leftout's acceptance among his classmates should result in greater potential for peer group affiliations with his more advantaged age-mates, thus aiding in compensating for the Leftout's maladjustment potential, based on inadequate affiliative relationships in the family.

Efforts should be made to build curricular content around the interests of the students. More curricular flexibility in the early school years seems indicated. So too is the use of such "unfit" materials as comic books,

sports pages of newspapers, trade and special interest books and maga-
zines, and so forth. Why destroy a Leftout's potential interest in reading
by requiring Dick and Jane in preference to Batman?

It is clear that care needs to be exercised in selecting the criteria
for defining "emotional maladjustment" among Leftouts. Cooperative
research efforts between educators and psychologists should be undertaken
in this area. In the absence of unambiguous criteria of emotional maladjustment, compensatory programs need to exercise extreme caution in
separating the "emotionally maladjusted" Leftout from his more advantaged age-mates, since peer group affiliations with them could serve
to help "cure" his problems.

Relative Status Deprivation
Among Teachers and Age-Mates

Theoretical Framework. In our society, attractive rewards are
freely available to some members and denied to others. Some highly
valued rewards are permitted only to those who have attained certain
levels of status by reason of age, education, social position, prestige, and
ethnic or racial identity. Barriers to attaining valued rewards may arise
from: (1) a relatively low social-class position, (2) ethnic or racial identity
which is devalued, (3) intellectual or physical limitations, (4) lack of
achievement motivation, (5) lack of skill and training, and (6) lack of
knowledge and experience.

The seeking of valued rewards is a powerful motivating force for
producing behavioral changes, in keeping with the perceived requirements
for their acquisition. Thus, the giving of rewards for socially acceptable
behavior and denying rewards (or punishing) for unacceptable behavior
will be effective in the socialization process.

Socialization to cultural value orientations and behavioral expectations begins in the family and, ideally, is strengthened by secondary contacts. The content of socially acquired value orientations and behavioral
expectations depends on what is taught in various subcultural groups and
which group or individuals are selected as the model for identification.
Thus, the significant others or reference groups with whom the Leftout
identifies may either support and strengthen the socialized values learned
in the family setting, or weaken and undermine their effects by devaluing
those things that he has been taught to value.

Social interaction must be perceived as mutually rewarding by the
individuals involved or it will cease. The more cohesive the group is, the
greater the influence they can exert over value orientations and behavioral
norms, and the greater the reward power they have over any member,
under the condition that conformity to the group's expectations is per-

ceived by the individual to be instrumental to their social acceptance of him. Social rejection is primarily associated with lack of knowledge of and conformity to the value orientations and behavioral expectations of the group in which an individual seeks social acceptance.

Interaction leads to social learning and shared norms. Rewarding social situations produce more interaction. Friendly, accepting situations stimulate the *incidental learning*[19] required for *acculturation*[20] and *social assimilation.*[21] The less interaction there is among persons, the greater the likelihood of conflicts in value orientations and behavioral expectations; the more conflict, the less interaction and communication of norms. Social rejection by the majority group in a heterogeneous school situation precludes the incidental learning required for acculturation and social assimilation by the Leftouts.

Synthesis. The Leftout may be disadvantaged in the area of rewarding social affiliations in the school situation, because he is more likely to suffer *status deprivation*[22] and he is more likely to be rejected by his teachers and more advantaged age-mates. Rejection by either has been shown to reinforce rejection by the other.

The bases of social status among elementary-school children have been shown to be: (1) social adaptability, (2) high intelligence, (3) well developed motor skills (especially among younger boys), (4) biologically appropriate sex-role identification, (5) friendliness and sociability, (6) physical attractiveness (as socially defined, including ethnic and racial characteristics of body build and skin color), (7) communication skills, including speech and dialectal patterns, (8) core-cultural value orientations toward lack of physical aggressiveness and the valuing of scholastic achievement, (9) cleanliness, careful grooming, and stylish mode of dress, and (10) time for and interest in participating in a variety of school sponsored extracurricular activities. Thus, the Leftout's status deprivation may be based on racial, ethnic, or social-class discrimination; inadequate

[19]*Incidental learning*—the process of learning by identification with or emulation of role models in the behavioral field, who are not aware of their instructional function; as opposed to intentional instruction. *Intentional instruction* refers to formal institutionalized means or deliberate attempts to influence socialization; may employ verbal communication or role models or both, but in this case the latter are aware of their instructional function.

[20]*Acculturation*—the process of learning the value orientations and behavioral norms of a group different from the one in which the individual was originally socialized.

[21]*Social assimilation*—the process by which an "outsider" is accepted as a genuine member of a group, with the full responsibilities and privileges accorded to any member.

[22]*Status deprivation*—an individual's perception of external limitations on his potential for personally defined prestige.

training and experience; or personality problems resulting from inadequate socialization.

The status deprivation problems of Negro Leftouts will differ from those of white Leftouts only insofar as they are *increased* by the factor of a skin color that serves as the basis for social discrimination. Social-learning variations, rather than racial factors, are more clearly the basis for differentiation among groups.

The elementary-school classroom functions in much the same way as the family, that is, as a primary social system in which needs are satisfied and aspirations developed. It serves as a mirror for the child's developing self-concept and as a touchstone for his value orientation and behavioral expectations. The elementary-school classroom has both a social group orientation and a task group orientation. Thus, the consequences of membership in the specific social system of a heterogeneous elementary school are partly determined by the child's academic status and partly by his status in interpersonal relationships with teachers and age-mates.

Socialization is achieved through the two jointly operating interactional processes of intentional instruction and incidental learning. Different goals in the school situation correspond to different socialization processes. Thus, academic achievement will be primarily obtained through intentional instruction by the classroom teacher, and knowledge of the means for social acceptance will be primarily obtained through incidental learning from age-mates. Nevertheless, the attitudes of the teacher toward social aspects, and the attitudes of peers toward academic aspects, are both influential for the Leftout's adjustment potential in the school situation.

The elementary-school classroom teacher has a significant influence on the Leftout's potential for total school adjustment, in that she has both formal reward power and social reward power. She can accept or reject him as a person and can help to influence and guide peer relationships. Thus, she is apt to be a significant other to the Leftout.

It has been shown that the child's perception of his social status is more closely related to levels of academic achievement expectation than is either measured intelligence or actual performance. Thus, if there is acceptance by the Leftout of the teacher and age-mates as significant others (contingent upon their acceptance of him) and if he finds the learning situation a rewarding one, then he will learn. If he does not accept the values and goals of his teachers and age-mates and if the learning situation is not intrinsically rewarding, then he will not learn.

Any child is automatically excluded from certain kinds of rewarding associations with adults because of his age and immaturity. It is only with his age-mates that he may find prestige, hierarchical status, and friendships based on equality. Thus, the peer group is the most common social reference group for school-age children. Many of the skills and values acquired during the socialization process are learned in peer groups. The influence of other children constitutes a major component of the social milieu to which the Leftout must adjust in a heterogeneous school situation.

We are suggesting that peer associations are rewarding. A child's social acceptability by his peers is an important influence in directing and modifying his value orientation and his behavior, if changes are instrumental to his social acceptance. We have suggested that it is probable that the Leftout, at least initially, seeks affiliative interactions with his more advantaged age-mates. However, the *quality* of the interaction is important. There is a significant difference between physical and social integration. Physical integration refers to simply being in the same place at the same time, whereas social integration refers to the closeness of shared value orientations and behavioral expectations. A heterogeneous school may be integrated without fostering social propinquity. Physical propinquity may still allow the Leftout to: (1) be ignored, (2) be rejected actively or when forced into association, (3) restrict his interaction with his more advantaged age-mates to minimal, formal, or problem-solving situations. Social propinquity is required for maximal general interaction.

The closer the normative orientation of children is, the more frequently will they interact under conditions of equality. The Leftout typically does not share value orientations and behavioral expectations under conditions of equality with his more advantaged age-mates and, thus, is likely to suffer status deprivation. Provocation to deviant behavior and values is apt to be strengthened by the Leftout's status deprivation in the heterogeneous school situation.

This author would argue that among Leftouts, the provocation force peculiar to rejection of the system, coalition with others like himself, and continued deviant behavior in the heterogeneous school situation is perception of status deprivation. This author would suggest that the greater the degree of perceived status deprivation the more likely are the Leftout's value orientation and behavioral norms to remain deviant.

Academic Consequences of Status Deprivation

Research evidence has suggested that teachers' responses to high status children differ from their responses to those with low status, in that they are more likely to negatively evaluate those children they perceive as being of low status. Rewards in the formal academic system are differentially distributed. Children receiving the greatest teacher approval are those who: (1) are most intelligent, (2) show the highest academic achievement, and (3) have the best over-all personality adjustment. Disadvantaged children typically receive fewer rewards in the formal system. For the Leftout, the discrepancy between his own status and that of his more advantaged age-mates may create severe conflicts and frustration. It is suggested that such conflicts and frustration may lead to: (1) a rejection of the demands of his teachers and more advantaged age-mates if he can achieve status elsewhere; or (2) dysfunctional anxiety and curtailment of his learning potential if his only way to potential status is through rewards in the formal system. Either of these is apt to be maladjustive for the academic demands of the heterogeneous school situation.

This author has suggested that prolonged failure to achieve academic status may result in a lowered self-concept of ability. Self-concept of ability functions quite independently of measured intelligence in influencing academic adjustment, and has been shown to be a better predictor of actual achievement potential. Thus, disparities in the reward system on the basis of status have consequences for future academic achievement potential, in that fewer rewards tend to lower the child's self-concept of ability. This is demonstrably maladjustive in the school situation.

We have suggested that status deprivation in the formal reward system makes informal rewards from peers especially important to the Leftout. However, *value climates*[23] among peer groups vary. Peer group differences in value climates may help or hinder in altering the Leftout's maladjustive value orientations and behavioral expectations, and influence both social and academic adjustment potential. Thus, if the Leftout finds himself in a value climate in which academic achievement is highly valued by his peers, his chances for successful academic adjustment are enhanced. On the other hand, if the Leftout seeks social status among peers whose value climate devalues academic achievement, this is maladjustive for academic adjustment in the heterogeneous school situation.

Our review of the literature has suggested that peers, as well as parents and other adults, influence the child's value orientation and behavioral expectations. Research evidence has shown that peer group affiliations are formed early in the child's school career and become more firmly established over a time. Thus, the value climate of the peer group may have important influences on the Leftout's school adjustment potential. It has been shown that academic maladjustment increases over a time,

[23]*Value climates*—a situational variable referring to the particular bases for awarding of prestige which are present in any given age, sex, grade, or socioeconomic group in any specific school or classroom.

resulting in a cumulative deficit in excess of the original level of the Left-out's comparative disadvantage. Therefore, not only is selection of the particular peer group important to academic potential, but the earlier the affiliation occurs and the length of time it remains established also influences academic potential. If the Leftout's status deprivation among teachers and more advantaged age-mates leads him to affiliations with peers who devalue academic achievement, then the earlier and more pro-tracted this affiliation is, the more maladjustive it is for academic demands in the school situation.

The range and scope of both achievement potential and social adjust-ment problems in heterogeneous schools is suggested to be greater because of: (1) contact chances with achievement-oriented peers—the juxtaposi-tion of norms and values, and (2) learning chances provided by the range of role models. The Leftout is typically caught in cross pressures between the norms of the different groups in a heterogeneous school situation. Cross pressures among conflicting normative expectations may create emotional strain for the Leftout. Severe and pervasive pressures may create incapacitating anxiety, which is maladjustive for academic adjust-ment.

Moderate strain may be functional in that it creates a desire to reduce the strain. One way of reducing the strain is to conform to the value orien-tations and behavioral expectations of teachers and more advantaged peers, which is adjustive in the school situation. However, insecurity in social relationships and inadequacy in achievement performance (leading to status deprivation) can influence the Leftout to allow the cross pressures to create extreme anxiety or be resolved by rejection of the value orienta-tions and behavioral expectations of his teachers and more advantaged age-mates. Either of these modes of dealing with cross-pressure strain is maladjustive for the academic demands of the school situation.

Social Consequences
of Status Deprivation

The peer group's direct influence is modified by: (1) the charac-teristics of the situation itself: (a) the physical setting, (b) the type of ac-tivity, (c) the size of the group, (d) the clarity of the task and associated expectations, and (e) the nature of the reward system; (2) individual varia-tions in susceptibility to influence created by (a) the strength of the reference group bond, and (b) individual personality needs; (3) the charac-teristics of the children doing the influencing; and (4) the impact that adults, for example, teachers or parents, may have on children's asso-ciations. Nevertheless, peer group affiliations are influential and important to the school-age child. As an agent of socialization, the peer group acts as: (1) one determinant of stability and acceptance in social relationships, (2) a contributor to the child's developing self-concept, and (3) an influence on developing value orientations and behavioral expectations.

Feelings of isolation from, or social rejection by, age-mates arise early in the school situation and from everyday experience. It is suggested that if the Leftout holds his classmates in the position of a reference group, then failure to establish status among them will have a negative effect on his social and emotional adjustment in the school situation.

A child's social status with his age-mates is of central importance in assessing his social adjustment to them. Research evidence suggests that once children have been brought together as a group in the school situation: (1) in general, group patterns of relationships are quickly established and remain relatively stable over a time; (2) there is little or no *group* difference in friendship fluctuation between boys and girls at any of the various age and grade levels found in the elementary-school situation; (3) there are considerable *individual* variations in the stability of dyadic friendships at all age and grade levels; and (4) the criteria by which acceptability is judged is similar within the groups but changes between age, sex, and sociocultural groups.

The Leftout may be deprived of status among teachers and more advantaged peers alike. Such status deprivations mutually reinforce one another. The child becomes aware of his own status deprivation through his rejection by significant others. This status deprivation may lead to a lowered self-concept (which is both academically and socially maladjustive), or he may respond in such a fashion that his behavior serves to further reinforce his rejection from the group. Deviant behavior is also both academically and socially maladjustive.

The Leftout is by definition a deviant. However, the persistence of deviant behavior can be accounted for in terms of social learning in the school situation. Children will most readily adopt the behavior and value orientations of those with whom they identify. Children conform most closely to the behavior of models: (1) who are friendly, that is, accepting of them, and (2) when conformity is instrumental in gaining social acceptance.

Response patterns to social norms, both deviant and nondeviant, can readily be transmitted through incidental learning and *vicarious reinforcement*.[24] Behavior that is reinforced is learned. Behavior that is ignored or punished is extinguished. The Leftout has little or no incentive to deviate from the expectations of his age-mates unless he cannot fulfill

---

[24]*Vicarious reinforcement*—a subtype of incidental learning; refers to learning of response consequences from observation of behavioral models without the observer's performing any overt responses himself or receiving any direct reward or punishment.

their expectations and is rejected by them, which punishes his affiliative seeking and redirects or extinguishes it.

Even incomplete knowledge or partial conformity to the normative expectations of his more advantaged age-mates, or both, may gain for the Leftout some degree of social acceptance. Once he is "in," the processes of acculturation and social assimilation can be fostered through learning in interaction. Imitation of the model's normative behavior is facilitated if that model receives rewards. Thus, if the Leftout's models are his more advantaged age-mates (who are more likely to receive rewards), his own learning is facilitated. On the other hand, the Leftout may refrain from making new deviant responses or from repeating already learned deviant responses if he observes that such behavior is not rewarded.

However, if the Leftout is deprived of status among his teachers and more advantaged age-mates, deviant behavior is an ideal solution to these problems of status deprivation, because deviance: (1) repudiates the value orientations of the reference group, which serves as the basis for the Leftout's self-evaluation of failure; and (2) at the same time rewards him with status among any peers who may share his problems. The literature suggests that persistence of deviant behavior results from intermittent positive reinforcement, such as would be derived from those behaviors and value orientations rewarded by peers when these are in conflict with those expected in the school by teachers and more advantaged age-mates. Among preadolescent children, clique boundaries are not rigid (although they solidify with increasing age), and it is possible for a Leftout to be socially accepted by his more advantaged age-mates if he has some knowledge of the prevailing norms, is willing to conform to them, and is socially adaptable, that is, changes to conform to changing value orientations and behavioral expectations. Thus, the Leftout's early affiliation with other status deprived children is maladjustive for the social demands of the heterogeneous school situation.

In general, clique boundaries have been shown to be less rigid in the early years. Thus, the Leftout has the greatest chance of acculturation and social assimilation when the group is newly formed. His chances for an acceptable social status among his more advantaged age-mates in general decrease: (1) the longer the group has been established, (2) the older his age-mates, and (3) the more stable the existing patterns of acceptance and rejection have become. Nevertheless, while social preferences are initially based on simple indices of value agreement, continued interaction necessitates more complex indices of agreement. Among children, the bases of social acceptance change over a period of time. Thus, the socially acceptable child has, as his primary characteristic, social adaptability. Therefore, even if the Leftout has acquired some limited acceptance among his more advantaged age-mates, his status may remain insecure if he fails to adapt to changing demands.

If there is failure to establish value agreement, interpersonal relationships will disintegrate. Continued social frustration and rejection are apt to result in: (1) social withdrawal from teachers and more advantaged age-mates, that is, the Leftout will change his reference group; or (2) emotional withdrawal, that is, he will exhibit a lowered self-concept and withdrawn, depressed symptoms. Either of these consequences of status deprivation are maladjustive for the social demands of the heterogeneous school situation.

High social status in the group is a source of positive self-evaluation for the child. Status deprivation is a source of dissatisfaction with himself, which may produce: (1) high motivation to change in the direction of the group's expectations under conditions of instrumentality, if no other group can offer comparable rewards; or (2) a lowering of self-concept if boundaries are perceived to be insurmountable. This author is suggesting that there is an interactional relationship between self-concept and social acceptance, such that: (1) an adequate self-concept is a prerequisite for social acceptance, and social acceptance increases the likelihood of positive self-evaluation, which, in turn, raises the level of the self-concept even higher; and that (2) an inadequate self-concept leads to social rejection, and social rejection increases the likelihood of negative self-evaluations, which, in turn, tend to lower the self-concept even more. Thus, we suggest that status deprivation is maladjustive for the social and emotional requirements of the heterogeneous school situation.

"Cures" for Status Deprivation

The kind of compensatory programs that have already been suggested should also aid in helping overcome the Leftout's status deprivation. In addition, the problems engendered by status deprivation indicate that the earlier such compensatory measures are taken the better.

It has been shown that social acceptance can be fostered if the Leftout has a classroom teacher who consciously attempts to reward him in some manner and who works at fostering social integration among all students. It is suggested that Leftouts are apt to be especially susceptible to the socializing influence of their teachers and age-mates because of: (1) their relatively greater dependency needs, (2) their relatively indefinite status, (3) their anxiety for acceptance (if not extreme), and (4) their relatively low levels of *self-esteem*.[25] This greater susceptibility to so-

[25] *Self-esteem*—refers to the amount of agreement between the child's self-description and his description of an ideal self, such that the higher the agreement level is, the higher the degree of self-esteem.

cial influence can be exploited to help overcome status deprivation. However, any radical change in an effort to correct the child's disapproved behavior in the school situation (either academic or social) will threaten whatever social and material rewards are associated with his deviant career, unless he perceives that he will be provided with satisfactory substitute rewards.

Research evidence indicates that children's susceptibility to influence efforts also varies with: (1) age—younger children are more susceptible to influence attempts; (2) sex—girls are more susceptible than boys; and (3) instrumentality—if conformity is made instrumental to achieving his goals, then the Leftout will be more susceptible to influence attempts.

Influence efforts are usually most successful in very small group situations, in which the members can relate frequently and intimately with one another. This would suggest partnerships in which a Leftout is assigned to work with one or a very few achievement-oriented classmates. If such work is to be graded, the grade should be based on the result of the group's efforts. This is also a good situation in which to use students who are one or two grades advanced, so that they may serve as role models and guides. If there is an age discrepancy that is not too great, children will be influenced fairly easily by other children.

Deliberate manipulation of group dynamics should go a long way toward welding a class together if care is taken to keep it group centered, not teacher centered. A student disciplinary board can be a very effective influence agent if the membership rotates and both rules and punishments are clearly understood and fair. A Leftout would probably be more likely to conform under this kind of a disciplinary policy. Furthermore, by serving his turn as a member of such a board, he could gain a sense of responsibility, a sense of involvement in making the rules, and a sense of authority and respect in enforcing them.

Social acceptance should be fostered if the Leftout can obtain help in developing some talent or special skill valued by his more advantaged age-mates. But compensatory measures, designed to help the Leftout develop such skills and talents and to foster his acculturation and social assimilation, are best taken during the earliest school years.

Leftout boys and girls should be especially encouraged to participate as equals with their more advantaged age-mates in school sponsored extracurricular activities such as sporting events, clubs, safety patrol, work groups that aid the teacher in cleaning up, rearranging, and so on. Tasks and activities should be numerous enough and carefully designed to adequately reward every child in the school. Such activities encourage competition with fair play, team work with responsibility, and help give the Leftout a sense of the security of belonging. At the same time, programs such as these help in educating the more advantaged child to accept cultural differences. The cardinal rule for all influence efforts should be to do it *through* the children, not *to* them.

Social acceptance should be fostered if the Leftout can be influenced by significant others to be adaptable to changes in his social environment. Since the bases of social acceptance among children change over a time, the socially rejected child has an opportunity for future acceptance if he possesses or develops skills, talents, or personality characteristics that can be exploited at a later date to overcome status deprivation. Thus, compensatory efforts should not stop with the earliest school years.

If deviant behavior is to be extinguished, it is best to ignore it, if possible, or to punish it if it is a gross violation of normative expectations. However, it is also necessary to supply guidelines to *approved* behavior by intentional instruction or incidental learning from role models or both. Because of the influence that peers have on the Leftout's value orientation and behavioral expectations, the more contact a Leftout has with appropriate role models from the majority group, the faster and more complete should be his acculturation. The more complete his acculturation is, the more complete his social assimilation. Thus, the Leftout who is brought into daily contact with his more advantaged peers has the best chance for learning the norms essential for academic and social success and for overcoming his status deprivation. Compensatory programs should not separate Leftouts from their age-mates, but should be designed to utilize more advantaged children as role models, for social influence, and as instructors for the value orientation and behavioral expectations required for an acceptable social status in the heterogeneous school situation.

Upward social mobility through academic achievement is probably more likely to result from experience in heterogeneous classrooms than in homogeneous classes. Heterogeneous classes are less likely to provide a common value climate and more likely to provide associations with teachers and age-mates that will facilitate the Leftout's achievement of social status. When children of diverse experience, training, and socioeconomic background are brought into contact in the heterogeneous school situation, the mingling of divergent and sometimes conflicting value orientations and behavioral expectations may be a source of frustration and disturbance for each group of children. At the same time, such heterogeneity is both: (1) a source of knowledge, developing tolerance, and understanding for the majority group; and (2) a source of the social learning required for upward mobility for the Leftout. In a heterogeneous public school, in general, both the acculturation of the Leftouts and their social assimilation should be most successful when: (1) the Leftouts are a relatively small minority, constituting not more than 25 percent of the school population; (2) when the Leftouts are from a sociocultural group that has been in the United States a relatively long time, and is not discriminated against because of race or religious and ethnic identity; and (3) when the Leftouts come from the same kind of community (rural or urban) as their more advantaged classmates. These factors ought to be considered when designing compensatory programs, so that relevant kinds of training for social acceptance can be built in as part of the goals.

Relatively Low Levels of Self-Esteem

Theoretical Framework. Personality and value orientations are open to modification throughout life by changing social influences and new experiences. Thus, the stability of personality is relative. Adjustive stability requires continual adaptation in response to new experiences or reinterpretations of old ones, in light of changed perceptions or demands for reorganization and reevaluation of value orientations and behavioral expectations. In short, socialization is ideally a continuous process.

One of the major products of the socialization process is that of knowledge of role expectations. Within any social system, each individual occupies one or more roles, which are accompanied by normative expectations as to how a person in that particular position should think, feel, and behave. The normative expectations accompanying various roles may be pervasive or delimited, complex or simple, clear or ambiguous, integrative or conflicting. Ambiguous or conflicting normative expectations are seen to create cross pressures that are apt to result in emotional strain and anxiety for the individual.

The closer the correspondence is between the value orientations and behavioral expectations of various socializing agents, the more adequately and rapidly socialization takes place. On the other hand, the more conflicts there are between the value orientations and behavioral expectations of the various agents of socialization, the slower, more anxiety prone, and inadequate is the socialization process apt to be.

Synthesis. We are suggesting that the Leftout, who is apt to be ill prepared to understand and cope with the value orientations and behavioral expectations of his teachers and more advantaged age-mates, is also apt to have a slow, difficult, and conflict-ridden time of socialization in the school situation. Such conflicts create frustrations and anxieties, which may result in an inadequate level of self-esteem. Thus, the Leftout may be disadvantaged in that he has a relatively lower level of self-esteem than his more advantaged age-mates.

The lack of successful adjustment to school seems to be based on: (1) lack of knowledge, experience, training, and motivation; (2) maladjustive value orientations and behavioral expectations; (3) repeated failures to achieve academic or social status, or both; and (4) a pessimistic evaluation of self, a low self-concept. These factors have been shown to have personality consequences in the form of a low or inadequate level of self-esteem.

Children low in self-esteem have been shown to be: (1) more persuasible, (2) more field dependent, and (3) more conforming than those with high levels of self-esteem. Thus, a low level of self-esteem may have adjustive consequences for the Leftout, in that pressures by his teachers and more advantaged peers toward conformity may be very effective in influencing his adjustment to the academic and social demands of the heterogeneous school situation. On the other hand, a low level of self-esteem may have maladjustive consequences, because the Leftout is also highly susceptible to social pressures from other status deprived children and to any cross pressures that may exist.

It has been suggested that the cross-pressured Leftout may choose between two general alternatives: (1) reject the value orientations and behavioral expectations of his teachers and more advantaged age-mates in favor of forming a coalition with others like himself; or (2) attempt to conform to the expectations of his teachers and more advantaged age-mates, in which case repeated academic and social problems are apt to have maladjustive emotional consequences. This author would argue that the direction actually taken will depend on other personality and situational variables. It is being suggested here that when the Leftout is unattracted to those doing the evaluating of his position, when negative academic and social evaluations among teachers and more advantaged age-mates are unimportant to him, when he knows what they expect of him but chooses not to conform, and when alternative status-giving positions are available to him, he is more likely to form a coalition with other disadvantaged children. We have already discussed the potentially negative consequences of this alternative in the last section.

On the other hand, it is suggested that when the Leftout *is* attracted to those doing the evaluating of his position, when academic and social evaluations among teachers and more advantaged age-mates are important to him, when he knows what they expect of him but cannot meet their expectations, or when their expectations are unknown to him, and when there seem to be few alternative means of achieving status, he is apt to evidence some emotional maladjustment in the heterogeneous school. Let us examine here the consequences of this alternative.

Academic, Social, and Emotional Consequences of Low Levels of Self-Esteem

The Leftout's self-concept—his feelings about himself, his place among his peers and teachers, and his academic ability—is influenced by many interacting variables: (1) his parents' evaluation of him, (2) his family's socioeconomic status and type of structural organization, (3) the value orientations and behavioral expectations of the subcultural group with which he chooses to identify, (4) his educational background and language skill, (5) his ethnic and racial identification, (6) his sex-role identity, (7) his degree of conformity to the value orientations and behavioral expectations of his teachers and more advantaged age-mates, (8) his degree of social acceptance and adaptability, and (9) his own experiences with academic success or failure.

It is being suggested that the more of these areas there are in which the Leftout is disadvantaged, the more likely he is to exhibit a low level of self-esteem. A low level of self-esteem is suggested to be maladjustive for the academic and social demands of the heterogeneous school situation, and to give rise to emotional maladjustment.

As we have seen, the more conflicts between the value orientations and behavioral expectations to which the Leftout has previously been socialized, and those demanded by the new situation of the heterogeneous school are pervasive (deep in quality) or extensive (many in quantity), the more likely he is to evidence severe anxiety symptoms and be functionally incapable of changing his behavior or adapting his value orientation to new demands. Severe conflicts have been shown to result in: (1) failure to achieve academically, (2) failure in interpersonal relationships, (3) erratic, aggressive, rebellious, deviant, disruptive behavior that is often defined as emotional maladjustment. All of these may serve to reduce the Leftout's already low level of self-esteem even further. This author would argue that those Leftouts who are upwardly mobile are more subject to emotional disorders and to decreases in self-esteem than those who are stationary—partly because of the increased normative cross pressures to which these Leftouts are subject.

The etiology of the Leftouts' maladjustive low levels of self-esteem would seem to include, then: (1) perceptions of inability to reach goals to which they aspire, which may result in frustration, anxiety, and self-disparagement (negative self-evaluation) and (2) downward readjustment of mobility aspirations. When the area of evaluation is academic achievement, and the Leftout accurately perceives what is expected of him by his teachers and achievement-oriented peers, but he is incapable of fulfilling these expectations because of a lack of background experience, training, or skill, and he feels he has failed, he is apt to come to evaluate himself in a less favorable way, that is, lower his level of self-esteem. When the area of evaluation is interpersonal relationships with the majority group, and the Leftout accurately perceives what is expected of him by his teachers and more advantaged age-mates, but he perceives that he has failed to gain social acceptance among them, he is apt to come to evaluate himself in a less favorable way, that is, lower his level of self-esteem.

This author is suggesting that the nature of the Leftout's self-concept is apt to have adverse consequences on his academic adjustment in the heterogeneous school situation, such that an inadequate level of self-esteem tends to be reflected in academic achievement in the form that the lower the self-esteem level, the more likely he is to fail. A low level of self-esteem is apt to have adverse consequences on the Leftout's social adjustment in the heterogeneous school in terms of his social acceptance, in the form that the lower the self-esteem level, the more likely he is to be rejected by others—including others like himself.

Low academic or social status may result in emotional maladjustment, especially: (1) social indifference (withdrawal), (2) rebelliousness (hostility), or (3) severe anxiety and depression. Any of these responses to the heterogeneous school situation are seen to be symptomatic of the Leftout's emotional maladjustment.

It is suggested that emotional maladjustment may both stem from and contribute to academic and social maladjustment. Emotional disturbance is seen to be maladjustive for the demands of the heterogeneous school situation in that it tends to be incapacitating for the Leftout's learning potential, either through intentional or incidental means.

It must be remembered, however, that this relationship between the Leftout's social and academic problems and the nature and extent of his emotional maladjustment is largely a theoretical one. The proper identification and classification of emotional maladjustment among elementary-age school children, the exploration of the relative impact of various suggested developmental antecedents, and the selection of appropriate treatment measures all represent primary areas for scientific investigation.

"Cures" for Low Levels of Self-Esteem

It is suggested that for the Leftout, an inadequate self-concept is more likely to exist because of his lack of prerequisite skills required for social and academic success. Thus, the kinds of compensatory programs already suggested should help to overcome the Leftout's low levels of self-esteem. The Leftout's self-concept is developed: (1) prior to and outside of school, especially through family contacts, (2) by teacher's attitudes toward him, (3) by his level of academic success, and (4) by his level of social success among his peers. Compensatory programs, which include the cooperative and active efforts of parents, teachers, and peers to raise the Leftout's self-esteem level, should have a positive influence on his school adjustment potential.

Self-esteem levels are also dependent on several personal variables. For the Leftout these include: (1) the importance to him of the specific area of focus of others' evaluations; (2) his knowledge of others' expectations and evaluations; (3) his perceptions of the quality of others' evaluations; and (4) his attraction to those doing the evaluating. Thus, compensatory programs must be designed to: (1) foster the Leftout's ego involvement; (2) offer specific training in core-cultural value orientations and behavioral expectations; (3) offer rewards and chances for positive evaluations; and (4) foster social acceptance of the Leftout with warm, supportive teachers and peers.

Our analysis indicates that the early identification of low levels of self-esteem and appropriate compensatory measures are crucial to the Leftout's potential for school adjustment. Thus, cooperation among psychologists and teachers to develop more accurate evaluative and predictive measures of level of self-esteem is indicated. So too is the need for more counselors at the elementary-school level both to work directly with the Leftout child and to help in the planning of effective compensatory programs. Every Leftout should have routine visits with a counselor, who would check on his personal progress, keep his record up to date, and work to check any developing maladjustment.

Compensatory programs should be designed to take advantage of the Leftout's existing skills and talents, as well as to offer him the means of developing new ones. If high academic standing is made the basis for permitting participation in nonacademic activities, then a Leftout may translate this to mean that he is not useful or valued if he is not "smart." The bad times, when his ego is suffering the most, are the best times to help a Leftout build his self-esteem. Small successes go a long way toward mitigating grand despair.

Placement in "special classes" is often equal to social demotion and exposure to a watered down curriculum. This places a Leftout at an even greater disadvantage and has negative consequences for his self-esteem. The school is in the business of motivating children, helping them learn, and communicating with them. The school is not in the business of labeling children or grading them for the job market. Continuous contact with his more advantaged age-mates under conditions of equality is the best setting for helping the Leftout overcome a low level of self-esteem.

Implied in much of the discussion of cures for a Leftout's real or potential maladjustment in the heterogeneous school situation, is the need to redefine the teacher's role and, concomitantly, to redefine the bases for training and selection of teachers. A large majority of states require four years of college for an elementary teaching certificate. Nevertheless, most states have to issue temporary certificates or provide for probationary status in order to fill their classroom needs. For the nation as a whole, these inadequately prepared teachers include about 5 percent of the labor force. However, in very large cities and in certain rural areas, the percentage is much higher. Many cities have a category called "permanent substitutes," and schools with large numbers of disadvantaged children are more apt to be staffed with teachers in that classification. Yet, it is the disadvantaged child who particularly needs a teacher who can provide continuity, who is experienced, and who is well trained to meet his special needs.

The particular problems of disadvantaged children in heterogeneous schools suggests the need for drastically better original training for teachers and continual inservice retraining programs for experienced teachers. Teacher education ought to provide a special program for teaching Leftouts, just as there are programs for teaching the physically or mentally handicapped.

Such a program should stress training in group dynamics, subcultural understanding, the dynamics of communication, and developmental psychology. Such a program should be designed so that student teachers could divide their time between academic training and participation in an elementary-school classroom, beginning in their *freshman year*. A training program such as this would give experienced teachers a whole new source of aides. At the same time, a program such as this would offer teachers-in-training invaluable experience in dealing directly with Leftouts.

Bibliography
and General Reference
Sources

Abrahamson, S., 1952, "Our Status System and Scholastic Rewards," *Journal of Educational Sociology*, **25**, 441–450.

Ausubel, D. P., 1958, *Theory and Problems of Child Development*. (New York: Grune and Stratton, Inc.)

Bandura, A., and A. Huston, 1961, "Identification as a Process of Incidental Learning," *Journal of Abnormal and Social Psychology*, **63**, 311–318.

Bandura, A., and R. H. Walters, 1963, *Social Learning and Personality Development*. (New York: Holt, Rinehart and Winston, Inc.)

Bedoian, V. H., 1953, "Mental Health Analysis of Socially Over-Accepted and Socially Under-Accepted, Overage, and Underage Pupils in the 6th Grade," *Journal of Educational Psychology*, **44**, 366–371.

Bennett, Jr., William S., and Noel P. Gist, 1964, "Class and Family Influences on Student Aspirations," *Social Forces*, **43**, 167–173.

Berelson, Bernard, and Gary A. Steiner, 1964, *Human Behavior: An Inventory of Scientific Findings*. (New York: Harcourt, Brace & World, Inc.)

Bernstein, B., 1961, "Social Class and Linguistic Development: A Theory of Social Learning," *Education, Economy, and Society*. (Eds.) A. H. Halsey *et al.* (New York: The Free Press), 288–314.

Bloom, B. S., A. Davis, and R. Hess, 1965, *Compensatory Education for Cultural Deprivation*. (New York: Holt, Rinehart and Winston, Inc.)

Bloom, R., M. Whiteman, and M. Deutsch, 1963, "Race and Social Class as Separate Factors Related to Social Environment." Paper read at American Psychological Association meeting, Philadelphia, Pa. September, 1963. Mimeo., reprints available.

Bonney, M. E., 1946, "A Sociometric Study of the Relationship of Some Factors to Mutual Friendships on the Elementary, Secondary, and College Levels," *Sociometry*, **9**, 21–47.

Bronfenbrenner, Urie, 1958, "Socialization and Social Class Through Time and Space," *Readings in Social Psychology*. (Eds.) E. E. Maccoby, T. M. Newcomb, and E. L. Hartley. (New York: Holt, Rinehart and Winston, Inc.)

———, 1961, "The Changing American Child—a Speculative Analysis," *Merrill-Palmer Quarterly*, **7** (2), 73–84.

Brookover, Wilbur, 1953, "Teachers and Stratification of American Society," *Harvard Educational Review*, **23**, 257–267.

Brookover, Wilbur, and David Gottlieb, 1961, "Social Class and Education," *The Social Psychology of Education*. (Eds.) N. L. Gage and W. W. Charters. (Boston: Allyn and Bacon, Inc.)

Brookover, Wilbur, Ann Patterson, and Shailer Thomas, 1962, "Self-Concept of Ability and School Achievement," Final Report of *Cooperative Research Project #845, U.S. Office of Education*. (East Lansing: Bureau of Research and Publications, College of Education, Michigan State University Press.)

Brookover, Wilbur, J. M. LePere, D. E. Hamachek, S. Thomas, and E. L. Erickson, 1965, "Improving Academic Achievement Through Student's Self-Concept Enhancement," Final Report of *Cooperative Research Project #1636, U.S. Office of Education*. (East Lansing: Bureau of Educational Research Services, College of Education, Michigan State University Press.)

Bruner, Jerome S., "The Cognitive Consequences of Early Sensory Deprivation," *Sensory Deprivation*. (Ed.) P. Solomon. (Cambridge, Mass.: Harvard University Press.)

———, 1964, "The Course of Cognitive Growth," *American Psychologist*, **19**, 1–15.

Burton, William H., 1953, "Education In The United States," *Harvard Educational Review*, **23** (Fall), 248.

Campbell, J. D., 1964, "Peer Relations in Childhood," *Review of Child Development Research*. Vol. I. (Eds.) Martin L. Hoffman and Lois W. Hoffman. (New York: Russell Sage Foundation), 289–322.

Carlson, Rae, 1963, "Identification and Personality Structure in Pre-adolescents," *Journal of Abnormal and Social Psychology*, **67** (6), 566–573.

Casler, Lawrence, 1961, "Maternal Deprivation: A Critical Review of the Literature," *Monographs of the Society for Research in Child Development*, **26** (2), 6, 28.

Charters, W. W., 1953, "Social Class Analysis and Control of Public Education," *Harvard Educational Review*, **23** (Fall).

Clark, K. B., and M. K. Clark, 1952, "Racial Identification and Preference in Negro Children," *Readings in Social Psychology*. (2d ed.) (Eds.) Swanson, Newcomb, and Hartley. (New York: Holt, Rinehart and Winston, Inc.), 551–560.

Cohen, Albert K., 1955, *Delinquent Boys*. (New York: The Free Press.)

Cohen, J., 1964, "Social Work and the Culture of Poverty," *Mental Health of the Poor*. (Eds.) F. Riessman *et al.* (New York: The Free Press.)

Coleman, James S., 1959, "Academic Achievement and the Structure of Competition," *Harvard Educational Review*, **29** (Fall).

——, 1960, "The Adolescent Subculture and Academic Achievement," *The American Journal of Sociology*, **65** (January).

Commoss, H. H., 1962, "Some Characteristics Related to Social Isolation of Second Grade Children," *Journal of Educational Psychology*, **53**, 38–42.

Cooley, Charles H., 1902, *Human Nature and the Social Order*. (New York: Charles Scribner's Sons.)

Cronbach, Lee J., 1960, *Essentials of Psychological Testing*, (2d ed.) (New York: Harper & Row, Publishers), 174.

Curry, R. L., 1962, "The Effect of Socio-Economic Status on the Scholastic Achievement of 6th Grade Children," *British Journal of Educational Psychology*, **32**, 46–49.

Davis, Allison, 1944, "Socialization and the Adolescent Personality," *Yearbook of National Social Studies in Education*. Vol. 32, Part I. (Chicago, Ill.: University of Chicago Press), 198–216.

——, 1948, *Social Class Influences Upon Learning*. (Cambridge, Mass.: Harvard University Press.)

——, 1957, "Acculturation In Schools," *American Minorities*. (Ed.) Milton L. Barron (New York: Alfred A. Knopf), 446–449.

Davis, A., and R. J. Havighurst, 1947, *Father of the Man: How Your Child Gets His Personality*. (New York: Houghton Mifflin Company.)

Deutsch, Martin, 1963, "The Disadvantaged Child and the Learning Process," *Education in Depressed Areas*. (Ed.) A. Harry Passow. (New York: Bureau of Publications, Teachers College Columbia University), 163–180.

——, 1964, "The Role of Social Class in Language Development and Cognition," (New York: Institute for Developmental Studies). Mimeo, reprints available.

Dreger, R., and K. Miller, 1960, "Comparative Psychological Studies of Negroes and Whites in the United States," *Psychological Bulletin*, **57**, 361–402.

Duffy, J. F., 1961, "The Effects of Induced Anxiety on Incidental Learning of Hi and Lo Anxious Subjects," Unpublished Ph.D. dissertation, University of Pennsylvania.

Eisenstadt, S. N., 1962, "Archetypal Patterns of Youth," *Daedalus* (Winter), 28–46.

Elkins, D., 1958, "Some Factors Related to the Choice-status of Ninety Eighth-Grade Children in a School Society," *Genetic Psychological Monographs*, **58**, 207–272.

Festinger, Leon, 1950, "Laboratory Experiments: The Role of Group Belongingness," *Experiments in Social Process.* (Ed.) J. G. Miller. (New York: McGraw-Hill, Inc.), 32–46.

Fink, M. B., 1962, "Self-Concept as it Relates to Academic Under-Achievement," *California Journal of Educational Research*, **13** (2), 57–62.

Fjeld, S. P., 1961, "The Communication of Values and Sociometric Choice," Unpublished Ph.D. dissertation, University of Missouri.

Flanders, N. A., and S. Havumaki, 1960, "The Effect of Teacher-Pupil Contacts Involving Praise on the Sociometric Indices of Students," *Journal of Educational Psychology*, **51**, 65–68.

Frazier, E. F., 1950, "Problems and Needs of Negro Children and Youth Resulting from Family Disorganization," *Journal of Negro Education*, **19** (Summer), 269–277.

Gold, Martin, 1963, *Status Forces in Delinquent Boys.* (Ann Arbor, Mich.: Institute for Social Research, University of Michigan Press.)

Goodman, M. E., 1952, *Race Awareness in Young Children.* (Reading, Mass.: Addison-Wesley Publishing Company, Inc.)

Gottlieb, D., 1964, "Teaching and Students: The Views of Negro and White Teachers," *Sociology of Education*, **37**, 345–353.

deGroat, A. F., and G. G. Thompson, 1949, "A Study of the Distribution of Teacher Approval and Disapproval Among 6th Grade Children," *Journal of Experimental Education*, **18**, 57–75.

Gross, Neal, 1953, "A Critique of 'Social Class Structure and American Education,'" *Harvard Educational Review*, **23** (Fall).

Gussow, J., 1965, "Language Development In Disadvantaged Children," *IRCD Bulletin*, **1** (5). (New York: Ferkauf Graduate School of Education, Yeshiva University.)

Hartley, R. E., 1959, "Sex-Role Pressures and the Socialization of the Male Child," *Psychological Reports*, **5**, 457–468.

Hernandez, D., 1963, "Is the Concept of Social Class Being Misused in Education?" *Journal of Educational Sociology*, **36**, 322–324.

Hieronymus, A., 1951, "Study of Social Class Motivation: Relationships

Between Anxiety for Education and Certain Socio-Economic and Intellectual Variables," *Journal of Educational Psychology*, **42**, 193–205.

Hollingshead, August B., 1949, *Elmtown's Youth*. (New York: John Wiley & Sons, Inc.)

Homans, George Caspar, 1950, *The Human Group*. (New York: Harcourt, Brace & World, Inc.)

——, 1961, *Social Behavior: Its Elementary Forms*. (New York: Harcourt, Brace, & World, Inc.)

Horney, Karen, 1945, *Our Inner Conflicts*. (New York: W. W. Norton & Company, Inc.)

Horowitz, F. D., 1962, "The Relationship of Anxiety, Self-Concept and Sociometric Status Among Fourth, Fifth, and Sixth Grade Children," *Journal of Abnormal and Social Psychology*, **65**, 212–214.

Horrocks, J. E., and M. E. Buker, 1951, "Friendship Fluctuations During Childhood," *Journal of Genetic Psychology*, **78**, 131–144.

Hovland, C. I., and I. L. Janis, (Eds.), 1959, *Personality and Persuasibility*. (New Haven, Conn.: Yale University Press.)

Hunt, Joseph M., 1961, *Intelligence and Experience*. (New York: The Ronald Press Company.)

Hyman, Herbert H., 1942, "The Psychology of Status," *Archives of Psychology*, no. 269. (New York: Columbia University Press.)

Jenkins, W., 1958, "An Experimental Study of the Relationship of Legitimate and Illegitimate Birth Status to School and Personal and Social Adjustment of Negro Children," *American Journal of Sociology*, **64**, 169–173.

John, V., 1963, "The Intellectual Development of Slum Children: Some Preliminary Findings," *American Journal of Orthopsychiatry*, **33**, 813–822.

Kagan, J., 1964, "Acquisition and Significance of Sex Typing and Sex Role Identity," *Review of Child Development Research*. Vol. 1. (Eds.) Martin L. Hoffman and Lois W. Hoffman. (New York: Russell Sage Foundation), 137–168.

Kahl, J., 1953, "Educational and Occupational Aspirations of 'Common Man' Boys," *Harvard Educational Review*, **23** (Fall), 186–203.

Kardiner, Abram, 1939, *The Individual and His Society*. (New York: Columbia University Press.)

Kelman, H. C., 1960, "Effects of Role-Orientation and Value-Orientation on the Nature of Attitude Change," Paper read at the meetings of the Eastern Psychological Association, April 15, 1960. Mimeo, reprints available.

Kitano, H. H., 1962, "Adjustment of Problem and Non-Problem Children in Specific Situations: A Study in Role Theory," *Child Development*, **23**, 229–233.

Kohn, M. L., 1963, "Social Class and Parent-Child Relationships: An Interpretation," *American Journal of Sociology*, **68**, 471–480.

Kohn, M. L., and E. E. Carroll, 1960, "Social Class and the Allocation of Parental Responsibilities," *Sociometry*, **23**, 372–392.

Lambert, Nadine, 1964, "The High School Dropout in Grade School," *Guidance and the School Dropout*. (Eds.) D. Schreiber and B. Kaplan. (Washington, D.C.: School Dropouts Project, National Education Association.)

Lavin, David E., 1965, *The Prediction of Academic Performance*. (New York: Russell Sage Foundation.)

LeShan, L., 1952, "Time Orientation and Social Class," *Journal of Abnormal and Social Psychology*, **47**, 589–592.

Lewis, Hylan, 1961, *Child Rearing Among Low Income Families*. (Washington, D.C.: Washington Center for Metropolitan Studies), pamphlet.

Lewis, Oscar, 1959, *Five Families*. (New York: Basic Books, Inc.)

——, 1966, "The Culture of Poverty," *Scientific American* (October), **215** (4), 19–25.

Loeb, M., 1953, "Implications of Status Differentiation for Personal and Social Development," *Harvard Educational Review*, **23** (Fall), 168–174.

Lott, A. E., and B. E. Lott, 1963, *Negro and White Youth*. (New York: Holt, Rinehart and Winston, Inc.)

Luria (Luriia), A. R., and S. Y. Yudovitch, 1961, *Speech and the Development of Mental Processes in Children*. (London: Staples Press, Ltd.)

Lynd, Robert, and Helen Merrell Lynd, 1929, *Middletown: A Study in American Culture*. (New York: Harcourt, Brace & World, Inc.)

Lynn, D. B., 1959, "A Note on Sex Differences in the Development of Masculine and Feminine Identification," *Psychological Review*, **66**, 126–135.

Lynn, D. B., and W. L. Sawrey, 1959, "The Effects of Father-Absence on Norwegian Boys and Girls," *Journal of Abnormal and Social Psychology*, **59**, 258–262.

McClosky, H., and J. H. Schaar, 1965, "Psychological Dimensions of Anomy," *American Sociological Review*, **30** (1), 14–40.

McDermott, J. F., S. I. Harrison, J. Schrager, and P. Wilson, 1965, "Social Class and Mental Illness in Children," *American Journal of Orthopsychiatry*, **35** (3), 500–508.

Macdonald, M., C. McGurie, and R. J. Havighurst, 1949, "Leisure Activities and the Socio-Economic Status of Children," *American Journal of Sociology*, **54**, 505–519.

McGraw, L. W., and J. W. Tolbert, 1953, "Sociometric Status and Athletic Ability of Junior High School Boys," *Research Quarterly of the American Association of Health and Physical Education*, **24**, 74–80.

Malpass, L. F., 1953, "Some Relationships Between Students' Perceptions of School and Their Achievement," *Journal of Educational Psychology*, **44**, 475–482.

Mead, George Herbert, 1934, *Mind, Self, and Society*. (Chicago, Ill.: University of Chicago Press.)

Merton, Robert K., 1957, *Social Theory and Social Structure*. (Revised ed.) (New York: The Free Press.)

Miller, S., 1964, "The American Lower Classes: A Typological Approach," *Social Research*, **31** (Spring).

Moynihan, D., 1965, "A Family Policy for the Nation," *America* (September 18), 11.

Mussen, Paul H., J. J. Conger, and Jerome Kagan, 1963, *Child Development and Personality*. (2d ed.) (New York: Harper & Row, Publishers.)

Nash, J., 1965, "The Father in Contemporary Culture and Current Psychological Literature," *Child Development*, **36** (1) (March), 275–293.

Neugarten, B. L., 1946, "Social Class and Friendship Among School Children," *American Journal of Sociology*, **51**, 305–313.

Newsweek Magazine (January 10, 1966), 45.

Newton, E., 1962, "The Culturally Disadvantaged Child in our Verbal Schools," *Journal of Negro Education*, **31** (Spring), 184–187.

Parsons, Talcott, 1951, *The Social System*. (New York: The Free Press), Chapter VII. (Paperback, 1964.)

Passow, A. Harry (Ed.), 1963, *Education in Depressed Areas*. (New York: Bureau of Publications, Teachers College, Columbia University.)

Piaget, Jean, 1951, *The Child's Conception of the World*. (New York: Humanities Press, Inc.)

——, 1954, *The Construction of Reality in the Child*. (New York: Basic Books, Inc.)

——, 1952, *Judgment and Reasoning in the Child*. (New York: Humanities Press, Inc.)

——, 1959, *The Language and Thought of the Child*. (New York: Humanities Press, Inc.)

——, 1948, *The Moral Judgment of the Child*. (New York: The Free Press.)

——, 1952, *The Origins of Intelligence in Children*. (New York: International Universities Press, Inc.)

Pope, B., 1953, "Socio-Economic Contrasts in Children's Peer Cultural Prestige Values," *Genetic Psychological Monographs*, **48**, 157–220.

Potashin, R., 1946, "A Sociometric Study of Children's Friendships," *Sociometry*, **9**, 48–70.

Riessman, Frank, 1962, *The Culturally Deprived Child*. (New York: Harper & Row, Publishers.)

Rogoff, N., 1961, "Local Social Structure and Educational Selection," *Education, Economy, and Society*. (Eds.) A. H. Halsey *et al.* (New York: The Free Press), 241–251.

Rokeach, Milton, 1960, *The Open and Closed Mind*. (New York: Basic Books, Inc.)

Rosen, B., 1956, "The Achievement Syndrome: A Psychocultural Dimension of Social Stratification," *American Sociological Review*, **21**, 203–211.

Rosen, B., and R. D'Andrade, 1959, "The Psycho-Social Origins of Achievement Motivation," *Sociometry*, **22**, 185–218.

Rosenbaum, M., 1963, "Psychological Effects on the Child Raised by an Older Sibling," *American Journal of Orthopsychiatry*, **33** (April), 515–520.

Schachter, S., 1951, "Deviation, Rejection and Communication," *Journal of Abnormal and Social Psychology*, **46**, 190–207.

Schorr, A., 1964, "The Non-Culture of Poverty," *American Journal of Orthopsychiatry*, **34**, 220–221.

Schrupp, M. H., and C. M. Gjerde, 1953, "Teacher Growth in Attitudes Toward Behavior Problems of Children," *Journal of Educational Psychology*, **44**, 203–214.

Schurr, Evelyn, 1964, "The Accuracy of Children's Judgments of the Playing Abilities of their Peers in Grades One Through Six," Unpublished Ph.D. dissertation, Illinois State University.

Sears, R. R., E. E. Maccoby, and H. Levin, 1957, *Patterns of Child Rearing*. (New York: Harper & Row, Publishers.)

Sears, R. R., L. Rau, and R. Alpert, 1965, *Child Rearing and Identification*. (Stanford, Calif.: Stanford University Press.)

Sewell, W. H., 1952, "Infant Training and the Personality of the Child," *American Journal of Sociology*, **58** (September), 150–159. (Bobbs-Merrill Reprint No. 257.)

Sewell, W. H., A. Haller, and M. Strauss, 1957, "Social Status and Educational and Occupational Aspiration," *American Sociological Review*, **22**, 67–73.

Siller, J., 1957, "Socio-economic Status and Conceptual Thinking," *Journal of Abnormal and Social Psychology*, **55**, 365–371.

Singer, A., Jr., 1951, "Certain Aspects of Personality and Their Relation to Certain Group Modes, and Constancy of Friendship Choice," *Journal of Educational Research*, **45**, 33–42.

Smith, G. H., 1950, "Sociometric Study of Best-Liked and Least-Liked Children," *Elementary School Journal*, **51**, 77–85.

Stendler, Celie, 1949, *Children of Brasstown*. (Urbana, Ill.: University of Illinois Press.)

Stevenson, H. W., and E. G. Stewart, 1958, "A Developmental Study of Racial Awareness in Young Children," *Child Development*, **29**, 399–409.

Sullivan, Harry Stack, 1953, *The Interpersonal Theory of Psychiatry.* (New York: W. W. Norton & Company, Inc.)

Sutton, R. S., 1962, "An Appraisal of Certain Aspects of Children's Social Behavior," *Journal of Teacher Education*, **13**, 30–34.

Thomas, William I., and Florian Znaniecki, 1918–1921, *The Polish Peasant in Europe and America.* 5 Vols. (New York: Alfred A. Knopf.)

Tiktin, S., and W. W. Hartup, 1965, "Sociometric Status and the Reinforcing Effectiveness of Children's Peers," *Journal of Experimental Child Psychology*, **2**, 306–315.

Toby, J., 1957, "Orientation to Education as a Factor in the Social Maladjustment of Lower-Class Children," *Social Forces*, **39**, 259–266.

Trager, H. G., and M. R. Yarrow, 1952, *They Learn What They Live: Prejudice in Young Children.* (New York: Harper & Row, Publishers.)

Tuddenham, R. D., 1952, "Studies in Reputation: I—Sex and Grade Differences in School Children's Evaluation of their Peers; II—The Diagnosis of Social Adjustment," *Psychological Monographs*, **66** (333).

Tuma, E., and N. Livson, 1960, "Family Socio-Economic Status and Adolescent Attitudes to Authority," *Child Development*, **31**, 387–399.

U.S. Department of Labor, Office of Policy Planning and Research, 1965, *The Negro Family: The Case for National Action.* (Washington, D.C.: Government Printing Office), March.

Walker, E. L., and R. W. Heyns, 1962, *An Anatomy for Conformity.* (Englewood Cliffs, N.J.: Prentice-Hall, Inc.)

Warden, S. A., 1964, "The Student Education Corps: A Case Study of a Partial Solution," *The American Adolescent.* (Eds.) D. Gottlieb and C. Ramsey. (Homewood, Ill.: The Dorsey Press, Inc.)

Warner, L., R. Havighurst, and M. Loeb, 1944, *Who Shall Be Educated?* (New York: Harper & Row, Publishers.)

Watson, R. I., 1959, *Psychology of the Child; Personal, Social and Disturbed Child Development.* (New York: John Wiley & Sons, Inc.)

Weiner, M., and W. Murray, 1963, "Another Look at the Culturally Deprived and their Levels of Aspiration," *Journal of Educational Sociology*, **36**, 319–321.

White, Robert W., 1948, *The Abnormal Personality.* (New York: The Ronald Press Company), 144–145.

Will, Robert E., and H. G. Vatter, 1965, *Poverty in Affluence.* (New York: Harcourt, Brace & World, Inc.)

Wilson, R. S., 1960, "Personality Patterns, Source Attractiveness, and Conformity," *Journal of Personality*, **28**, 186–199.

Wolf, R. M., 1964, "The Identification and Measurement of Environmental Process Variables Related to Intelligence," Unpublished Ph.D. dissertation, University of Chicago.

Yarrow, L. J., 1964, "Separation from Parents During Early Childhood," *Review of Child Development Research*. Vol. I. (Eds.) Martin L. Hoffman and Lois W. Hoffman. (New York: Russell Sage Foundation), 89–136.

Bloom, B. S., A. Davis, and R. Hess, 1965, *Compensatory Education for Cultural Deprivation*. Holt, Rinehart and Winston, Inc., 383 Madison Avenue, New York, N.Y. 10017.

Based on working papers contributed by participants in the Research Conference on Education and Cultural Deprivation. Paperback; 179 pages; $1.75. 115 pages of annotated bibliography.

IRCD Bulletin, Project Beacon, Ferkauf Graduate School of Education, Yeshiva University, 55 Fifth Avenue, New York, N.Y. 10003.

A bimonthly publication from the Information Retrieval Center on the Disadvantaged. One or two short essays and four to six pages of bibliography. Subscription: $1 per year.

Poverty and Human Resources Abstracts, G. C. Morningstar (Ed.), The Institute of Labor and Industrial Relations, University of Michigan. Wayne State University, University of Michigan, P.O. Box 1567, Ann Arbor, Michigan 48106.

Published bimonthly. Review article, annotated bibliography, and recent legislative developments; related to all aspects of poverty and human resources. Annual subscription: $30 loose leaf, $40 bound. Single Issues: $6 loose leaf, $7.50 bound.

Research Relating to Children: An Inventory of Studies in Progress, U.S. Childrens Bureau, Federal Security Agency, Social Security Administration, Washington, D.C.

Clearinghouse for Research in Child Life. Research proposals and author abstracts.

Indexes

Name Index

199

Subject Index